A Funny Thing Happened on the Way to the Agora
Ancient Greek and Roman Humour

R. Drew Griffith and Robert B. Marks

Legacy Books Press

Published by Legacy Books Press
RPO Princess, Box 21031
445 Princess Street
Kingston, Ontario, K7L 5P5

www.legacybookspress.com

First published in 2007 by Legacy Books Press
1

ISBN-13: 978-0-9784652-0-9

This book is typeset in a Latin725 BT 10 point font.

Printed and bound in the United States of America and the United Kingdom.

This book is printed on paper. We tried to get steel, but it was too expensive.

To the students of CLST 205, Queen's University.
And to Beth and Oriane.

And with special thanks to A.R. George, George Clark, and Michael Greenhalgh.

Table of Contents

Preface

By Professor L.Z.A. Pscytt, Professor of Classics, Miskatonic University,
Arkham, Massachusetts

It is with great pleasure that I have accepted the responsibility of
providing a preface for this wonderful book. When my good friend, Professor
Robert Drew Griffith, asked me to write the beginning of the book on a
subject for which he is the top of the field, I was honoured. I didn't even need
to wait for the book to arrive, why I just had to pick up my tape recorder and
start dictating. Indeed, I'm sure that once the manuscript of the book arrives,
it will be a masterpiece that will do Griffith and his university proud.

Now, what is humour? Well, humour is what do you mean my wife is on
the phone, can't you see I'm dictating... oh, whatever, no I can't speak to her
now, no, I really don't want to hear – oh dear God in Heaven, she wants to
do what? Tell her that she can't, look she's a seventy-year-old woman who
weighs two hundred pounds – the sight of her in a leather bikini would make
the blind run screaming in terror, I don't care if it's a costume party, I'm not
going with it, no I don't want to look like a porn star, yes, I'm going with the
fluffy bunny costume, well it's a hell of a lot better than a leather bikini, now
I'm trying to dictate a preface to this bloody book, will you leave me in peace?
I'll call my wife later!

Now, as I was saying, humour is whatever we find funny.

Part I
Funny Stuff

POET
Tell, O Muse, of Odysseus, the man who returned home from
Troy to slay the suitors annoying his wife, but only after blinding a
Cyclops, avoiding the sirens, sleeping with Circe, watching his
men get killed by the Sungod, and being trapped by Calypso.

MUSE
Look, do you want to tell this story?

– Evadne Noel, *The Odyssey: Breadbox Edition, Book I*

Chapter I – What is Humour?

The word "Humour"

There are many types of humour in the world. American humour is markedly different from British Humour, which is different from Canadian humour.[1] Then there is slapstick, word-play, political humour, and debatable humour (such as when a certain co-author tries to tell jokes). We take it for granted that the word refers to comedy.

But is that true? What is the real meaning of the word "humour"? This question itself requires some justification. It is a habit of thought of the philologist or professional "lover of words" to believe that words really matter, that in the words of Martin Heidegger, "speech speaks" or in those of Friedrich Nietzsche, we are trapped in the "prison-house of language."[2] These philosophers meant that we do not, as we so confidently say, speak English; rather English speaks us in the sense that it constrains us to say what has already been said before. Imagine it this way – we can only understand a concept that we have words for. For example, the seven-headed tentacled monster from the dawn of time with a penchant for Harry Potter books can only exist in our minds because we have the words to express it in our lexicon. If we didn't have the word "tentacled," to take just one example, we could never even begin to grasp the concept, or at least the monster with tentacles, and the poor creature would have a dreadful time picking up the next Harry Potter book. Different languages offer different constraints, and we can learn a lot about a culture by paying attention to the words they use.

"Humour" was originally a medical term. Greek medicine was very primitive, because Greeks thought the worst thing you could wish on anyone was that their body be mutilated after death. After all, everybody knew that whatever a body experienced between the moment of death and that of a proper burial the soul would experience for all eternity as well. They never said, "Go to Hell!," because they thought we would all go to Hades after we died; instead they said, "Go to the crows!," inviting them to die and be pecked at by birds or eaten by wild dogs.[3] The Romans, in a similar vein, said, "Go to the cross!" (The modern equivalent, perhaps, is "To the curb!") Because they were adverse to mutilating the body, ancient physicians could

---

[1] In 2000 the Cuban government created the *Premio Nacional de Humorismo*. Wouldn't the world be a better place if every country took humour this seriously?

[2] M. Heidegger (P. D. Herz trans.), *On the Way to Language* (New York and San Francisco 1971) 124, F. Jameson, *The Prison-House of Language* (Princeton 1972).

[3] Greek even has a word, *skorakizein*, which means "to tell someone to go to the crows."

not perform dissection,[4] and so they had to guess at what went on inside us (and, apparently believed that the anatomy of animals like cows and pigs weren't worth studying, even if you were going to eat them afterwards anyway). To do so they advanced the theory that the human body is a microcosm of the universe. Since they thought that the universe was made up of four elements – earth, air, fire and water[5] – they concluded that the body must have four elements also.

Given all the spit, snot, blood, semen, vomit and so on that oozes and drips out of the body, ancient physicians were pretty sure that the body's four elements must all be liquid, so they called them *chumoi* in Greek or *humores* in Latin. The latter word is related to our "humid" and the "aqueous humour" in our eyeballs. The four humours are phlegm (which is spit), bile (which is stomach acid), blood (which is, well, blood) and black bile (also known as *melaina choler*). If you were healthy, you had an equal measure of these four juices, and thus a good temper(ament), using that word in the sense of "measure," as in J. S. Bach's *Well-tempered Klavier*.

If things got out of whack and one humour came to be more abundant in the body than the others, you were sick, and were said to be "humorous." The physician treating you would try to restore the balance of the humours, usually by draining out some of your blood by cutting one of your veins or by applying a leech. This had the obvious effect on the patient, made the doctors feel like they were doing something useful, and made the leech farmers and gatherers very happy people.

The humours didn't just affect your physical well-being, though, but your mental state as well. (Our species is Homo Sapiens, "Humans the wise," and it's no accident that the word "sapiens" is related to the liquid-words "sap, seep, sip, sop, soap, sup" and "soup.") Too much phlegm and you become withdrawn, too much bile and you get a permanent case of rage, making you unsafe for highway driving, too much blood and you are permanently happy – sounds good, but supposing you're at a funeral and can't stop laughing – and too much black bile and you fall into a depression. If any of these things happens, you will begin to behave in an automatic way without reference to the ever-changing circumstances of the world around you, and you will quickly become a social nuisance.

When this occurs, people will laugh at you. This is partly an automatic response to anyone who is humorous, but it is deliberate as well. People don't like being laughed at, and will moderate their behaviour to avoid it. In this way the laughter of one's neighbours is to the psychologically humorous person what blood-letting is to the physically humorous. Laughter really is, as we put it – though we usually mean something very different when we say

---

[4] The first public dissection of a cadaver was performed by Herophilus of Chalcedon in Alexandria around 300 B.C.

[5] Empedocles frs. 346 and 347 (Kirk, Raven and Schofield). Early scientists wasted a lot of time on this issue. Anaximenes fr. 140 , for instance, argued that everything was really air (fire is hot air, water is wet air, earth is really compressed air, etc.).

it! – the best medicine.

Humour and Laughter

From what we said above we can reach three conclusions. First, humour resides in the personality. It is not something situational, but instead a part of the very makeup of a person or character. This means that the first principle and soul of tragedy is plot, as Aristotle says in his *Poetics* (6.19). This could explain the plotlessness of many comedies.

Second, humour results in a loss of subtlety, or a flattening out, or a mechanization of behaviour. Such mechanization lends itself to expression in repetition, as with clowns, and in replication with many people behaving in the same annoying way. For example, in an episode of *The Simpsons* Homer plays with a hospital bed while saying "Bed goes up, bed goes down." Tragic heroes like Antigone can also be unyielding, but they know what they're doing, while comic figures are unaware of their own "flatness."[6]

Third, humour is associated with certain identifiable and categorizable types. The Greeks called these "characters." This is usually a positive word for us, such as when we so often say, "Studying Classics helps you build character," but the Greeks meant something less flattering by it. The word comes from an old Hebrew or Arabic word, *charash*, meaning "to plough." The Greeks used it to describe scratching something into metal objects, and then the minting process whereby stamps turned out an endless succession of identical coins. A lot of comedy hinges on the characters, or stock types, such as the grumpy old man, the miser, and the boaster, repeated endlessly, just like the coins. From Classical literature these passed into the Italian *Commedia dell'arte* with its Harlequin, Columbine and Pierrot, and thence into the English *Punch and Judy* show.

Although the idea of the four humours goes back to antiquity, the use of the word "humorous" to describe someone weird and funny is a modern

---

[6] The Victorian mathematician, Edwin A. Abbott published in 1884 an allegorical fantasy entitled, *Flatland: A Romance of Many Dimensions* (rpt. Oxford 1974). The inhabitants of the eponymous world of Flatland live in two dimensions, as though upon a single sheet of paper. Each night the novel's hero, A Square, goes home to the house he shares with his wife and retires for the night after locking the door. Now A Square's house is designed to keep out burglars who operate, like himself, in two dimensions. It has, therefore, a floor, a roof and two walls. It neither requires nor has side-walls, for everyone in Flatland is, well, *flat,* with no thickness, or in other words no sides. One day out of the blue a three-dimensional intruder enters A Square's house through one of the "missing" side walls. A Square, who can look only in front, up, down, or behind, does not see this three-dimensional being as he approaches from one side, and is wholly unaware of his presence until his body suddenly intersects the plane of Flatland, at which moment he becomes palpably present in A Square's living room, before departing again as surprisingly and as effortlessly as he had come. This allegory may suggest why "humorous" people seem so comically feeble to the rest of us.

development.[7] When the ancients wanted to cover more or less the same semantic field they could speak of comedy (but that was for them a theatrical genre), or satire (this word is related to "satisfy" and describes a dish, the *lanx satura*, composed of odds and sods, a bit like "farce" which is the French word for "stuffing"). Mostly, though, the Greeks and Romans would call humour the ridiculous – that which makes you laugh.

It is very interesting that English describes a humorous situation from the perspective of the individual, "he or she is humorous, i.e. has an imbalance of humours," while the ancients describe it from the perspective of society, "he or she is ridiculous, i.e. we laugh at him or her." We can relate this difference to three important distinctions between ancient and modern world-views.

First, in contrast to ourselves, the ancients privileged the effect of an action over the intention. While we would say, "It's the thought that counts," the Athenians would go as far as to put an inanimate object on trial for murder and throw it into the sea if convicted (Arist. *Ath. Pol.* 57.4; they weren't completely nuts; this was their answer to our coroner's inquest, and was designed to prevent similar accidents from happening in the future – but it's still about as far as you can get from the thought being the thing that counts).

Second, following from the fact that effects are usually effects *on other people*, the ancients privileged the needs of society over those of the individual. People can be expended – we will all die anyway – whereas Rome the eternal city will go on forever, regardless of what those pesky Huns may think. Canada has a Charter of Rights and Freedoms; the ancients had laws enforcing the *obligations* of citizens. Magistrates walked the market in Athens on days when parliament was sitting, carrying a rope dipped in red dye. Anyone found with a dye-stain on their clothes (and who had therefore had been shopping instead of attending the town-hall meeting) was subject to a fine (Ar. *Ach.* 22, Pollux 8.104). Citizens could be ostracized to prevent their acquiring too much political power, regardless that this involved trampling all over what we would consider to be their rights.

Third, and finally, the backbone of society is its customs and traditions, and the ancients preferred these to an individual's originality and creativity. "Innovation" and "thinking outside the box" would not have been big buzz-words in Greece and Rome, even if they had been translated into Greek and Latin. In light of these three differences between ancient and modern ways of seeing the world, it is not surprising that the ancients spoke of humour from the perspective of society as "the ridiculous."

This whole question of individual versus public perspective that we've been considering hinges on the fact that jokes enforce boundaries with an inside and an outside. We see this when we tell "in-jokes" that can be appreciated only by those who are "in the know." We see it even more clearly when we laugh *at* someone, that is when the ridiculous is transformed into ridicule and derision. And in the ancient world this transformation happened

---

[7] The earliest example in the *Oxford English Dictionary* is from 1705.

all too often. In other words, a very important element in humour is aggression.

Humour and Aggression

Even physiologically, laughter is aggressive, requiring as it does that we bare our teeth. The vocabulary of humour also contains a thinly veiled aggression (for example, "I'm pulling your leg," or "it burns!").[8] The level of aggression varies in part at least according to the butt of the joke. When we poke fun at ourselves, the aggressive aspect is minimal, which is why it's a good ploy to use when beginning a speech to capture the goodwill of the audience (Dem. 23.206, Ar. *Vesp.* 567). As one turns to ridicule other people, and then finally one's audience, the level of aggression rises. There is a limit, however, to how aggressive humour can become. In general, no one laughs at total, unchecked aggression, as in rape, murder or mutilation (although there are some B-movies, such as *Army of Darkness*, that managed to make that sort of humour work to some degree).

We can see the limits of aggression in humour when we look at tickling, that familiar physical provocation to laughter. Charles Darwin noted that tickling has rules.[9] He established four of these, which have interesting ramifications for our subject:

(1) First, you cannot tickle yourself. Auto-tickling is impossible, because it lacks the vital element of *surprise*.
(2) Second, you can't tickle just any old body-part, but only those areas that are not normally touched, or are touched only by the constant pressure of a flat surface. The belly or the soles of the feet are ideal. This is apparently because there needs to be some *recontextualization* in order to provoke laughter.
(3) Third, when you tickle someone, you have to put your heart into it, tickle him with gusto and keep moving your fingers around all over the place. The attack constituted by the tickling has to be *at once total and nil*.
(4) This leads to the final point, namely that you can tickle only your friends. You can't tickle total strangers, or your enemies, because the invasion of their personal space will then be a real threat and not a bogus one.

Plato recognizes this paradox that humour is at once aggressive and harmless when he says in the *Philebus* 48a-50b that we experience both pain and pleasure when we watch a comedy – pain, because the spectacle of a comic character ignoring the Delphic maxim "know thyself" is morally and

---

[8] On this whole subject, you might want to consult Conrad Lorenz, *On Aggression*, M. K. Wilson trans. (New York 1963).

[9] C. Darwin, *The Expression of the Emotions in Man and Animals.* 1872, ed. P. Eckerman (New York and Oxford 1998) 197-99.

aesthetically repugnant, and pleasure, because the comic hero is perforce weak, and therefore harmless (whereas an equally un-self-aware person, if endowed also with political power and the scope to bring other people down with him, would be not funny, but terrifying). This distinction between weak and strong, common-man and king, maps onto the distinction between comedy and tragedy.

We can see this better by understanding how the Greeks imagined the world. It was something like this:

$$\frac{\text{GODS}}{}$$

$$\frac{\text{US} \qquad\qquad \text{HEROES}}{}$$

ANIMALS

Note that the humanistic Greeks did not hesitate to put us humans at the centre of the world; "Man is the measure of all things," as Protagoras said (80 B 1 Diels-Kranz), and Archimedes also declared: "Give me a place to stand, and I will move the earth."(Pappus 8.11) The boundary between god and human is death, for we will all die eventually; but gods never will (heroes are humans who have *already* died; the closest thing we have to the Greek hero in the modern day is an Orthodox Christian or Roman Catholic saint, although the only heroes we hear about are the great ones). The boundary between human and animal consists of the two qualities that allow us to live in communities and make us, in Aristotle's words (*Pol.* 1253a3), "the political animal" ("political" itself being a Greek word from *polis*, for "city"). The first of these is shame (Greek *aidos*, Latin *pudor*), or the capacity to respond to the public pressure of praise and blame with corrective action, which made ancient Greece and Rome – in contrast to our own "guilt-culture" – a "shame-culture."[10] The second quality is justice. The Greek idea of justice centred on reciprocity, "giving to each person his due," in Simonides' words (642 *PMG*), or in practical terms helping friends and harming enemies.

The powerful who have nothing else left to strive for are sometimes seduced into trying to cross the boundary between god and human by failing to know themselves, defying death and acting as though they will live forever, all of which are VERY bad ideas. Greeks called such acts *hubris*. Hubris ends inevitably and often painfully in failure, and is the subject-matter of tragedy. Those at the lowest end of the social spectrum are sometimes tempted to defy the boundary that separates us from animals, trying to get something for nothing (i.e. unjustly) without caring who sees them do it (i.e. immodestly). This is what we call comedy.

---

[10] E. R. Dodds, *The Greeks and the Irrational* (Berkeley and Los Angeles 1964) 28-63.

Chapter II – Why is it Funny?

Humour and the Intellect

When it comes down to it, comedy is based on character. A funny situation just isn't funny unless it catches a certain kind of character a certain way. For example, two racers in a road rally disguised as medics while racing in an ambulance making bizarre excuses to a police officer while trying to explain why they were speeding is funny. An ambulance stopped on the side of the road by an upstart cop while somebody is dying in the back is not.

Clearly there are some situations in which the antics of a character are funny and others in which they are not. Where do we draw the line between them? Thomas Hobbes wrote:

> *Sudden Glory*, is the passion which maketh those *Grimaces* called LAUGHTER; and is caused either by some sudden act of their own, that pleaseth them; or by the apprehension of some deformed thing in another, by comparison whereof they suddenly applaud themselves.[1]

Not surprisingly, Hobbes' biggest insight into laughter is the idea of, well, surprise (indeed, he uses the word "sudden" three times in this little sentence). He also capitalizes on the notion of laughter being at the expense of somebody else's misfortune, of which the simplest example is physical deformity. This is certainly in keeping with a lot of ancient literature. Take, for example, this speech of Thersites from *Iliad* 2.225-77, which begins after describing the ugliness of Thersites, and how he has managed to annoy almost the entire Greek army:

> "Son of Atreus, what are you whining about and demanding now?
> Your tents are full of bronze, and many women
> are in those tents – choice ones, whom we Achaeans
> give you first of all, whenever we sack a citadel.
> Or do you still lack gold, which someone of the horse-taming
> Trojans may bring from Ilium as a ransom for his son,
> whom I might have bound and led away, or another of the Achaeans.
> Or is it a woman, so you might mingle with her in love
> and lock her up far from here? It's not right
> that, being a king, you lead the sons of the Achaeans into misfortune.
> You weaklings, shame on you! Achaeanettes, Achaeans no longer,
> let's go home in our ships, and let this one
> chew on his prizes here in Troy, so he might see
> whether we ourselves also help him or not –
> he who even now has dishonoured Achilles, a big man,
> better than him, for he's snatched and keeps his prize, having taken her himself.
> But Achilles has not much bile in his heart, but gives her up;
> or else, son of Atreus, you would have just committed your last outrage."

---

[1] T. Hobbes, *Leviathan* 1651, C. B. Macpherson ed. (Harmondsworth 1968) Part 1, Chapter 6, p. 125.

So he spoke, wrangling with Agamemnon, shepherd of the people,
did Thersites. Swiftly beside him stood godlike Odysseus,
and looking askance at him reproached him with a word:
  "Thersites, with no judgement of words, though being a shrill public
    speaker,
shut up. Don't wish to contend alone with kings:
for I say no other mortal is worse than you,
as many as have come with Atreus' son under Ilium.
So don't hold up your mouth and harangue the kings,
and bring rebukes to them and keep an eye on our homecoming
...."
  Just so he spoke, and with his staff the nape of his neck and two shoulders
he struck. And the other was bent double, and a moist tear fell from him,
and a bloody welt stood up out from under his nape
from the golden staff. He sat down and quivered,
and they, grieved though they were,[2] laughed sweetly at him,
and thus would one say, looking at another nearby:
  "Wow! Indeed Odysseus has done ten thousand good things,
leading good counsels and marshalling the war;
but now he has done this much the best thing among the Argives,
he who has checked this slanderous word-flinger out of assemblies.
Not indeed will his manly heart urge him back again
to quarrel with kings in reproachful words."

Now Thersites' speech is not very different from that of Achilles in the previous book of the *Iliad* (the last line, in fact, is lifted verbatim from it), but there Homer invites us to sympathize with Achilles' position. The difference here is that Thersites is no Achilles and he lacks the self-awareness to realize it, even though everybody else does. Therefore it is appropriate to humiliate and mock him, thus causing a comedic reversal of fortune that brings him down from the lofty heights on which he has placed himself to a new knowledge of his limitations and his place in society.

We call this rejoicing at the misfortunes of others using the German word *Schadenfreude*. The Greeks called it *epichairekakia*, and the most famous description of the phenomenon in the ancient world comes from the Roman author Lucretius. Here is his *The Nature of Things* 2.1-13:

Sweet it is, when winds stir up the surface of the high sea
to watch from land the great struggle of another;
not because there is delightful pleasure that someone is being harassed,
but because to see evils from which you yourself are free is sweet.
Sweet again to watch great contests of war
marshalled on the plains without yourself a share of the danger.
But nothing is finer than to hold what learning makes:
the well fortified, calm precincts of the wise,
whence you can look down and everywhere see others
wandering and errantly seeking the path of life:
striving with the mind, contending in rank,

---

[2] They were sorry that they had apparently lost the war, not that
Thersites has been humiliated.

and working day and night with surpassing effort
to rise to the heights and acquire material wealth.[3]

Immanuel Kant defined laughter as "an affection arising from a strained expectation being suddenly reduced to nothing."[4] He picks up on Hobbes' notion of surprise, but adds the idea of expectation, in other words a gap in knowledge between the (ignorantly) expected outcome and the real outcome, stressing also the greatness of the one and the triviality of the other. For example, if one is a diabolist attempting to summon the devil, one has expectations that the devil will be a massive, powerful being – it is therefore surprising and funny if the devil turns out to be five inches tall with a proclivity towards starting fights with bunny rabbits. This corresponds to a type of joke that the ancients called contrary to expectation (*para prosdokian*). This is clear in two examples. The first is from Aristophanes' *Frogs* 852-55, as Dionysus says:

> Hey, shut up, much-honoured Aeschylus!
> But, wretched Euripides, set yourself
> out of the way of the hailstones, if you're smart,
> lest with forehead bashed in by his wrath with some verbal
> masonry, you pour forth your Telephus.

Telephus was a notoriously terrible play by Euripides in which the title character, a stately Trojan king, appeared on stage – to the shock of the audience – in rags. So in place of an expected horrible thing (Euripides' brain oozing out), something trivial appears – the ragged king, or even worse, the play.

This second example is from Petronius *Satyricon* 54:

> Just when Gaius was saying these things, the boy fell onto Trimalchio's [arm].[5] The slaves shouted; no less did the guests – not because of so nauseating a person, whose very neck-bones they would have happily seen broken, but because of the bad ending to the dinner, if they would have to weep for a dead stranger...
> Nor did my suspicion stray far: in fact, in place of punishment, there came a decree of Trimalchio, whereby he ordered the boy to be free, so no-one would be able to say so great a man had been injured by a slave.

---

[3] German scholars call this rhetorical structure "a and b, but more so c" a *Priamel*, or "preamble." This particular example has been often parodied, cf. Byron, *Don Juan* I. cxxii-cxxvii, and Lautréamont, *Les Chants de Maldoror* II. xiii (see H. Juin ed. Paris, 1973 page 106 with note on page 420).

[4] I. Kant, *Critique of Judgement* 1790, J. C. Meredith trans. (Oxford 1952) Part I, Book II, Chapter 54.

[5] "Arm" or some such word has fallen out of the original text.

Humour and Ignorance

Charles Baudelaire once said something to the effect of: "The wise man does not laugh without trembling... The wise man par excellence, the incarnate Word, never laughed. In the eyes of him who has all knowledge and power, nothing comic exists."[6] This particularly emphasizes the notion of ignorance as a necessary part of humour.

While the Hebrew God is omniscient (Jeremiah 1.5, Acts 15.18), the Greek gods were not, permitting such divine *faux pas* as Demeter eating Pelops' shoulder in ignorance, or Zeus choosing thighbones wrapped in fat over Grade A sirloin at the world's first sacrifice. They therefore can, and do, laugh. Like others of their qualities, their laughter is special. Homer calls it *asbestos*, not "flame-proof and hazardous to everybody's health," as we mean by the word, but "inextinguishable."

There is a perfect illustration of the role of ignorance in humour in this passage from Apuleius *Metamorphoses* 2.31-3.10,[7] which also demonstrates a long-windedness that would make any politician proud:

> When Thelyphron first set out this tale, my fellow-drinkers, drenched in wine, again renewed their laughter. Meanwhile they called for drinking the usual toasts to Laughter. As Byrrhena explained to me: "Tomorrow," she said, "marks a solemn day established from the earliest cradle of this city, on which day we alone of mortals propitiate the most holy god, Laughter with a hilarious and joyful ritual. You will make it more pleasant for us by your presence, and I hope that from your own wit you might provide something funny to honour the god, so that we might more greatly and more fully satisfy so high a power."
>
> "Well," said I, "so be it, just as you command. And I wish, by Hercules, to find some material in which so great a god may be more richly clothed." After these words, at the suggestion of my slave, who was reminding me of the late hour, and being myself already far gone in drink, I carefully stood up, and, having said farewell to Byrrhena, with unsteady footsteps betook myself upon my homeward way.
>
> But as we went along the first street, by a sudden gust the torch on which we were relying was blown out, so that scarcely escaping the gloom of the unwelcoming night, with toes stubbed on cobbles, exhausted, we returned to our lodging.[8] While we were still drawing near – look! – three so-and-sos, lively and with pretty huge bodies, were rushing against our door with the greatest force, and not in the least perturbed by our presence, but jumping up all the more often in a contest of strength, so that to us – and to me in particular – they seemed not without reason to be robbers, and most savage ones at that. Next,

---

[6] C. Baudelaire, "De l'essence du rire" (1855) pages 975-93 in Y. G. le Dantec, Pléiade edition (Paris: Gallimard, 1961).

[7] This passage may have been the inspiration for Cervantes, *Don Quixote* Part 1 Chapter 35.

[8] Greeks, of course, had no streetlights. Streetlights were first installed on the Arcadian Way in Ephesus (in modern Turkey) during the Roman period.

I immediately drew from my side the sword that I am wont to carry fastened to my tunic for such occasions. Without hesitating, I flew into the midst of the robbers, and I plunged it very deeply into them, one by one, as I encountered each assailant, until at last before my very feet, punctured by deep and many wounds, they breathed out their last breaths. So having contended, when the house had been opened by [the servant-girl] Fotis, who had been awakened by all the commotion, panting and bathed in sweat, I crept in and immediately, as one exhausted not by a fight with three robbers but by the slaughter of Geryon,[9] handed myself over at one and the same moment to bed and to sleep.

....

Dawn, shaking her lovely pink arm, with purple reins was driving her car into the sky, when night handed me over to day, plucked from carefree slumber. Angst flooded my mind at the recollection of the night's crime. Then, with legs crossed and hands woven over my knees in an interlocking row of fingers, sitting back upon my couch, I wept copiously, already imagining the court and trial, already the sentence and finally the executioner himself. "How could I happen upon some judge mild and lenient enough that he would be able to pronounce me innocent, bathed as I am in the gore of triple slaughter, and smeared with the blood of so many of his fellow-citizens?..."

Repeatedly going over these things in my mind, I was bewailing my misfortunes. Meanwhile, the outer doors began to be struck, and the door to my room echoed with repeated shouting; without delay, when the house had been laid open, every part of it began to be filled with a huge influx – magistrates and their attendants, and the multitude of a jumbled crowd – and immediately two lictors[10] by order of the magistrates threw their hands upon me and began to drag me off, though I was plainly not resisting. As soon as we stood in the alley, immediately the whole citizen-body poured forth in public in a great press and followed us. And though I was walking sad with head cast down toward the ground – nay rather toward the very underworld –, nevertheless out of the corner of my eye I saw something worthy of great wonder: for among so many thousands of people thronging about me, there was nobody at all, who wasn't busting a gut laughing. However, when we had wandered around the whole main square (in the manner of those by whose cleansing atonements people expiate the threats of evil omens by leading prisoners round the forum), having been led round every corner, I was placed in the court and its dock. With the magistrates already sitting on the raised dias and the town-crier already shouting repeatedly for silence, everyone demanded as with one voice, because of the multitude of the throng, which was endangered by an excess of crowding, that the trial be moved to the theatre. No delay, when the populace running as one filled the enclosure of the seating-area with remarkable speed. Even the lobby and the whole balcony were closely packed, many clinging to the pillars, others hanging off statues, and not a few half visible looking in through windows and down from rafters, for all were neglecting the danger to their safety in their marvelous eagerness to see me. Then the public attendants led me forth across the middle of the stage like some sacrificial victim and stood me in the midst of the orchestra.

So again, urged on by the ample shouting of the town-crier, a certain senior

---

[9] A mythical monster with three bodies, killed by Hercules.

[10] The attendants assigned to a magistrate as a sign of the dignity of his office.

accuser leapt up, and, when water had been poured into a jug that had a pipe narrowly fitted into it instead of a stopper to measure the time of his speaking, and from which it was flowing out drop by drop, he thus addressed the people:

"No small matter, and one especially regarding the peace of the whole city, and one that will benefit from being made a serious example of is dealt with here, most worthy fellow-citizens. Wherefore, it befits you singly and collectively to look out with greatest care for the public welfare, lest any nefarious murderer, who has committed such bloody slaughter as this man has cruelly perpetrated, go unpunished. Nor should you think that I am motivated to be severe out of private animosity or personal hatred. For I am prefect of the night-watch, and to this day I think no-one is able to fault me in any way for my diligent work. So I will set forth in good faith the matter itself and what things were done in the night. When already for almost a third of my watch I had gone round observing the doorways one by one of the whole city with scrupulous care, I spotted this most cruel young man, with dagger drawn, unleashing slaughter everywhere, and already men three in number killed by his savagery lay before his very feet breathing their last, their bodies quivering in a pool of blood. And this man, rightly touched in his conscience by so great a crime, immediately fled, and having slipped into some house under cover of darkness, laid low the whole night through. But by the providence of the gods, which allows no deed of wrongdoers to go unpunished, before yon fellow could give us the slip with hidden flight, waiting until morning, I took care to lead him before the most heavy sentence of your judgement. So you have a criminal made sinful by such slaughter, a criminal caught red-handed, a foreign criminal! Therefore, calmly pass against this non-native the sentence for his crime as severely as you would avenge yourselves upon one of your own citizens."

My accuser, having spoken so bitterly, checked his savage voice, and immediately the town-crier ordered me to begin, if I had anything I wanted to say in response. But at that point in time, I could do no more than weep – not, by Hercules, thinking so much of the sullen accusation, as of my own wretched conscience. But, however, a boldness misbegotten from heaven led me to say this:

"I do not myself fail to recognize how hard a thing it will be for him who is charged with murder, when three bodies of your citizens are laid out before you, no matter how truthfully he may speak and to whatever fact he may confess, to persuade so great a multitude that he is innocent. Yet if your humanity will have accorded me a little public hearing, I will easily teach you that I wrongly face capital punishment, not for my own fault, but because of rational indignation, and by a chance circumstance your great outrage against this crime.

"For when I was bringing myself home from dinner later than usual, pretty drunk – for I will not hide my so obvious crime – before the very doors of my host – I refer here to your good fellow-citizen, Milo –, I saw these most savage robbers seeking entrance and wanting to tear the house-doors off their mangled hinges, with all the door-bolts (which had been most carefully pulled to) already violently thrust back, debating amongst themselves the murder of the inhabitants. Finally one of them, quicker of hand and taller of body, incited the others with these words: 'Come on, lads. Let's attack the sleepers with brave hearts and bold strength. Let all delay, all hesitation be put from your breasts. Let Slaughter stalk, with dagger drawn, though the whole house. Whoever lies sleeping, let him be stabbed; whoever tries to fight back, let him be wounded. That way we'll get away safe, if we leave no one safe inside the house.' I admit, gentlemen, that to put to flight these wild robbers and to scare them off, having judged it the duty of a good citizen, and at the same time fearing dreadfully both for my host and for myself, armed with my little sword, which always accompanies me because of dangers of this kind, I approached. But in short these barbarians, huge men, did not take flight, and when they saw me armed, still boldly stood their ground.

"The battle-lines were drawn. First, the leader himself and strong standard-bearer of the others attacked me with strength then and there, and grabbing me by the hair with both hands and forcing me backward, moved to kill me with a stone. When he ordered one to be handed to him, with a sure hand I struck him, and luckily knocked him down. And soon the second, as he clung by his teeth to my feet, I slew with a well-placed blow between the shoulders. I killed the third as he rushed at me thoughtlessly by stabbing him in the chest. So when the peace had been restored, and the house of my host and the common safety were protected, I trusted that I would be not just unpunished, but indeed publicly praised, who had never been prosecuted even for the smallest crime, but well respected in my own country and always valuing my innocence above all commodities. Nor can I understand why I now undergo this charge of just vengeance, since I acted against the vilest robbers, when no-one is able to show either that personal animosity pre-existed between us – and certainly none of those robbers was ever known to me – nor can any booty be clearly shown, in the desire for which so great a crime may be thought to have been committed."

Having said these things, again with tears springing up, and with hands stretched out in prayer, I was sadly begging now to these people, now to those for public pity and for some sign of mercy. Yet when I believed that they would all have been sufficiently moved by humanity and affected by pity through my tears, having appealed to the eye of the Sun and Justice, and recommending my present case to the providence of the gods, having lifted my face a little higher, I saw absolutely the whole populace happy – they had given themselves over to laughter – and no different was that good host and relative of mine, Milo, absolutely undone by laughter. Then in silence, "See his faithfulness!" I said to myself, "See his conscience! I who am both a homicide for the safety of my host and am lead to death-row, but he isn't happy yet, that he not only doesn't offer me the comfort of standing by me, but he even laughs at my death!"

While these things were happening, some woman ran through the middle of the theatre, teary and crying, clothed in a black dress and holding an infant to her breast, and right behind her an old hag covered in filthy rags, and both with equally sad weeping, and both shaking olive branches, who having poured over the stretcher on which the bodies of the murder-victims lay covered, with loud wailing they lamented mournfully: "For public pity, for the common law of humanity," they said, "take pity on these wrongly slain youths, and give to our bereavement and loneliness the comfort of vengeance. Surely help this poor little man abandoned by Fate in his early years, and from the blood of this robber appease your laws and public order!"

After these things, the magistrate who was in charge rose and said to the people such things, "From the crime, which must be earnestly vindicated, not even he who committed it can distance himself, but only one source of comfort remains for us: that we ask about the other henchmen in so great a crime. For it is not worthy of belief that a single man could have killed three such strong youths. Therefore the truth must be extracted by torture. For indeed the slave who accompanied him fled in secret and the matter has come to this point that under questioning he should indicate his comrades in crime so that the fear spread by so dire a gang might be suppressed."

No delay, when according to the Greek custom, fire and the wheel and every type of whip was brought in. My wretchedness was completely increased, nay rather doubled, to see that I wouldn't at least be allowed to die intact. But that hag who had destroyed everything with her weeping, said, "Best of citizens, before you nail yon robber – destroyer of my poor sweeties – to the cross, let him uncover the bodies of the slain, so that by the contemplation of their beauty and at the same time of their youth, more and more roused to righteous indignation, you will be outraged as fits the crime."

These things having been said, there was applause and immediately the magistrate ordered me myself to unveil with my own hand the bodies that were laid out on the stretchers. Though I hesitated and long delayed to revisit my former crime with a new revelation, the lictors forced me by order of the magistrates so insistently that finally thrusting my very hand from beside me they stretched it to its own ruin over the very bodies. Then overcome by such necessity, I gave in and, though against my will, with the cloth pulled back I revealed the bodies. 'Good gods: what crime is this? What portent?' Though already numbered among the property of Proserpina, and slaves of Orcus, suddenly I was frozen, stunned in the opposite state, nor am I able to explain the effect of this new image upon myself. For those corpses of slaughtered men, were three inflated wineskins, punctured with holes and, so far as I recalled my wrestling-match of the previous night, gaping in just those places in which I had wounded those 'robbers'.

Then that laughter that barely and with cunning had been suppressed, was freely kindled among the people.

The humour in this passage works on a number of levels. First, there is the ignorance of the narrator, leading to a slow build-up to the revelation of the practical joke. Then there is the build-up itself, which is comical. The trial does not take place in a courtroom, but is instead moved to a theatre, the wrong place for a trial, but precisely the right place for a show. The narrator, in his fear and confusion, does not notice any of this. Finally, there is the revelation of the true identities of the "victims," during which time the practical joke is revealed using the old comic trope of indirection.

There is also a religious aspect to this passage. The process of taking the narrator, accusing him of a crime he did not commit, and publicly placing the blame upon him is the beginning of a *Pharmakos*, or *scapegoat*, ritual, where, after a process of accusation, an individual "cleanses [the community] and is hit by wet noodles" before being sent into exile (Hipponax fr. 5 West, *IEG*).[11] In this case, however, the ritual is not completed. The narrator is not exiled from the community, although he does beat a hasty retreat from the festival.

Humour, the Body and the Emotions

Theories of the roles of ignorance, surprise, and expectation are all well and good, but they seem too cerebral to account for the physiological fact

---

[11] J. Bremmer, "Scapegoat Rituals in Ancient Greece," *HSCP* 87 (1983) 299-30.

that when something strikes us as funny, we have a physical reaction: we laugh. Let's face it – most people don't go through a process of evaluation of the humorous merits of a joke based on intellect, levels of ignorance, development of character, and intensity of humour before laughing – or at least, if they do, they don't get invited to too many parties.

This bothered Darwin's friend Herbert Spencer a lot (the former, not the latter, although if he was the sort who didn't get invited to too many parties, that might have bothered him too). He thought about the physiology of laughter and chose as his example an incident from his own life. He once went to a Shakespeare-in-the-park performance of *Romeo and Juliet*. Just at the great balcony scene where Romeo is calling to his beloved to appear on the balcony a goat wandered out of the park and started chewing on Romeo's rear. The audience burst out laughing, which had deleterious consequences for the performance of the tragedy (though the goat may very well have gone on to great things, or at least been gratified). Why did they react this way? Spencer wrote:

> Under any considerable tension, the nervous system in general discharges itself on the muscular system in general, either with or without the guidance of the will... In a man whose rear impels him to run, the mental tension generated is only in part transformed into a muscular stimulus: there is a *surplus* which causes a rapid current of ideas... The muscular actions constituting [laughter] are distinguished from most others by this, that they are *purposeless*. In general, bodily motions that are prompted by feelings are directed to special ends, as when we try to escape a danger, or struggle to secure a gratification. But the movements of chest and limbs which we make when laughing have no object... [Laughter occurs when] a large mass of emotion had been produced... The channels along which the discharge was about to take place are closed. The new channel opened... is a very small one... The excess must therefore discharge itself in some other direction.[12]

This theory of laughter as arising out of emotional tension deprived of its natural object accords well with the stories of Hephaestus' antics in *Iliad* 1 (see chapter VI) and Iambe's jests in the *Homeric Hymn to Demeter* (see chapter IX).

While Spencer enlarged the appreciation of humour to include the body, Freud enlarged it to include the emotions or what he called the Unconscious, that huge body of psychic matter of which we are not normally conscious, but which makes its presence felt through the imagery of dreams or those lapses of speech that we call, after their discoverer, "Freudian slips." In 1905 Freud wrote a book on jokes, which is obviously a subset of humour, except in the cases of terribly unfunny individuals. In this work he outlined three techniques of jokes.

(1) First there is condensation, in the sense of compression, exemplified by the title of Seneca's work *Apocolocyntosis,* "the 'Pumpkinification' of Claudius," (as opposed to *Apotheosis,* "the Deification of Claudius") in which

---

[12] H. Spencer, "The Physiology of Laughter," *MacMillan's Magazine* 1 (March 1860) 395-402 = *Essays* (London 1901) vol. 2 pages 146-47.

the Roman idea of deified emperors, the Stoic ideal of the spherical god, and the popular perception that Claudius was a clod all fuse together into one comic nonce-word suggesting a godlike emperor who could easily double as a beach ball.

(2) Then there is the multiple use of the same material. This is well illustrated by this excerpt from Petronius' *Satyricon* 36, which is a perfect illustration of the multiple use of the same material, most commonly known as the multiple use of the same material:

> No less than we, Trimalchio also pleased with this sort of joke, said, "Carve'er!" The server immediately appeared and, having gestured to the orchestra, carved the hors d'oeuvres so that you would think a gladiator was fighting to the accompaniment of an organist.[13] Nevertheless, Trimalchio carried on in a very slow voice: "Carve'er, Carve'er!" I, having suspected that the word so often repeated referred to some witticism, did not blush to ask this of him who sat beside me. And he, who had often seen jokes of this sort, said, "Do you see him who is carving the hors d'oeuvres? His name is 'Carver', so as often as he says, 'Carve'er', by the same word he both calls him and commands him."

(3) Freud's final joke strategy is the double meaning. We see this in Seneca's *Apocolocyntosis* 4.3:

> His last word heard among men was this, when he let slip a louder noise from that part by which he found it easiest to speak: "Oh no! I think I shat myself!" I bet he did. He certainly shat on everything else.

A more complicated example of the same phenomenon is in the Milesian tale of the Widow of Ephesus that Eumolpus, the wretched poet, tells his fellow travellers to calm their fears during a storm at sea. The story is as follows (Pet. *Sat.* 111-12):[14]

> There was a certain lady of Ephesus of such famous virtue that she drew women even from nearby nations to see her. Well, when this lady buried her husband, not content to follow the funeral-procession in the usual way with disheveled hair and naked breast, and weep in front of the crowd, she followed the body even into the tomb, and began to watch over the corpse that had been placed in an underground vault in the Greek manner and wept night and day. Neither her relatives nor her neighbours were able to stop her from torturing herself this way, and from driving herself to death through starvation. The magistrates at last, having been snubbed, departed, and this woman of singular example, widely mourned, was already spending her fifth day without food. Beside the wretched woman, a most faithful maid-servant sat and at once shed

---

[13] Ctesibius invented the pipe-organ in the third century B. C., but somehow it worked with water rather than air. He called it the "water-flute" (*hydraulos*) in Greek, which is the origin of our word *hydraulic*.

[14] See D. McGlathery, "Petronius' Tale of the Widow of Ephesus and Bakhtin's Material Bodily Lower Stratum," *Arethusa* 31 (1998) 313-36, with bibliography.

tears with her in her mourning and, whenever the lamp placed in the tomb went out, relit it. There was one subject of talk in the whole town. People of every rank admitted that this alone was a true example of virtue and love, when meanwhile the governor of the province ordered thieves to be nailed to crosses along the little road on which the lady had recently bewailed the corpse. So the next night when the soldier who was guarding the cross lest someone should take down one of the bodies for burial, remarked to himself a light shining rather brightly among the tomb-stones, and heard the groans of one mourning, and from human weakness yearned to know who or what was causing it. So he went down into the tomb, and shocked at the sight of the most beautiful woman, as though at a ghost or the shades of Hell, stood stock-still. Then, when he saw the lying man's corpse, and considered her tears and face without makeup, having realized what was going on, namely that the woman was not able to bear her yearning for the dead man, he brought his little dinner into the tomb and began to exhort the mourner not to carry on in completely useless sorrow and to tear her breast with groaning that could get her nothing: all people will have the same end, and come to the same dwelling, and the other things by which wounded minds are led back to health. But she ignored him, cast his words of comfort aside and beat her breast more violently and placed her torn-out hair upon the body of the lying man. The soldier did not give up, however, but tried with the same argument to give food to the poor woman, while the maid-servant, certainly broken down by the smell of his wine, first stretched out her hand, won over by the inviting man's hospitality, and then, refreshed by drink and food, began to tackle her mistress' stubbornness, and said, "What good will it do you if you die of starvation, if you bury yourself alive, if you give up your ghost unasked, before the Fates condemn it?[15]

Thinkst thou that this ash or buried shades can tell?[15] Don't you want to live again? Don't you want to cast off this womanly error and enjoy the pleasant light as long as will have been granted? The very body of the man lying here ought to urge you to live." No-one is unwilling to listen when they are urged either to eat food or to live. So the woman, having suffered dry abstinence for so many days, broke her stubbornness, and stuffed herself with food no less avidly than the maid-servant who had given in first. You know the rest, what a full stomach usually tempts people to. With the same blandishments with which the soldier had caused the woman to want to live he now laid siege to her very virtue. The young man did not seem unattractive or ineloquent to the virtuous woman. The maid suggested that she should show him some gratitude, and also said:

"Wilt thou struggle even against a pleasing love?" Need I say more? The woman did not even withhold that part of her body, and the conquering soldier persuaded her of that too. So they lay together not just on that one night on which they made their honeymoon, but also on the next and on the third day, naturally having shut the doors of the tomb, so that anyone, whether friend or stranger, who might come to the tomb would think that the most modest woman had expired over her husband's body. For the rest, the soldier, delighting both in the woman's looks and in their secret, bought whatever good things were within his means, and brought them to the tomb immediately on that first night. So when the relatives of one of the crucified men, having seen that the

---

[15] This episode is based on Dido's conversation with Elissa in Vergil, *Aeneid* book 4. That a Greek slave can aptly quote from Latin epic poetry may be part of the joke here.

watch had been relaxed, took down the hanged man by night and gave him the last rites. The soldier was by-passed while he was shirking his duty, and when the next day he saw one cross without a corpse, terrified of torture, explained to the woman what had happened. He would not wait for the judge's sentence, but would with his own sword exact the penalty for his desertion. So she should prepare a space for one about to die and let the fateful tomb be for her lover as well as her husband. The woman, no less sympathetic than virtuous, said, "May the gods not allow me at the same time to witness two funerals of the two men most dear to me. I would rather hang the dead than kill the living." Following this utterance, she told him to take her husband's body out of its coffin and nail it to that cross that was vacant. The soldier followed the very clever woman's plan, and the next day the people wondered how a dead man had gone to the cross.

This story ends with a pun in Latin: "go to the cross!" – meaning "go to Hell!" or "drop dead!" So, not only has the dead man managed to get up onto the cross, the pun suggests he has dropped dead again (which is hard to do). Freud concludes that:

> ...all these techniques are dominated by a tendency to compression, or rather to saving. It all seems to be a question of economy: brevity is the soul of wit. (pp. 41-42) The purposes of jokes can easily be reviewed. Where a joke is not an aim in itself – that is, where it is not an innocent one – there are only two purposes that it may serve, and these two can themselves be subsumed under a single heading. It is either a hostile joke (serving the purpose of aggressiveness, satire, or defence) or an obscene joke (serving the purpose of exposure) (pp. 96-97).[16]

Many classical examples come to mind, but for a great example of aggressive humour take Catullus 36. Catullus and his girlfriend, Lesbia have had a fight. He sent her some lampoons he had written at her expense. She vowed that if ever they got back together again, she would burn them, the works – she said – of the world's worst poet. Now reconciled, the couple faces a problem: how honestly to fulfill the vow, given that there's a much worse poet out there than Catullus:

> *Annals* of Volusius, used toilet-paper,
> fulfill a vow for my girlfriend,
> for she vowed to holy Venus and
> Cupid, that if I came back to her
> and stopped brandishing fierce lampoons,
> she would give some very choice writings
> of the worst poet to the slow-footed god[17]
> and burn them on unlucky logs.
> And the worst girlfriend thought she
> was making a witty vow to joking gods.

---

[16] S. Freud, "Jokes and their Relation to the Unconscious (1905)," *Standard Edition of the Complete Psychological Works* volume 8 (London 1960), with some help from Polonius (Shakespeare, *Hamlet* II.ii.90).

[17] Vulcan, god of fire, slow-footed, because he was lame.

....
But you, meanwhile, come into the fire
full of the countryside and ineptitude,
Annals of Volusius, used toilet-paper!

When one looks at the humour of Greeks and Romans, it quickly becomes clear that there is very little we could teach them about toilet humour. In fact, they could probably teach us a thing or two. As an example of obscenity take this passage from Aristophanes' *Clouds* 1088-1108. Two Arguments, the Lesser and the Stronger are (what else?) arguing. The topic of the debate is whether or not it hurts to have a radish shoved up your ass.[18] Well, it would, says Lesser Argument, unless you were an asshole. He then goes on to show that for most people, therefore, it wouldn't hurt a bit:

Lesser Argument: Come, tell me,
    who are our lawyers?
Greater Argument: Assholes.
L   I believe you.
    Now, who are our tragedians?
G   Assholes.
L   You're right!
    And who are our politicians?
G   Assholes.
L   Well then,
    do you see how foolish you were?
    Look at who most of the audience are.
G   I'm looking.
L   What do you see?
G   By the gods –
    many more assholes!

So just why is laughing fun? Why do we enjoy humour? Freud has a good form-follows-function answer:

> The pleasure in the case of a tendentious joke [i.e. one with an ulterior motive of aggression or obscenity] arises from a purpose being satisfied whose satisfaction would otherwise not have taken place... (The factor inhibiting this satisfaction may be external, e.g. fear of offending someone powerful, or internal, i.e. psychical, e.g. good taste and breading.) [B]oth for erecting and for maintaining a psychical inhibition some "psychical expenditure" is required. And, since we know that in both cases of the use of tendentious jokes pleasure is obtained, it is therefore plausible to suppose that *this yield of pleasure corresponds to the psychical expenditure that is saved.*

This analysis, by focussing on the saving of repression and on license, relates to the two loci of much of ancient humour, the public festivals of Dionysus, wherein one might find the comedies of Aristophanes and

---

[18] Yes, you heard correctly, a radish shoved up your ass. For more on this and related themes, see Chapter IX.

Menander, and the private symposia, exemplified in Plato's and Xenophon's *Symposia* and the Trimalchio-episode of Petronius' *Satyricon*, in which special license was granted to break normal social taboos. It is when we look here that we find one of the true foundations of all ancient humour – society, and how an individual relates to it.

Chapter III – A Funny World

Humour and Society

The interplay between the individual and society changes from culture to culture. In the modern day and age we have the concept of the "tyranny of the masses," but we are a society that values individual rights over the rights of society, and frequently over common sense. In the ancient world, the idea of the individual taking priority over society was a comical one. Humour was, in the end, grounded firmly in society.

Two opposing theories that root humour in society are of particular note. Let us begin with the French philosopher Henri Bergson. Bergson was born in the year in which Charles Darwin published his *Origin of Species*, and the entire life's work of this long-lived and prolific author can be seen as a response to the philosophical challenges posed by Darwin's theory of evolution (it can also be seen as a collection of letters formed into words that contain meaning, but this tends to be a less productive approach).

It is possible to read Darwin's theory as depicting the earth as a factory in which two arbitrary forces, chance random mutation and natural selection, exist in a Malthusian world of competition for limited resources in which living things, humans included, are just raw material fed into a machine that spits out at the end of the assembly-line every so often a new species, and refuses to offer a warranty, or even a return policy, when that snazzy third arm just refuses to work properly. This determinist view horrified Bergson, and he developed the idea that there is in all living things, and *a fortiori* in humans, a life-force, which, being French, he called the *élan vital*, which responds to the changing needs of new situations, modifying and adapting to each. Thanks to this force, we are not just raw material, putty or pawns, but active agents in the process of species-creation, and in the world as a whole.

In 1900 Bergson published his book, *Laughter*, which locates humorous behaviour in failures to listen to this life-force, and posits laughter as society's corrective to such behaviour. In its own way this theory nicely expresses many of the ancient ideas about humour that we have seen so far. Bergson writes:

> The comic will come into being, it appears, whenever a group of men concentrate their attention on one of their number, imposing silence on their emotions and calling into play nothing but their intelligence.[1]

This idea of the social nature of humour is linked to the readily observable fact that, unlike Snidely Whiplash from *Rocky and Bullwinkle*, we seldom laugh when we are alone. St. Augustine describes in his *Confessions* some forbidden fruit that, like Adam and Eve (on whom see Chapter IV), he and his friends stole when they were boys, and adds to it a reflection on this

---

[1] H. Bergson, *Laughter: An Essay on the Meaning of the Comic* 1900, C. Brerton and F. Rothwell trans. (New York 1911) 8.

aspect of laughter (2.4, 9):

> Surely, Lord, your law and the law written on the hearts of men, which no sin erases, punishes theft; for what thief can stand a thief? Not even a rich one one driven by poverty. But I wanted to commit a theft, and I did it compelled by no need except for a lack of, and distaste for righteousness, and bursting with wickedness. For I was going to steal what I had lots of, and much better too. Nor did I want in the event to enjoy what I had sought out by theft, but the theft and the sin itself. There was a pear-tree near our vineyard heavy with fruit, seductive neither in shape nor in taste. We most vile teenagers came in the depths of night to shake down and carry them away, until which time we had prolonged our fun like a plague in vacant lots.[2] From there we carried off a great weight of them not to our own banquets, but just to throw to the pigs; even if we ate a few, what was done by us was pleasant to us in so far as it was not right (*eo liberet, quo non liceret*)[3]...
>
> What was that state of mind? Surely indeed it was plainly and excessively bad, and woe to me that I had it. But, however, what was it? Who understands his own errors? There was laughter as of a tickled heart, because we were deceiving those who did not know what was being done by us, and would violently have objected. Therefore, why did it delight me in so far as I was not doing it alone? Is it indeed that no-one easily laughs alone? No-one does so easily, yet however laughter sometimes conquers men even alone and singly, when no-one is present, if something very ridiculous happens upon their sense or their thought. But I would not have done it alone; I would not at all have done it alone.

Bergson goes on to say that "A comic character is generally comic in proportion to his ignorance of himself" (page 16). This reminds us of the Aesopic fable of the faults of men (Phaedrus 4.10):

> Jupiter has placed on us two packs, one full of our vices he has given us behind our backs, one heavy with others' he's hung before our chest. For this reason we aren't able to see our own, but as soon as others err, we blame them.

Moreover, Bergson writes that "*Something mechanical encrusted on the living,* will represent a cross at which we must halt, a central image from which the imagination branches off in different directions" (pages 37-38). By "something mechanical" Bergson refers to an action that has become mechanical, and by being mechanical, draws our attention to the person performing that action, such as continuing to laugh long after a joke has ceased to be funny. This idea is well illustrated by *Iliad* 6.466-81, in the last conversation between Hector and his wife Andromache:

> So speaking, glorious Hector reached out to his son,

---

[2] This is an echo of one of Cicero's speeches against Cataline, whose conspiracy fatally weakened the Roman republic. Augustine is pretty impressed by the magnitude of his own theft!

[3] A pun that Dante would plagiarize in his description of Semiramis (*Inf.* 5.56): *che libito fè licito in sua legge.*

and immediately the child leaned back into the bosom of his shapely nurse
crying, shocked at the sight of his own father,
frightened by the bronze and the horse-hair crest,
when he saw it nodding dreadfully from the top of his helmet.
His own father laughed, as did his lady mother.
Immediately glorious Hector took from his head the helmet
and placed it brightly shining on the ground.
Yet he at least, when he had kissed his own son and swung him in his arms,
said, praying to Zeus and the other immortals:
"Zeus and you other gods, allow that this one –
my child – may become, as I surely am, outstanding among the Trojans
and likewise good in strength and rule over Ilium with force:
and sometime may one say, 'This one is much better even than his father'
when he comes home from war. And may he bring gory booty
having killed a warlike man, and may his mother feel joy in her heart."

If ever there were something mechanical encrusted on the living it is an
ancient war-helmet, and this is not just a physical thing, but a habit of mind,
for Hector has forgotten to leave his work at the office, so to speak, and has
brought his military mentality with him back from the battle-field into the
bosom of his family. (This is clear from the prayer for his son that ends this
quotation: he cannot even conceive of praying with Thomas Paine, "If there
must be trouble, let it be in my day, that my child may have peace."[4] No:
Hector knows only how to hope for yet bloodier victories for the boy.) When
we first see him and Andromache laughing, we might think that they are
laughing at the baby who does not recognize his own father, and this is
certainly plausible – Greeks did not find babies cute, but thought that they
were idiots; in fact the word for baby, *nepios* (literally "in-fant," "not
speaking") comes as early as the *Iliad* to mean "idiot." Soon, however, we see
that it is Hector who is laughed at, for he is the one behaving inappropriately
by dressing as a warrior while in the bosom of his family, and the laughter
has the desired corrective effect, because he immediately takes off the
offending helmet, and sets it on the ground.

Again Bergson writes that "This rigidity is the comic, and laughter is its
corrective" (page 21). We see this constant repetition of a single kind of
behaviour even in inappropriate circumstances in Catullus' poem 39 on one
of his girlfriend, Clodia Metelli's, other lovers, Egnatius:

Egnatius, because he has white teeth,
smiles everywhere he goes. If he has come to
the court, where a lawyer is provoking a tear,
the guy smiles; if by the pyre of a dutiful son
they are mourning, when the bereft mother bewails her only son,
the guy smiles. Whatever it is, wherever it is,
whatever is going on, he smiles: he has this sickness,
neither elegant, I think, nor urbane.
So I've got to point it out to you, good Egnatius:
if you were a city-slicker Sabine or Tiber-dweller,

---

[4] T. Paine, *The American Crisis* No. 1 (Dec. 19, 1776).

or a poor Umbrian, or fat Etruscan,
or a black Lanuvian, or a toothy man
from beyond the Po (to add my own people to the list),
or anyone at all, who washes their teeth cleanly,
I would still not want you smiling everywhere,
for nothing is more inept than inept laughter.
But you're a Spaniard. In Spanish lands
what each one has pissed he uses in the morning
to scrub his teeth and rosy gums[5]
so that, the more polished are your teeth,
the more piss we know you've drunk!

As to the use of laughter as a corrective, there are many examples of that, such as the stories of Ares and Aphrodite or that of Archilochus and Lycambe (also known as the stories-that-are-not-appearing-in-this-chapter).

Bergson's theory makes good sense, and explains a number of passages of ancient literature, but it is based on the presupposition that society is always right and the deviant individual always wrong, and in need of correction. But what if society isn't right, and it is the non-conformist individual who is?

Sicilian playwright Luigi Pirandello thought that society, and its most basic manifestation – the family – was a trap. Once one became ensnared in society's web, the essence of one's person was subdued, one's individuality lost. If this is so, then we must welcome the behaviour of characters in the Theophrastean sense as liberators from suffocating convention. We catch a glimpse of this anarchic point of view in Pirandello's 1908 essay *On Humour:*[6]

Yes, an epic or dramatic poet may represent a hero of his in whom opposite and contrasting elements are shown in conflict, but he will *compose* a character from these elements and will want to represent him as consistent in every action. Well, the humorist does just the opposite: he will *decompose* the character into his elements and while the epic or dramatic poet takes pains to picture him as coherent in every action, the humorist enjoys representing him in his incongruities.

Perhaps Pirandello's most famous play is *Six Characters in Search of an Author* (1921). This play begins in a theatre with a theatrical troupe rehearsing for a performance of a play by Luigi Pirandello. They are interrupted by a group of six characters who burst in and demand to take over the stage so that their story can be told. It emerges that they have been going around for some time in search of an author, and we see their scenes performed over and over again as they try to establish for the actors their story. One of the characters in the play says to the stage-manager:

---

[5] This was apparently true; see Diod. Sic. 5.33.5 and Strabo 3.4.16.

[6] L. Pirandello 1908 *On Humor*, trans. A. Illiano and D. P. Testa. (Chapel Hill, 1960) 143.

A Character, sir, can always ask a man who he is. Because a character really has his own life, as shown by his traits, for which reason he is always "somebody," while a man – I'm not talking about you in particular, but a man in general – can be nobody.

This celebration of being a character as a positive virtue, and breaking the norms and conventions of society as a noble mission recalls the ancient philosopher Diogenes. Diogenes Laertius (no relation) says this of him (*Diog.* 20):

> Diogenes, son of the banker Hicesius of Sinope: Diocles says that when his father ran the public bank and had corrupted the coinage (*paracharazantos to nomisma*), he went into exile. But Eubulides in his *On Diogenes* says that Diogenes himself did this, and was exiled along with his father. Moreover, Diogenes says about himself in his *Pordalus* that he corrupted the coinage.[7]

It's not really clear what Diogenes did to the money that got him into trouble, but the verb *paracharasso* is related to the verb *charasso*, which was the source of the word "character." Also, the word used here for "coinage" (*nomisma*) can also mean "customs," so Diogenes built a new character on the customs of his society (or perhaps drew moustaches on the faces of the coins – anything is possible).

When he arrived as an exile in Athens, Diogenes fell under the sway of Socrates and his eccentric (*atopos*) indifference to the needs of the body – as in the story, which we will consider in Chapter VIII, of his refusal to have sex with Alcibiades, despite that young man's great beauty. Diogenes preached a doctrine that happiness comes from self-sufficiency (*autarkeia*), and since it is easier to be self-sufficient by training oneself to limit one's wants rather than by increasing one's wealth, Diogenes led the simplest life he could, living in the marketplace in a barrel (the ancient equivalent of living in a cardboard box over a heating-grate). One day someone passed his barrel as he was masturbating and called him a dirty old man. He replied that if he could stop his hunger-pangs by rubbing his stomach, he'd do that too (Diog. Laert. 6.46).[8] This flouting of modesty led Plato to call him the Dog (*kuon*, related to our word "hound"), dogs being the symbol par excellence of shamelessness. It is from this nickname that the title of Cynic comes, which applies to Diogenes and his followers (Diog. Laert. 6.40).

Diogenes had various humorous adventures usually associated with witty quips (*chreiai*). Among the most famous are two stories. He once walked around in broad daylight with a lit lamp claiming that he was looking for an honest man (Diog. Laert. 6.41). Another day, Alexander the Great came to him as he was sunbathing in the Craneum and asked him what he,

---

[7] R. B. Branham, "Defacing the Currency: Diogenes' Rhetoric and the Invention of Cynicism," *Arethusa* 27 (1994) 329-59.

[8] This may, in part, be a parody of the Epicurean ideal of self-sufficiency (*autarkeia*).

Alexander could do for him. Diogenes replied, "Get out of my sun" (Diog. Laert. 6.38).

Humour and the Underdog

On the other hand (or, since this is a third theory, one of the feet), René Girard analysed society in terms of mimetic desire, the process whereby we want what our neighbour wants simply because he wants it. This is different from jealousy, where we want what our neighbour already has, because in mimetic desire we both love our neighbour (hence our imitation of him – the sincerest form of flattery – in wanting what he wants) and hate him, as he is our rival in the quest for the longed-for goal. Whenever there is a crisis in society, say a drought or a plague, then the stress caused by mimetic desire becomes unbearable, and society has to find a scapegoat to blame, and to thrust out of the community. This doesn't actually solve any of the problems caused by the crisis, but it makes everybody feel a lot better (well, except for the poor scapegoat, but he doesn't count – after all, he's to blame for it all, and therefore justly tossed out).

Girard's favourite text for illustrating this tendency is Sophocles *Oedipus Rex* in which, according to him,[9] Oedipus is actually innocent of killing the former king (who is not, again according to Girard, his father) and of sleeping with his mother. He is convicted of these crimes – but it might just as well have been Creon or Teiresias who was convicted of them – because there is a plague, innocent people are dying, and *someone* has to pay.

Girard begins his essay "Perilous Balance: A Comic Hypothesis,"[10] by reading Molière's *Bourgeois gentilhomme* and noting that the way in which the various teachers whom the title-character, M. Jordan, has just hired for himself, seek to accuse each other of quackery (a phenomenon that will be more fully explored in Chapter VI) in order to get for themselves the exclusive attention of this wealthy burgher whose sudden desire for education is the springboard of the action, mirrors the attempts in Sophocles' tragedy of Creon, Oedipus and Teiresias to accuse one another of regicide (murder of the previous king), and therefore of causing the plague.

If this comedy is structured so much like the greatest of all tragedies, Girard asks, what is the relationship of comedy to tragedy, laughter to tears? Are they equal but opposite, yin and yang, like the paired masks that are their emblems? Or is comedy derived from tragedy – it certainly is historically more recent – with the series of moocher (flatterer and buffoon), quack, sucker and ironist parodically mirroring the tragic series of persuader (tempter, seducer), hubristic hero, imperilled community, and temperate adviser? Or, finally, does comedy include tragedy as part of itself, in much the same way that Desmond Morris says that in terms of the evolution of our

---

[9] But he is wrong, see R. D. Griffith, *The Theatre of Apollo* (Montreal and Kingston 1996) 29-44.

[10] *MLN* 87 (1972) 811-26.

species we cried until we laughed?[11] Girard opts for the third of these answers.

We cry when we are in crisis. Indeed tears are, at the physical level, an attempt to expel a foreign particle from the eye. When we cry from sadness our eye is enacting a metaphor, trying to drive out an unwanted emotion through physical action. Laughter, with its unseemly convulsions, is also a result of crisis, but it is a greater, more threatening crisis, because one who laughs is always at risk of being enveloped in the pattern that she is laughing at, as when in a skating rink a skater falls on the ice and others, laughing at her misfortune, loose their own balance and fall in turn, causing the people around the rink to laugh and then slip on the ice outside the rink that somebody forgot to clear off, and thus causing a multi-million dollar lawsuit. In comedy there is no place of refuge for the disinterested observer; we are all potential butts of comic jest.

This is well exemplified in the *Odyssey*. In that poem Odysseus laughs only once, and that silently, to himself. This is in 9.413-19 when the other Cyclopes have just gone away from Polyphemus' cave, having concluded that they cannot help him, since Nobody is blinding him. Odysseus says:

> So they spoke as they went away and my own heart laughed,
> because my name and blameless stratagem had tricked him.
> But the Cyclops, groaning and suffering sufferings,
> groping with his hands, took the stone from the door
> and placed himself in the doorway spreading his hands,
> so that he might perhaps catch someone sneaking out the door with the sheep,
> for he hoped perhaps that I was stupid enough in my heart.

In contrast to Odysseus' circumspection, the suitors of Penelope laugh readily. Compare 18.90-107, which describes the boxing match between Odysseus (disguised as a beggar) and the suitor's real pet-beggar, Irus:

> Then much-suffering, god-like Odysseus pondered
> whether to strike so that his soul would leave him fallen there,
> or to strike him lightly and just stretch him on the ground.
> And to him, as he thought, it seemed better
> to hit lightly, so the Achaeans wouldn't suspect.
> They both put up their dukes. Irus struck
> his right shoulder, and Odysseus struck his neck under the ear
> and crushed the bones within. Purple blood came out his mouth,
> and he fell to the dust, bleating, and struck it with his teeth,
> kicking the ground with his feet. Yet the suitors, happy,
> put up *their* hands and died laughing.[12] Yet Odysseus
> dragged him out through the porch, having seized him by the foot, so he would go to
> the courtyard and the doors of the verandah, and he propped him up,

---

[11] D. Morris, *The Naked Ape* (New York 1967) 116.

[12] Compare "I was withered from laughing" Aristophanes *Frogs* 1089-90.

leaning against the courtyard-fence, and put a sceptre in his hands.[13]
And having addressed him, he spoke a winged word:
"Sit here now, keeping pigs and dogs at bay,
but do not be lord of strangers and beggars at least,
since you're a pest, or some greater misfortune may befall you."

The idea of the suitors dying laughing comes all too literally true in 20.338-58, in which Telemachus dares to stand up to them:

Thoughtfully in turn Telemachus addressed him:
"No, by Zeus, Agelaus, and by my father's sufferings,
– who perhaps has died far from Ithaca, or who is still wandering –
I'm not putting off my mother's wedding, and I tell her
to marry whomever she wants, and I'll be giving undescribable gifts.
But I am ashamed to drive her against her will from the halls
with a harsh word. May God not bring that to pass!"
So spoke Telemachus. And among the suitors Pallas Athena
stirred up unquenchable (*asbestos*) laughter, and their wits she dashed aside.
They were already laughing with other people's jaws
and were already eating meat defiled with blood, and their eyes
filled with tears, and their hearts were thinking of weeping.
Among them Theoclymenus, the seer spoke:
"Oh wretches, what is this dreadful thing you suffer? By night
your heads and faces and knees beneath are veiled,
groaning has been kindled, your cheeks are tear-streaked,
and the walls have been sprinkled with blood and the beautiful tie-beams:[14]
the forecourt is full – full too the hall – of ghosts
coming up from the gloom of Erebus, and the sun
has died out of the sky, and an evil fog run over us."
So he spoke, and they all laughed sweetly at him.

Indeed, very shortly after this macabre episode Odysseus slays them all.

The idea of expulsion, so central to Girard's understanding of the world, has a comic aspect, because crises are often resolved by the expulsion, through laughter of (or more often, at) a scapegoat. This may be true in the case of Thersites, which we considered in the previous chapter, who pays with his humiliation for the anxiety of all the Greeks.[15] Encolpius in Petronius *Satyricon* began the wanderings that are the subject of this novel after having served as a scapegoat in Marseille after the wrath of Priapus, the ithyphallic scarecrow god, was visited upon that city, if we can trust a comment of the ancient Roman scholar, Servius (on Verg. *Aen.* 3.57):

---

[13] Irus is no longer a real human being; he has cartoonishly become an inanimate object for Odysseus to arrange like a doll.

[14] Compare the scene in Bela Bartok's opera *Bluebeard's Castle* where the castle-walls bleed.

[15] That at least is the view of W. G. Thalmann, "Thersites: Comedy, Scapegoats and Heroic Ideology in the *Iliad*," *TAPA* 118 (1988) 1-28.

Sacred: that is "accursed." It is derived from the French. For as often as the citizens of Marseille suffered a plague, one of the homeless would volunteer to be fed for a whole year at public expense, and on pretty fine foods. After this, decked out with a *bouquet garnis* and sacred clothes, he was led round the town with curses, so that he might absorb within himself the evils of the whole city, and then he was cast out. One reads of this in Petronius.

As previously mentioned, this custom, or something very like it, may underlie the festival of Laughter episode of Apuleius' *Metamorphoses* recounted in Chapter II, where Lucius says:

> However, when we had wandered around the whole main square (in the manner of those by whose cleansing atonements people expiate the threat of evil omens by leading prisoners round the forum), having been led round every corner, I was placed in the court and its dock. With the magistrates already sitting on the raised dias and the town-crier already shouting repeatedly for silence, everyone demanded as with one voice, because of the multitude of the throng, which was endangered by an excess of crowding, that the trial be moved to the theatre.

Humour Against Authority

On yet another hand... er... foot, Mary Douglas takes as the starting point of her essays "Do Dogs Laugh?" and "Jokes"[16] a fieldwork study by F. Barth of a Norwegian fishing community.[17] Barth describes the fishing operation he observed in this way:

> The statuses involved in these operations are defined by contract: a *skipper* with right of command on the vessel, including the direction of the course and the decision to lower the net-casting boats, a *netboss* who, once the boats have been lowered, has the right to command and direct the casting and drawing from his small motor launch, and finally two groups each of six *fishermen* who perform the manual work....
>
> The *netboss* acts out a very different role [from the *skipper*]: he is spontaneous, argues and jokes... [H]is joking behaviour is a constant denial of any claim to authority on the bridge in challenge of the skipper and is in this respect in marked contrast to the institutionalized pattern of gross and continual cursing and assertion of authority on his part during the net-casting operation.

This social situation makes Douglas think of the role of humour in inverting social structures, not specific ones necessarily, but the very principal of social structure as such. Just as political cartoonists do not rejoice when a given government is defeated at the polls (actually, they are more apt to lament their fate, because now they have to find creative ways to lampoon

---

[16] In *Implicit Meanings* (London 1975) 83-114.

[17] F. Barth, *Models of Social Organization* = *Royal Anthropological Institute Occasional Paper* 23 (Glasgow 1966).

the new leaders instead of relying on the familiar old jokes), so jokes in general do not aim at political revolution. In that sense they are frivolous, but create an "exhilarating sense of freedom from form in general." This social inversion mirrors the inversion of control of the conscious over unconscious mind noted by Freud, as well as the inversion of control of the mind over the body noted by Spencer.

We will see one ancient political joke in Chapter IX in the women's milling song from Lesbos, but for the moment we'll recount it here (*Carm. Pop.* 869 Page):

> Grind, mill, grind,
> for Pittacus always grinds
> as he rules over great Mytilene.

This is a political poem with multiple meanings. The first is in regards to Pittacus oppressing his people, where Pittacus continues to "grind on" in laying on the oppression. A second possible meaning is sexual, suggesting that even Pittacus "grinds on," or has sex – which itself reverts back to the political, as through his oppression he is screwing his population.

Let's now look at two other examples – one Greek and one Roman.

First the Greek. Thucydides 4.28 describes events in 425 B.C., a year in which the war with Sparta was going very badly. There was a powerful politician named Cleon who was the son of a tanner, and brought the coarse language of his background into the political arena that had hitherto been used to more refined modes of speech. This was a refreshing change, and Cleon won some popularity. Cleon tried to capitalize on his popularity by lambasting one of the generals, Nicias, for his continued lack of success. Thucydides picks up the story at the point at which Nicias suddenly turns the tables on him by offering to swap places with him:

> Now Nicias – when the Athenians were beginning to make a clamour against Cleon, asking why he didn't sail right now, if it seemed so easy to him at least – and at the same time seeing himself being blamed, told him to take whatever force he wanted, and see what would happen on his own watch. First of all, Cleon, thinking this was given to him in word alone, was ready, but when he realized that the other was really handing over power, started to back-peddle, and said that not he himself, but rather Nicias was the general. Now he was afraid, and scarcely believed that Nicias would dare to give power to him. But immediately Nicias issued an order, in which he stood aside from the command in Pylos, and called the Athenians as his witnesses. And they, as crowds love to do, the more that Cleon tried to escape from sailing and to back out of the things that he had said, the more they told Nicias to hand over power, and shouted at Cleon to sail, so that, not being able any longer to be set free from the things that had been said, he submitted to sailing, and coming forward, he swore that... within twenty days he would either bring back the Spartans alive, or else die trying. And some degree of laughter fell on the Athenians at his light talk, and the wise among them were glad, considering that they had happened upon one of two good things – either they would be free of Cleon (which they were rather

expecting), or, if they were deceived in their expectation, the Spartans would be defeated by them.

Cleon makes his arrangements, and in a truly politically savvy move, chooses a general named Demosthenes, who is already planning a landing, to help lead the troops. Now, contrary to all probability, and possibly one or two laws of physics, Cleon succeeded in capitalizing on the planning-work already done by Demosthenes and returned victorious within the stated twenty days. Aristophanes was furious and in 424 staged the *Knights,* in which a man named Demus (i.e. the sovereign People of Athens) has two slaves, Nicias and Demosthenes, and acquires another one, a tanner named Paphlagon,[18] who steals the cakes baked by the other two slaves and serves them to his master as his own handiwork. Here are lines 40-70 of the play (Demosthenes is speaking):

> We two have a master,
> rustic in temperament, a bean-chewer,[19] irascible,
> Demus of the deme Pnyx: dyspeptic little gaffer,
> a bit deaf. Last month he
> bought a slave, a Paphlagonian tanner,
> a most villainous and slanderous fellow.
> This man, this leather Paphlagonian, when he learned
> the old man's nature, falling down before our master
> wheedled, fawned, flattered, deceived
> with the ends of leather scraps, saying such things as these:
> "Oh Demus, having judged one case, get in
> your bath, gulp, gnaw, get your pay.
> Do you want me to set your dinner-table?" Then having snatched up
> whatever thing one of us may have prepared, the Paphlagonian
> makes a gift of it to our master. Why, the day before yesterday,
> a loaf of bread I'd kneaded into a Spartan cake at Pylos, he most villainously ran
> round and somehow snatched,
> and he served up the loaf kneaded by me.
> But us he drives away, and doesn't let anyone else
> serve our master, but holding a leather thong
> he stands by while he eats, shooing away the speakers.
> He chants oracles, and the old man wants the Sibyl.
> And when he sees that he's gone crazy,
> he works his skill: he outright slanders
> those within with lies, and then we get whipped.
> The Paphlagonian runs round begging from the slaves,
> disturbing, getting gifts, saying these things:
> "Did you see Hylas flogged because of me?

---

[18] Paphlagonia was a country on the Black Sea in present-day Turkey. The word sounds rather like *paphlazein*, "to splutter."

[19] Beans were the ancient equivalent of chewing-gum: only slack-jawed yokels chewed them. But there were also used to draw lots for public office (those who got white ones were chosen, those who got black ones lost).

If you don't please me, you'll die today!"
And we give him things. Otherwise, having eaten
eight times as much from our master, we shit![20]

Now let us turn to Rome. Among the children of Ap. Claudius Pulcher were a son, P. Clodius Pulcher, and a daughter, Clodia. It was she who married Q. Caecilius Metellus Celer, and, as lover of C. Valerius Catullus earned the nickname "Lesbia." Catullus went to Bithynia in 59 to take over the family business, whatever that was (quite possibly an import-export) from his brother who had died there unexpectedly. Out of sight, out of mind – Clodia took up with M. Caelius Rufus. At about the same time Metellus died suddenly. Caelius was very young, ambitious and tried to make a name for himself by attacking Herennus, who was defended by one M. Tullius Cicero (Caelius lost). Then Caelius grew tired of Clodia and moved on, a move that sent Clodia into a fury. She was outraged, for *she* left other men – she was never *left* by them – and Clodia accused Caelius in 56 of trying to poison her. Now Caelius knew a good lawyer when he saw one, and hired Cicero to defend him.

Here is Catullus' poem 79:

Lesbius is handsome (*Lesbius est pulcher*). Why not?
  Lesbia prefers him to you and all your clan, Catullus.
But, however, this handsome man would sell Catullus, clan and all
  if he could get three kisses from his friends.

This poem works by a kind of mathematical analogy. If Lesbia is Clodia, then Lesbius is Clodius, who really is not just *pulcher*, "handsome" but Pulcher – that's his name.[21] This is apparently one of the "hate poems" that Catullus wrote about Lesbia/Clodia after their rupture. In it he accuses the siblings of incestuous feelings for one another. This rumour was wide-spread if we trust Cicero's letters to his friend Atticus, in which he calls Clodia *boopis*, "ox-eyes," Homer's epithet for Hera. (Hera married her own brother, Zeus).[22] Here is a letter that Cicero wrote to Atticus (*ad Att.* 2.12) from the Three Taverns on 18 April 59 B.C.:

Oh your two sweet letters given to me at one time! How I can repay *ces bonnes nouvelles*, I don't know, however I freely confess that I'm in your debt.[23]

---

[20] Even today in Greece, "come and eat it" means "come and take the beating that's coming to you."

[21] Romans hadn't yet figured out the difference between upper-case and lower-case letters.

[22] R. D. Griffith, "The Eyes of Clodia Metelli," *Latomus* 55 (1996) 381-83.

[23] Both Cicero and Atticus spoke fluent Greek, and often threw Greek words into their letters to one another. I here translate such words by French. (RDG)

Mais voici la coïncidence: I had just gotten off the road from Antium to Appia at the Three Taverns on the day of the feast of Ceres, when my friend Curio ran into me coming from Rome. At the same moment a slave with letters from you. He asked me whether I had heard anything new. I said no. "Publius is seeking the tribunate of the people." "What are you saying?" I asked. "And he is very hostile to Caesar," he says, "and wants to rescind all those laws of his." What of Caesar?" I ask. "He denies that he ever stood for the adoption of that man." Then he gave vent to his own and Memmius' and Metellus Nepos' hatred. Having hugged the young man, I sent him away, and hurried to the letters. Where are they who speak *de vive voix?* How much better I could see from your letters than from his talk what was happening – about the daily cud-chewing, about the plans of Publius, about the bugle-calls of *celle aux grands yeux* [*boopis*], about Athenio the standard-bearer, about the letters sent to Gnaeus, about the conversation of Theophanes and Memmius. And then how much expectation you've given me about that *outré* dinner! My curiosity is *vorace*, but I can tolerate that you do not write me about *ce dîner*... I would rather be right there to hear you talk about it.

Always one to recognize a good case, Cicero decided to put off his former rivalry, and defended Caelius on the charge of attempting to poison Clodia. He won (again), and Clodia disappears from the historical record forever. His speech for the defence survives; here is a brief excerpt (*Cael.* 61-63) in which Cicero paints the prosecution account (which, sadly, does not survive) as a Keystone Kops adventure:

Still there is nothing said about where the poison came from or how it was procured. They say it was given to Publius Licinius, a modest young man of good character, one of Caelius' friends. The slaves, they say, had instructions to go to the Senian baths.

But, however, where the poison came from and how it was prepared we are not told. They say it was given to Publius Licinius, a modest and good lad, and friend of Caelius; it was agreed with the slaves that they should come to the Senian baths; Licinius was to come to the same place and the box containing the poison was to be handed over to him. Here first I ask, what benefit was there that it be brought into that place? Why didn't the slaves come to Caelius' house? If that great habit of Caelius – his great friendship with Clodia – remained, what suspicions would there be if the woman's slave was seen at Caelius'? But now if there had been a feud, if that habit had been broken, if discord had arisen, "hence those tears": this surely is the cause of all these crimes and accusations.

"Not at all," my opponent says, "When the slaves had revealed to their mistress the whole affair and Caelius' crime, the ingenious woman advised them to promise everything to Caelius, but so that the poison might be caught red-handed being handed over by Licinius, she ordered the Servian baths to be chosen as the place, so that she could send her friends there who would hide, then suddenly when Licinius had come and the poison had been handed over, they would jump out and catch the fellow."

All which things, gentlemen of the jury, have a super-easy means of refutation. Why indeed had she chosen especially the public baths? In which I cannot see what hiding-places there could possibly be for men in togas. For if they were in the lobby of the baths, they couldn't hide, but if they wanted to fly into the pool-area, they couldn't very comfortably do so in shoes and clothes, and perhaps wouldn't even have been let in – unless of course the powerful woman (using that two-quarter trick of hers) had made herself a friend of the bath-man.[24] And indeed I was waiting expectantly to hear who these good men would be said to be, who were witnesses of the poison being caught red-handed, but who have so far not been named. But I don't doubt that they are very serious people, who firstly are friends of such a woman, and then who accepted the mission of squeezing themselves into the baths, for she, being however powerful, would never have gotten anyone except from the most honest people, and people most full of dignity. But why do I speak about the dignity of these witnesses of yours? Consider their bravery and diligence, "They were hiding in the baths." Outstanding witnesses! "Then they rashly jumped out." Moderate men! So indeed you make your story up. When Licinius had come, he was holding a box in his hand, and was trying to hand it over – had not yet handed it over – when suddenly, these witnesses, famous, though with no name, fly out, but Licinius, when he was already stretching out his hand for the purpose of handing over the box, drew it back and by that sudden on-rush of men, gave himself in flight. Oh great power of truth! Which defends itself easily by itself against the cunning, skill, cleverness, of men, and against the fabricated trickery of all.

Catullus, perhaps pleased that Cicero had humiliated the woman who abandoned him, wrote this poem to Cicero (49):

Most eloquent of Romulus' descendants,
as many as are and were, Marcus Tullius,
and as many as will be in other years,
greatest thanks Catullus gives you,
the worst poet of all –[25]
as much the worst poet of all
as you are the best lawyer of all.

This sounds like quite a compliment if we read the last line as meaning "you are the best of all lawyers." But Cicero had worked both against Caelius and for him, and was known for switching sides in other cases as well. It is possible, then, that the last line means rather "you are the best lawyer of all people, because switching sides as often as you do, sooner or later you'll wind up defending everybody."[26]

These are just a couple of examples of humour used as an attack against figures in authority.

---

[24] Caelius in his turn accused Clodia of having poisoned Metellus, calling her a two-penny Clytaemnestra (Quintil. 8.6.53); Clytaemnestra had murdered her husband in a bath, making a clean break of it, as it were.

[25] Remember from the last Chapter the poem to Volusius in which Catullus also called himself "the worst poet."

[26] So K. Quinn, *Catullus: The Poems* 2nd ed. (London 1973) 235.

Modern Theories of Humour: Bringing it Together

While ancient theories of humour concentrate on the *humorous character*, modern theories tend to emphasize that there must be some *situation* – preferably embarrassing – in which that character gets his comeuppance. Although there are many possible examples, we'll look at a list, which is probably not exhaustive, of five sorts of situation that will achieve this effect, namely loss of bodily control, being naked in public, getting stuck somewhere and having to be rescued, getting drunk and doing improbable things, and getting caught running away.

Humour often seems to arise out of loss of control over bodily function. We see this in everything from Aristophanes' hiccup-attack in Plato *Symposium* 185c-e to those Aristophanic characters who defecate out of fear, giving new, well, original meaning to the phrase "getting the shit scared out of you." Examples of this phenomenon are many, such as Trygaeus feeding his own dung-beetle while flying on his back (yes, you heard correctly...) in *Peace* 149-79, but let us consider *Frogs* 479-85, in which the slave Xanthias tricks his master Dionysus into thinking that the boogey-monster, Empusa is about to get them. Dionysus says *enkechoda* "I've shit myself!," which sounds rather like *ekkechutai*, "I've poured a libation" and so he follows up with "call the god!" Here is the passage:

Xanthias:	Hey you, what have you done?
Dionysus:	I've shit myself. Call the god![27]
X	Oh ridiculous one, won't you stand up quick,
	before someone else sees you?
D	But I'm fainting!
	Put a sponge over my heart.[28]
X	Here, take it. Put it on yourself.
D	Where is it? *(He wipes himself.)*
X	Oh ye golden gods, *that's* where you keep your heart?
D	Well, it got scared, and crept
	up my nether hole.[29]

Another bodily function hard to control is the male erection, which causes so much trouble for Cinesias in Aristophanes' *Lysistrata* 829-953. It's almost completely unconscious, and in a society that doesn't wear underwear, about as subtle as a flying brick and as stiff as one. Here is a poem by Catullus (32) on the same problem (apparently quite a large one, considering the amount of sex he's asking for at length):

---

[27] Dionysus, of course, is himself a god.

[28] You have to know that the Greeks used sponges for toilet-paper. How lucky that Xanthias just so happens to have some on hand.

[29] Like the wandering womb that causes hysteria in women.

Please, my sweet Ipsitilla,
my darling, my clever one:
ask me to come to you at noon.
And if you do ask,
give me some help.
Let no-one bolt the door-sill,
nor let it please you to go out,
but may you stay at home and get ready for me
nine fuckings in a row.
Whatever you're doing, ask me quick,
for I lie here after breakfast full and on my back,
poking a hole in my trousers.[30]

Another embarrassing problem is being naked in public. We will see several examples of this, such as Sophocles and his cloak in Chapter V, Iambe "mooning" Demeter and Hippoclides dancing away his marriage in Chapter VIII, and we've already seen Diogenes masturbating in his barrel earlier in this chapter. Here are two more famous examples, starting with *Odyssey* 6.115-47:

Then the princess threw a ball to her maid,
but she missed the maid, and it landed in a deep eddy.
They shouted loudly, and god-like Odysseus awoke,
and sitting up, pondered in his heart and in his mind:
"Oh me, oh my, to the land of what people have I come now?
Are they perhaps both violent and wild and not just,[31]
or lovers of strangers, and do they have a god-fearing mind?
For the female shout of girls has just come over me,
of nymphs, who inhabit the steep crags of the mountains
and springs of rivers and grassy meadows.
So am I now perhaps near men of mortal speech?
But come, I myself will go and see."
So speaking, god-like Odysseus got up from the bushes
and from a thick tree a branch he broke off with his stout hand
– a leafy one, so that with it round his body he might hide his man's genitals.[32]
And he stepped to go like a mountain-nourished lion trusting in its strength,
which comes rained on and blown on, and with its two eyes
it blazes. Yet it comes among the cattle or sheep
or among the wild deer, and its stomach orders it

---

[30] Well, literally, "in my tunic and cloak." Only barbarians wore pants. See Vergil *Aeneid* 11.777. Catullus is lying in bed already dressed, so as to take immediate advantage of Ipsitilla's invitation when it comes.

[31] We have just witnessed Nausicaa's lovely picnic and know that she is no savage, but Odysseus has not.

[32] A parody perhaps of the suppliant's branch, ancestor of our white truce-flag, often carried by refugees.

to try to go even into the well-built house of the flocks.[33]
So Odysseus was going to mingle with[34] the
fair-haired girls, naked though he was, for need compelled him.
Terrible to them he seemed, ill-used by the brine,
and they ran, one here, one there over the jutting shingle.[35]
Alcinous' daughter alone remained: for in her heart Athena
had put courage, and took the fear from her limbs.
She stood her ground before him. Odysseus debated
whether to supplicate the fair-faced girl, having grasped her knees
or, standing where he was, with gentle words
to supplicate her, that she show him the city and give him clothes.
To him it seemed in his heart to be better
to supplicate her standing there, with gentle words,
so that the girl might not be angered at heart by him grabbing her knees.[36]

(There follows the speech in which Odysseus compares Nausicaa to a tree, which will be considered in Chapter V.)

Then there is the well-known story about the inventor Archimedes as told by Vitruvius (9.preface.9-10):

> While many and various were the wonderful discoveries of Archimedes, out of all of them indeed that one which I will set forth seems to have been accomplished with infinite cleverness. Hieron greatly excelled in royal power at Syracuse, when (things have gone well for him) he decided that a golden crown should be placed in a certain temple as a votive-offering to the immortal gods, he commissioned its making with a worker's fee, and weighed the gold for the contractor on a scale. The latter, on time, presented the work, carefully made by hand, to the king, and the weight of the crown on the scale seemed to match. After a rumour was spread that, some gold having been subtracted, an equal weight of silver had been mixed during the crown-making, Hieron, incensed that he had been made a fool of, but finding no means whereby to expose the theft, asked Archimedes to take upon himself consideration of the problem. Then he, when he had agreed to do so, came by chance to the baths, and there, when he was getting into the tub, he realized that as much of his body as was sitting in it, just so much water overflowed the tub. When this offered thereby the means of solving the problem, he did not delay, but jumped up from the tub with glee, and, going home naked, cried in a loud voice that he had truly found what he was seeking; for as he ran he kept shouting in Greek *eureka, eureka!*

If Archimedes in this anecdote becomes a type of the absent-minded professor, the same is true of Thales getting stuck somewhere and having to

---

[33] This is a battle-field simile that has gone awol from the *Iliad*.

[34] "Mingle with" (*mixesthai*) is often used of sexual intercourse.

[35] Being seen running away is itself funny; see below.

[36] We can all agree that he made the right choice. Among other things, in order to take hold of the princess' knees, Odysseus would first have to set down his branch.

be rescued, like Winnie-the-Pooh in Rabbit's hole. Thales predicted an eclipse of the sun (Hdt. 1.74) and ever after was the Greek equivalent to Albert Einstein – the ultimate scientific genius (Ar. *Nub.* 180, *Av.* 1009), although likely with better hair. Socrates tells the following story about him in Plato's *Theatetus* 174a-b:

> Just so, Thales, when studying astronomy and looking upward, fell into a well, and some witty and beautiful Thracian slave-girl is said to have mocked him,[37] since he preferred to know the things in the sky, but didn't see what was beneath him and beside his feet.[38]

Note in this story the comic reversal whereby the maidservant is smarter than the genius Thales.

The title character in Menander's *Curmudgeon* (*Dyscolus*) also falls down a well in Act Four and has to be rescued. Here too, as in Thales' case, a pretty girl is present. She doesn't mock him (she is, after all, his daughter), but her good looks are a distraction that impedes the rescue-efforts. In fact, the old man has alienated so many of his neighbours in the first three acts that most of them want to drop things on top of him rather than rescue him. He gets out in the end, albeit with something of a headache. Here are lines 666-90, Sostratus speaking:

Gentlemen, by Demeter, by Asclepius,
by the gods – never in my life
have I seen a man more timely drowned
– almost! What a sweet pastime!
For Gorgias, as soon as the old man fell in,
immediately jumped into the well, and I
and the girl up above did nothing, for
what could we do? Except that she was pulling out
her hair, weeping, beating her breast violently.
And I, just like a precious nurse-maid, by the gods,
stood beside her. I kept begging her not to do
these things, I kept supplicating her, looking
at her portrait, not at what was going on. The man stuck down there
mattered less than nothing to me, except that always
hauling him up – this annoyed me greatly.
By Zeus, I almost murdered him,
for the rope, as I was looking at the girl,
I let go of maybe three times. But Gorgias was an Atlas
– and not just any one either. He held on, and finally barely
pulled him up. Just as he got out,
I came here, for I couldn't control myself
any more. I almost went up to the girl

---

[37] Humiliation is worse when, as is almost always the case, it happens in front of an attractive member of the opposite sex.

[38] Pindar often encourages us to pay attention to what is to hand, or as he himself put it, "to foot."

and kissed her....

In Aristophanes' *Thesmophoriazusae* 689-783 Euripides' nephew Mnesilochus is unmasked by the women as an interloper in a women's only festival, and threatened with imminent death. He has to rescue himself by parodying two of his uncle's most notorious plays (sadly both now lost). First, modelling himself on the hero of *Telephus*, he seizes a woman's baby and threatens to slit its throat if they don't let him go. The baby turns out to be a wineskin in a diaper; he does slit its "throat" and the women rush up with glasses to catch its "blood." Thus foiled, he takes a leaf from the *Palamedes* in which the hero writes messages on oar-blades (the ancient answer to our "message in a bottle"). Mnesilochus has no oars of course, so he rips hunks of wood off the backdrop, writes on them and throws them onto the ground.

People often do embarrassing things under the influence of alcohol. We might think of the story of Hippoclides dancing away his wedding that will be mentioned in Chapter VIII, but which for now is yet another story known as not-appearing-in-this-chapter, or the drunken antics of Fortunata and Scintilla in Petronius' *Satyricon* 67. The best example of all, however, comes from Timaeus of Tauromenium (566 F 149 *FGrHist.* = Athen. 2.37b-c). He says that:

> There is a certain house in Agrigento called "the trireme" for the following reason. Some young men got drunk in it, and came to such a degree of madness when warmed by the unmixed wine[39] that they thought they were sailing on a trireme, and that there was a storm raging at sea.[40] And they became so far out of their wits that they threw all the furniture and mattresses out of the house as though into the sea, thinking that the captain was telling them to lighten the ship on account of the storm. Many people gathered and carried off whatever was tossed outside, but not even then did the youths snap out of their madness.

These young men violate modesty by bringing outside what belongs indoors (compare the Cinesias-and-Myrrhina episode of Aristophanes' *Lysistrata* or the citizens who, in a fit of communistic zeal, bring all their belongs to the assembly in Aristophanes' *Assembly Women*).

Finally we have someone caught running away. We will come in Chapter XI to the story of Eurystheus hiding from the hell-hound, Cerberus – whom he has asked Heracles to bring to him. For now let's stick to military desertion. Desertion in battle was a serious business. Legend tells of the Spartan mother who stood at the doorway as her son went off to battle, handed him his shield and said, "with it or on it" (Plut. *Mor.* 241F). People believed to have thrown away their shields in battle could be mercilessly ridiculed, assuming they survived throwing away their shields in the first

---

[39] Greeks and Romans mixed their wine with water and so made "spritzers." Unmixed wine was called *methu* (the Vikings' "mead"). People who drank it tended to act like Vikings.

[40] Our word "nausea" comes from the Greek word for "ship."

place (which is slightly suicidal in the middle of a battle). All we know about a certain Cleonymus is that Aristophanes accused him repeatedly of throwing away his shield. Here is *Clouds* 348-55:

> Socrates: [The Clouds] become whatever they want.
> If they see some long-haired wild man
> of those shaggy people, like Xenophantes' son,
> they mock his craze by making themselves like women.
> Strepsiades: And if they see the embezzler of public
> funds, Simon, what do they do?
> So   To show his nature they suddenly become wolves.
> St   So that's why, when they saw Cleonymus, the shield-thrower
> yesterday,
> seeing that he's so cowardly, they became deer.
> So   Yes, and now, because they saw
> Cleisthenes, for this reason they have become women.

(You might compare *Birds* 290, where a bird is mistaken for Cleonymus – we know it's a mistake, because the bird still has *his* crest.)

A truly shameless person could, like the good soldier Schweik, contrive to be so incompetent in battle as never to have actually to serve, and could even *boast* of having lost (and quite possibly thrown away) his shield in battle. This would be funny, as it is absolutely shameful behaviour, and yet is being held up with pride. In phalanx warfare, once everybody's shields were linked in formation, the shield a hoplite carried into battle would protect not only him, but also the person beside him (in Medieval warfare a similar formation was called a "shield wall"). Therefore, throwing your shield away not only places you in danger, but also endangers the person beside you as well as weakening the entire formation. Here is Archilochus fr. 5 West:

> In my shield some Thracian is rejoicing. Beside a bush I left it
> – blameless armour! – against my will,
> but *myself* I saved. What do I care about that shield?
> Let it go: I'll get another one no worse.

This apparently became a stock feature of the lyric poet's persona, as in Horace *Odes* 2.7.1-16:

> Oh often brought with me right to the
> final hour, when Brutus led the rebellion –
> who has given you back as a Roman
> to your ancestral gods and the Italian sky,
>
> Pompey, foremost of my companions,
> with whom often the lingering day with wine
> I broke, having crowned
> our glistening hair with Syrian bay-oil?
>
> With you Philippi and the fast flight
> I underwent, my shield improperly left behind,

when broken courage and threatening men
    shamefully touched the ground with their chins.

Me through the enemy swift Mercury
bore, terrified, on the thick air;
    you back into battle's boiling strait
       an engulfing wave did bear.

The joke here is that Archilochus and Horace are boasting about behaviour of which the ought to be ashamed.

If men escaping battle for fear of their lives is funny, women escaping the blockade of the acropolis in *Lysistrata* pages 409-413 for fear of sexual abstinence, which because of a truly sadistic co-author won't be covered until Chapter X, is probably funnier. At the very least, it's far easier on the eyes for a male audience, and infinitely more entertaining. For an analysis of humour, however, these five categories help to frame the classical character that we will soon be examining.

Chapter IV – The Earliest Humour

Ancient Egyptian Humour

Humour is, perhaps, universal. Although senses of humour may vary, one would be hard-pressed to identify a society that doesn't use humour to some degree or another. Identifying this humour, on the other hand, can be on the difficult side, not because of the humour being obscure, but because the farther back in history one goes, the less written documentation exists.

However, this does not mean that there isn't some evidence of humour. If nothing else, our ancestors were passionate graffiti artists – they would write on absolutely everything that wasn't moving (no doubt after learning that woolly mammoths don't make good writing surfaces for various reasons, not the least of which being getting them to stand still long enough to be written on). So, while the oldest forms of written humour may be scarce, visual humour can be found.

Patrick Houlihan has identified a number of examples of ancient Egyptian humour, some samples of which are listed below:[1]

1.   *Tomb-chapel of Nefer at Saqqara, Dynasty V (Houlihan p. 19)*

Workmen push a newly constructed boat into the water under the direction of an overseer. A baboon has seized an overseer's staff and is "shouting orders" of his own. Is this a depiction of a scene from real life, or a commentary from the workers' perspective on the nature of the overseer? And what does the baboon think of all of this, anyway?

---

[1] P. Houlihan, *Wit and Humour in Ancient Egypt* (London 2002).

2.   *Dynasty V or VI (Houlihan p. 22)*

A baboon in the role of steersman of a ship. Apparently the ancient
Egyptians thought that baboons were funny. No record exists of what
the baboons thought of ancient Egyptians.

3.   *Tomb-chapel of Wep-em-nofret at Giza, Dynasty V (Houlihan p. 28)*

One sculptor is roughing out with chisel and hammer on the stone wall of the chapel a human figure on a bas-relief, while his colleague finishes of another with a pumice-stone. The dialogue runs:

> First Speaker (on the left):
>   "Many these days the sky puts forth, and this statue is not complete!"
> Second Speaker (on the right):
>   "Endure your amount of work. Surely you don't think that this is wood!"

4.   *Dynasty XVIII (Houlihan p. 46)*

A man has drunk too much wine at a party and vomits. The woman sitting behind him wipes his head with a towel. It's sometimes amazing how old toilet humour really is.

5. *Tomb-chapel of Intef, Great Herald to the King (TT 155) at Thebes, mid-Dynasty*
    XVIII (Houlihan p. 49 and inside back cover)

An overseer directs bearers carrying wine amphorae to a store-room. The
door-keeper of the store-room is caught napping. The dialogue spoken
by each man is as follows (left to right):

> He says, "Go you! [We are] towards being scorched."

> "Look! (The) numbers (are) heavy."[2]

> "It's true."

> He says, "He (is a) drunkard with wine."

> He says, "(The) servant is spending the night."

> "I have not slept sleep!"[3]

---

[2] This might mean either, "the numbers (of jars) are heavy" or "the
numbers (of men) are heav(il)y laden."

[3] These are my translations, following T. Säve-Söderberg, *Four Eighteenth
Dynasty Tombs = Private Tombs at Thebes* (Oxford, 1957) 18 with plate XV
(RDG).

6. *Satyrical papyrus, possibly from Deir el Medina, Ramesside period (Houlihan p. 64)*

Animals engaged in human activities; a lion and a gazelle play *senet* (an Egyptian form of chess). This and the next two examples are reminiscent of Aesop. The humour here lies in the essential incongruity of things incapable of human activity actually performing it.[4] No doubt the Egyptians would have laughed their hindquarters off at a Disney cartoon.

7. *Cairo Museum (Houlihan p. 66)*

A mouse is attended by three cats: one offers her a drink, the other arranges her wig, the third carries her baby mouse in a "snuggly." Again, this is humour through the natural world being perverted in some way. There is a double reversal here: animals behaving like people and cats serving mice.

---

[4] Two cupcakes are in an oven. One says, "My, it's hot in here!" The other says, "Holy shit! A talking cupcake!"

8.   *(Houlihan p. 82)*

A cat herds ducks. Top right (just outside of the picture) there is a nest of their eggs.

Mesopotamian Humour

It is in Mesopotamia that we find what may be the first literary canon. Thousands of clay tablets have been recovered from the ruins of the various city states, and along with the king- and god-lists archeologists found epics and mythological cycles.

The majority of these tablets are written in Akkadian, the language of Babylonia, and there is a continuity that is difficult to find elsewhere. The civilization of the Mesopotamian city-states lasted over two millennia, and while the culture and language did change to some degree, it was still the same culture, and it is likely that the sense of humour did not shift dramatically.

But what did the Mesopotamians find funny? In his paper *Humor and Cuneiform Literature*, Benjamin R. Foster notes that:

> In a stratified society jokes will cluster around types of people who violate ethics or mores or who have an exaggerated sense of their own importance: the man who takes advantage of his position to make misery for others, who commits a gaff or oversteps the bounds of public decency or expected modesty, or who makes a fool of himself by a slip of the tongue or logic. In Mesopotamia cowardice, conceit, ambition, bad manners, deficient education, and inordinate desire provided the background for humorous remarks.[5]

---

[5] B. R. Foster, "Humor and Cuneiform Literature," *JANES* 6 (1974) 69-85 at 85.

The perfect example is the *aluzinnu*, a fool or prankster figure from the badly damaged *Aluzinnu* texts. But, despite the difficulty involved in dealing with an incomplete text and the fact that nobody is quite sure what exactly an *aluzinnu* is, what he does is quite clear. There is no skill beyond him (according to the *aluzinnu*), and he has traveled all over the known world (according, again, to the *aluzinnu*). His skills are demonstrated in their effectiveness – when performing an exorcism, he proceeds to burn down the entire house, relieving the homeowner of the burdens of the demons and any other maintenance issues he might have had, or ever will have. The *aluzinnu* is a master chef, suggesting a diet involving food like spoiled oil on onions, and donkey dung in bitter garlic.[6] He is a textbook comic character, as Foster notes, drawing on M. L. Ricketts:

> ...a prankster who is grossly erotic, insatiably hungry, inordinately vain, deceitful, and cunning toward friends and foes; a restless wanderer upon the face of the earth; and a blunderer who is often the victim of his own tricks and follies.[7]

So, ancient Babylon and Sumeria certainly had the comic archetype. Furthermore, it extended as far as the epic. In the tenth tablet of the standard Babylonian epic of *Gilgamesh*, Uta-napishti tells Gilgamesh that (tablet X, lines 272-277):

> What is given to the fool is [beer] sludge instead of [*fine*][8] ghee,[9]
>   [he chews] bran and grist instead of [*bread*][10]
> He is clad in a *mašhandu*-garment,[11] instead of [*a warm cloak,*][12]
>   instead of a belt, a cord of [*coarse rope*][13]
> Because he has no advisors [...,]
>   (because) he has no words of counsel [......]

---

[6] For a more detailed look at the *aluzinnu*, see Foster, pages 74-79. On his role as chef, see L. Milano, "Food and Identity in Mesopotamia: A New Look at the *Aluzinnu*'s Recipes," 242-56 in C. Grotanelli and L. Milano eds., *Food and Identity in the Ancient World* (Padua, 2004).

[7] Foster, 78.

[8] Insertion mine (RBM).

[9] A sort of butter product used in cooking.

[10] Insertion mine (RBM).

[11] A kind of rough blanket or garment used for warmth by those who can't get anything better.

[12] Insertion mine (RBM).

[13] Insertion mine (RBM).

As the above passage suggests, combined with the *aluzinnu* text, the Babylonian sense of humour seems to have been based at least in part around ignorance, in the sense of "not knowing any better," and what follows from it (such as not being able to get a decent coat to keep you warm, because nobody told you that you need one, or burning down a house during an exorcism because you don't know what you're doing). In the instances where people laugh, they are often laughing at an ignorant statement or action. In the story of Adapa, one of the seven antediluvian sages and the son of the god Ea, Adapa has broken the wings of the south wind in the hopes of tricking the gods into giving him immortality. His father, knowing the ways of the gods, tells him to go and seek out the gods Dumuzi and Gizzida so that they will take him to the greater god Anu. Once he is there, if he tells Dumuzi and Gizzida that he is mourning their absence, they will laugh at him and then put in a good word – but there is a warning. The gods will offer him the bread of death and the water of death, and he must not eat or drink either.

When Adapa goes to Dumuzi and Gizzida, they laugh at him as he expected. But, Anu has outwitted Ea and Adapa – instead of bringing him the bread and water of death, he has the gods bring Adapa the bread and water of eternal life, both of which Adapa refuses to consume. When Anu sees this, he laughs at Adapa, declares what has happened, and sends Adapa home with his mortality intact. Anu is most certainly laughing at the actions Adapa takes through his ignorance, and it is very likely that Dumuzi and Gizzida are laughing for the same reason, although there is a possibility that they are laughing in delight at the flattery Adapa has delivered to them.

In the stories of Gilgamesh (which will be dealt with in greater detail shortly), Gilgamesh himself laughs at the old men trying to dissuade him from going into the cedar forest to fight Humbaba (Pennsylvania tablet [OB III], lines 197-202):

"......
Huwawa,[14] his voice is the Deluge,
    his speech is fire and his breath is death.
Why do you desire to do this thing?
    An unwinnable battle is the ambush of Huwawa."
Gilgameš heard the speech of his advisers,
    he looked at his friend and laughed...

Gilgamesh is laughing because he knows what the old men don't – he and Enkidu are perfectly able to carry out the task, and in their concern the old men have made themselves into comic figures, worrying for no good reason.

Ignorance can be feigned as well in Babylonian literature. In the third tablet of *Atraḥasis*, the Mesopotamian flood myth, the god Enki is faced with a dilemma – the gods are about to flood humanity out of existence as a last resort to stop them from making too much noise, and they have sworn Enki

---

[14] An older name for Humbaba.

to secrecy. So, instead of warning his servant Atrahasis, Enki chooses to wait until Atrahasis is home, and then warns Atrahasis' hut, shouting out detailed instructions on how to build a boat and survive the deluge.

The ignorance appearing in *Atrahasis* turns the gods themselves into comic characters, very similar to the *aluzinnu*. Having railed against humanity for making too much noise and then bringing in a flood to wipe them out, the gods then find themselves starving because there's nobody left to make sacrificial offerings to them. When Atrahasis makes an offering of his own, the gods are described as gathering around the smoke like flies.

It is in *Gilgamesh*, the best known Babylonian epic, that we see two truly comic figures, shades of the *aluzinnu*, if not *aluzinnus* themselves, although they become more serious as the epic goes on. The first is Gilgamesh himself, who has absolutely no control over his lusts and urges. He cannot leave the men alone, and is constantly either fighting or playing some sort of sporting event with them (scholars are uncertain which), and his sexual appetite is such that he cannot leave the women alone either, and is constantly trying to sleep with them. A Sumerian tablet details Bilgames (the Sumerian name for Gilgamesh), in the middle of dancing with a group of women, stopping to go and have sex with a complete stranger who has just meandered by. And all of this is happening while he is the king of Uruk, and should know better. Gilgamesh is even abusing his power for his libido, having declared that he gets to sleep first on their wedding nights with all the women who get married.[15]

The second comic character is Enkidu, the nemesis created by the gods to keep Gilgamesh occupied, so that he won't have the energy to terrorize his own city. Enkidu is created to be a giant, hairy man, who is strong and godly. And, having just come into the world, Enkidu does the one thing that is the exact opposite of the heroic ethos – he grazes on grass and frolics with the gazelles, frightening a nearby hunter, who can't make head nor tail of him. While Gilgamesh is comical because he doesn't know to control his human lusts, Enkidu is comical because he doesn't know to control his animal nature, or to even make it into a heroic nature.[16]

One of the things that ignorance leads to is overreaction. When the hunter who can't figure out what to do about Enkidu talks to his father, he is told to fetch Shamhat the sacred prostitute from Uruk, a command that is seconded by Gilgamesh once the hunter arrives in the city. There are two ways in which this is a funny situation. The first is that the hunter, a man, terrified of Enkidu (who is busy impersonating inoffensive herbivores), sends a woman to deal with him. However, this is overshadowed by the overreaction involved – rather than try to talk with Enkidu to find out if he's some sort of wacky naturalist, or even to shoot him with an arrow and see what happens, the hunter and Gilgamesh move directly to having the

---

[15] This custom is called the *ius primae noctis* or *droit de seigneur*... Sounds less offensive in Latin or French, doesn't it?

[16] A gazelle impression may be brave, but it isn't heroic.

representative of the sex goddess Ishtar deal with the problem. It's not unlike using a sledgehammer to crack open a peanut.

Enkidu is seduced by Shamhat and becomes civilized through six days and seven nights of sex[17] – and the animals no longer recognize him as one of their own and they flee at the sight of him. He is still prone to overreacting and inappropriate behavior due to ignorance, however. When the shepherds who have taken him in go to sleep, Enkidu stands watch (The Pennsylvania tablets [OB II], lines 110-116):

> He put on a garment, / becoming like a warrior,
>   He took up his weapon / to do battle with the lions.
> (When) the shepherds lay down at night,
>   he massacred all the wolves, / he chased off all the lions.

While the shepherds are probably grateful for the total solution to the wolf problem that Enkidu has presented, wiping out ALL of the wolves is just a bit above and beyond the call of duty, regardless of how much of a howling good time Enkidu has had. Enkidu's inappropriate behavior is the cause of his learning about Gilgamesh and that he practices the *ius primae noctis* – while having sex out in the open with Shamhat, he notices a man hurrying somewhere, and Enkidu interrupts the sex in mid-thrust to ask the man where he is going. The wedding that the man tells Enkidu about is where Enkidu meets Gilgamesh, and the friendship that forms between them removes the ignorance of both, and changes them into dramatic characters – Enkidu becomes a wise and beloved friend, and Gilgamesh becomes a great ruler.

When Enkidu dies, both return to being comic characters to some degree. Enkidu, on his death bed in tablet VII, curses the sacred prostitute Shamhat for bringing him into civilization, prompting the sun-god Shamash to reprimand him for cursing her unjustly. He then recants his curse, turning it into a blessing.

Once Enkidu dies, Gilgamesh returns to inappropriate behaviour, although the fact that it arises out of grief rather than ignorance prevents it from being entirely comical. But, there is one humorous situation that arises from Gilgamesh's wanderings. Terrified of following Enkidu into death, Gilgamesh is seeking the gods so that he may gain immortality. In order to do this, he must first cross the Waters of Death, and to do that, he needs to find Ur-shanabi, the boatman of the immortal Uta-napishti. The ale-wife, who runs the divine bar on the shores of the river at the edge of the world, points the boatman out, also pointing out that the Stone Ones are repairing the boat. Rather than just introducing himself, Gilgamesh draws his weapons and attacks Ur-shanabi, in the process breaking the Stone Ones to bits and dropping them into the river. Once Ur-shanabi has calmed Gilgamesh down and gotten him to explain the situation, the boatman tells the hero that he can't do anything without a new means of propulsion, since it was the Stone

---

[17] Ancient epic heroes do nothing small.

Ones that powered the boat (Standard Babylonian Epic – tablet X, lines 156-158):

> Your own hands, Gilgameš, have prevented [your crossing.]
> You have smashed the Stone Ones, you have dropped [them in the river,]
> the Stone Ones are smashed and the cedar is not [stripped.]

Tablet XII of the standard Babylonian *Epic of Gilgamesh* presents an odd comic situation – one seemingly unrelated to the story, and even at variance to the plot of the poem as it is told in the other tablets. Enkidu is going down to the Netherworld to recover a ball and mallet for Gilgamesh. Gilgamesh warns his friend not to do various things that will attract the attention of the spirits there – and upon entering the underworld, Enkidu proceeds to do every single thing that Gilgamesh warned him against, including making noise, kissing and striking family members, and throwing sticks at the spirits. In short, Enkidu enters the Netherworld and immediately goes on a rampage.

While Gilgamesh and Enkidu present comic figures at the beginning and towards the end of the poem, the gods remain a humorous force throughout. This is particularly true of Ishtar, the goddess of sex and war. In Tablet VI of the standard Babylonian epic, Ishtar decides that she wants to seduce and marry Gilgamesh, but the king rejects her, listing a long line of former husbands who have come to a bad end (this is a far cry from the lusty Gilgamesh of the first couple of tablets, who would try to have sex with anything without a penis). Ishtar hears this from Gilgamesh, and leaves in a fury – and promptly goes up to her father, Anu, with tears in her eyes, telling him that the nasty Gilgamesh has hurt her feelings.

So far we have dealt with Mesopotamian character-based humour, but as Foster noted, there are at least two other types of humour that appear in the cuneiform texts. The first is parody. One possible example is *The Rulers of Lagash*, which appears to be a parody of the King-Lists – but with imaginary names and impossibly long reigns.[18] Foster also notes an example of a love poem where the poet compares his beloved's complexion to a gecko and her skin to a cooking pot, which plays on the ancient literary device of comparison to flattering things, but uses very unflattering comparisons instead.[19] This leads us to the next type of humour that Foster notices, which is the abuse text, most examples of which involve two people trading insults, although it can be a third-person monologue:

> Those of the abusive category are not really debates as there is no defense of a position and no reference to the opponent's argument. Each interlocutor confines himself to abusing the other with clever turns of phrase.[20]

---

[18] Foster, 82.

[19] Foster, 79. Greek examples can be found in Chapter V.

[20] Foster, 80.

There is a temptation to see the ancient civilizations of the Fertile Crescent as being filled with gravitas, but that is clearly not the case. Like human beings in general, the Sumerians, Babylonians, and Assyrians loved to laugh, and the literature they committed to clay tablets in cuneiform writing has a number of comical moments and characters. The cuneiform literature of ancient Mesopotamia would have a tremendous impact on a number of other cultures,[21] due in part to the interaction between Mesopotamia and a group of nomads that had recently settled in the Levant – a group known as the Hebrews.[22]

Hebrew Humour

While the Egyptians wrote on the walls and the Babylonians on clay tablets, the ancient Hebrews left a written record in their holy book. Let's consider two passages from the Hebrew Bible, one that involves laughter, indeed the most famous laugh in the "Old Testament," and the other that happens to be quite funny. The first is Genesis 18.1-15:

> Yahweh appeared to [Abraham] at the oaks of Mamre as he was sitting in the door of the tent in the heat of the day. He lifted his eyes and he looked, and voila!: three men standing beside him. He looked, and he ran to meet them from the door of the tent, and he bowed down all the way to the ground.[23] He said, "Sir, May I please find favour in your eyes. Do not pass by from before your servant! Let be taken a little of water. Wash your feet, and be supported under the tree. I will take a morsel of bread. Restore your hearts, and afterward pass by. Since for this you passed by to your servant."
> They said, "Do as you have spoken."
> Abraham hurried toward the tent to Sarah and said, "Hurry: three *seahs*[24] of fine flour. Knead, and make pitas!"
> To the herd ran Abraham and took a son of the herd, tender and good, and gave to the boy and he hurried to do [what was necessary] to it. He took yogurt and milk and the son of the herd that he had "done," and gave before them, and he took his stand before them under the tree, and they ate.
> They said to him, "Where's Sarah, your wife?"[25]
> He said, "Voila! In the tent."
> He said, "I will come back, come back to you at the season of the living [i.e. in the Spring], and voila! There will be a son to Sarah, your wife."

---

[21] Including Greek; see e.g. W. Burkert, *Babylon, Memphis, Persepolis: Eastern Contexts of Greek Culture*. Cambridge, Mass. and London 2004.

[22] Who, among other things, would incorporate the flood story of Atrahasis into the Book of Genesis.

[23] Apparently, they don't get many visitors in Mamre.

[24] A unit of measurement = 12.148 litres.

[25] That the strangers know of Abraham's wife's existence – much less her name – is the first sign that these are no ordinary passers by.

Sarah heard at the door of the tent, and it[26] was behind him. (Abraham and Sarah were old and gone in years, and there had ceased to happen to Sarah the way according to women [i.e. menstruation].) Sarah laughed (*the Hebrew verb is* **tsahaq**) within herself[27], saying, "After I am worn out, will pleasure[28] come to me? And my Mister is old!"

Yahweh said to Abraham, "Why did Sarah laugh, saying, 'Yeah right! I'll give birth, and I'm old!'? Is a thing beyond Yahweh's power? At the appointed time I will return to you at the season of the living, and to Sarah there will be a son."

Sarah lied, saying, "I didn't laugh," because she was afraid.

He said, "No, you laughed."

In the fulness of time, Sarah did give birth to a son whom she called **Yitshaq** (in English, Isaac) after her disbelieving laughter.

This passage, though concerned with laughter, is not apt to strike us as funny, whereas our second passage – a very famous one – is pretty amusing, and has one of the same Walt Disney talking animals the Egyptians loved so much. It is Genesis 2:4b-10 and 2:15 - 3:24, which describes, among other things, the coming of civilization:

On the day when Yahweh (God)[29] created earth and heaven, all the shrubs of the field were not yet upon the earth, and all the plants of the field did not yet grow, because Yahweh (God) had not caused it to rain on the earth, and humankind did not exist to work the ground. But mist would go up from the earth to cause all the face of the ground to drink.

Yahweh (God) formed into a human dust from the ground [*adamah*], and blew into its two nostrils life-breath, and the human [*adam*] became a living being.[30] Yahweh (God) planted a garden in Eden in the east, and put there the human he had formed. And Yahweh (God) caused to sprout from the ground every tree beautiful for seeing and good for eating, and the tree of Life in the middle of the garden, and the tree of the Knowledge of Good and Evil. A river

---

[26] Presumably "the door," unless this "it" is a scribal error for "she."

[27] Compare Odysseus' silent laugh at his Nobody-trick (*Od.* 9.413). That Yahweh hears Sarah's silent laugh is further evidence of his omniscience.

[28] Sexual pleasure, of course. The word she uses is almost identical to the name of the Garden of Eden.

[29] This is still early on in the Bible (the second chapter), and we might not have figured out that Yahweh *is* God, so the author kindly reminds of this fact, and reminds us, and reminds us...

[30] God made man out of the ground because of a pun. O.k., but what if *adamah* had meant "tinfoil," would he have made our species out of that material?

came out of Eden to cause the garden to drink, and from there it divided and became four heads...[31]

And Yahweh (God) took the human and caused him to dwell in the garden of Eden to work it and to watch over it. Yahweh (God) gave orders to the human, saying:

"From every tree of the garden you may really eat, but from the tree of the Knowledge of good and evil – don't eat from it, because in the day of your eating from it, you'll really die."[32]

And Yahweh (God) said,

"No good the human's being alone! Let's make for him a helper useful to him."

So Yahweh (God) formed from the ground all living things of the field, and all birds of the sky, and caused them to go to the human to see what he would call them, and all the human called them – each living being –, was its name. The human called the names of every beast and bird of the sky and of every living thing of the field. But for Adam[33] there was not found a helper suitable.[34] So Yahweh (God) caused to fall a deep sleep on the human, and he slept, and He took one of his ribs, and the flesh closed back into place. And Yahweh (God) built the rib[35] he'd taken from the human into a woman, and brought her to the human.

The human said:[36]

"Finally! Bone of my bones; flesh of my flesh.

This shall be called 'woman' (Hebrew *ishsha*), for from 'man' (*ish*) has this been taken."

(That's why a man leaves his father and mother and clings to his woman, and they become one flesh.) Both were naked – the human and his woman – yet they weren't ashamed by one another.[37]

---

[31] We now embark on a learned footnote about the names, etc. of the four rivers.

[32] This turns out not to be, strictly speaking, true. The day that Adam eats from the tree marks the beginning of his status as a mortal rather than the actual moment of his death. Then again, what's a day here and there to the everlasting Yahweh?

[33] Now for the first time in the story, the article ("the") disappears from the word *adam*, "human", and it becomes the proper name, Adam.

[34] This is a pretty trial-and-error method for an omniscient God to use in finding out that Adam likes girls.

[35] Yes, that's what it really says, "built" (Hebrew *yibhen*), as though out of Tinker Toys,

[36] Apparently still in naming-mode.

[37] Being naked in public and not knowing it is a comic theme (e.g. Hippoclides dancing away his wedding; Archimedes shouting *eureka*).

The snake was clever beyond all living beings that Yahweh (God) had made.[38] He said to the woman, "So! God says you can't eat from any tree in the garden?"

The woman said to the snake, "From the fruits of [every] tree of the garden we may eat, but from the fruit of the tree that's in the middle of the garden, God said, 'you may not eat of it, and you may not touch it, lest you die.'"[39]

The snake said to the woman, "You won't really die, for God knows on the day you eat from it, your eyes will be opened, and you'll be like God, knowing good and evil.

The woman saw how good the tree was for eating,[40] and that it was a desire to the eyes, and that the tree was pleasant for contemplation.[41] So she took from the fruit, and ate, and gave also to her man with her, and he ate. The eyes of both of them were opened, and they knew they were naked. So they sewed together leaves of a fig-tree, and made for themselves grass-skirts.[42]

Then they heard the voice of Yahweh (God) walking up and down in the garden in the breeze of the day, and the human and his wife hid from the face of Yahweh (God) in the branches of a tree of the garden. Yahweh (God) called to the human, saying to him:

"Where are you?"[43]

---

[38] What appears at first to be an enormous non-sequitur (it will make sense later, trust us) is explained by the fact that "naked" and "clever" sound the same in Hebrew. It's as though our author had said, "Speaking of naked/clever people..."

[39] The serpent bypasses Adam and approaches Eve, who has at best only hearsay knowledge of the divine commandment (she wasn't born when it was given and neither the snake nor the woman are on a first-name basis with God). Note too that he exaggerates God's commandment (God forbade the eating of only *one* tree). In denying the serpent's allegation, Eve does not return to God's original commandment, which sounds pretty paltry beside the impressive prohibition uttered by the serpent, but decides to improve upon it (God Himself said nothing about Adam and Eve *touching* the tree).

[40] Eve must have very good eyesight if she can *see* that the fruit *tastes* good.

[41] Does this mean "it gives pleasure when you contemplate it," or "it pleases you by increasing your powers of contemplation"?

[42] What is the great wisdom that the couple gain by eating the fruit of the impressively named "Tree of the Knowledge of Good and Evil"? They realize they have no underwear; remember that "clever" and "naked" are homonyms in Hebrew. We readers have known this all along. They then get some fig-leaves (cf. Odysseus and his shrubbery in the conversation with Nausicaa).

[43] In Hebrew, *ayyekhah*? This word always reminds us of T. S. Eliot's poem *The Waste Land* Part V, "What the Thunder Said". Eliot kindly tells us in a footnote that what the thunder said in *Upanishad* 5.2 is *Datta, dayadhvam, damyata* ("Give, sympathize, control"). It's hard to ignore

He said, "Your voice I heard in the garden, and I was afraid, because I'm naked. So I hid."

He said, "You caused you to know you're naked? From the tree that I ordered you not eat, did you eat?"

The human said, "The woman, whom *you* gave me: she gave me from the tree, and I ate."[44]

Yahweh (God) said to the woman, "Why did you do this?"

The woman said, "The snake caused me to be confused, and I ate."

Yahweh (God) said to the snake,
"Since you've done this,
    cursed are you[45] before all beasts
        and before all living beings.
    On your belly shall you walk
        and dust shall you eat
all the days of your life.[46]
    Enmity I will put between you
        and the woman,
    and between your seed
        and her seed.
    She shall strike your head
        and you shall strike her heel."

To the woman He said,
"They'll be really great: your pains and pregnancies.
    In pain you'll bear sons,
and yet for your man will be your longing,
    and he'll rule over you."

To Adam he said,
"Since you listened to the voice of your wife,
    and ate from the tree that I forbade you
saying, 'Don't eat from it',
    Cursed be the ground for your sake.[47]
In pain shall you eat from it all the days of your life.
    Thorns and thistles shall it cause to sprout for you.
You'll eat herbs of the field.

---

thunder, isn't it?

[44] We love this line. It is not Adam's fault, it's the woman's. Well, it's not really the woman's fault, either. It's God's – after all he was the one who gave Adam the woman in the first place!

[45] No longer *'arum*, "clever", but now *arar*, "cursed."

[46] Before now snakes had legs, you see. Note that the punishment fits the crime; a serpent who has sinned in the matter of food (the apple) is punished in a matter of food (he will eat dust).

[47] Yahweh stops short of cursing Adam himself, as he had the snake, but he curses the ground (*adamah*), whence Adam derives both his substance and his name.

    In the sweat of your brow shall you eat bread,
til you return to the ground,
        for from it were you taken,
    for dust you are,
        and to dust you shall return."

Now, the human called the name of his woman, "Eve," for she was the mother of all living (Hebrew *hay*). Yahweh (God) made for Adam and for his woman tunics of skin and put some clothes on them.[48]

Yahweh (God) said,

"Look, the human has become as one of us, knowing good and evil. What if he stretches out his hand, and takes also from the tree of Life, and eats, and lives forever...?"[49]

So Yahweh (God) sent them from the garden of Eden to work the ground from which he was taken. And he drove out the human, and caused to dwell in the east of the garden of Eden cherubs and the flame of their sword that kept on turning, to watch over[50] the way to the tree of Life.

This is comparable to, and possibly inspired by, the aforementioned taming of Enkidu at the beginning of the epic of Gilgamesh by the sacred prostitute Shamhat.[51]

It is notable that both stories, while expressing the idea of the dawn of civilization through the actions of the woman (is it any wonder we call wives "our better halves?"), deal with the process in a fairly tongue-in-cheek way. The humour in both cases, however, strikes a balance between the situational and the character-based, while the Greek and Roman humour that would follow in the west depended almost entirely on characters instead.

---

[48] Let's cover up a bit more of Eve than those grass-skirts are doing. This is a general admission narrative!

[49] Creepy theremin music here, instead of words. This rhetorical device is called "aposiopesis."

[50] The same verb (Hebrew *shamar*, "to watch over") that described the human's original function is now used of the Cherubs. Not for the last time in history was a human job outsourced to robots.

[51] It is worth noting that it is likely that by coupling with her, Enkidu is performing a sacred marriage, and therefore gaining his wisdom through a mythological act.

Part II
Real Characters

"He started it," said Rincewind simply.

Bravd and Weasel looked at the figure, now hopping across the road with one foot in a stirrup.

"Fire-raiser, is he?" said Bravd at last.

"No," said Rincewind. "Not precisely. Let's just say that if complete and utter chaos was lightning, then he'd be the sort to stand on a hilltop in a thunderstorm wearing wet copper armour and shouting 'All gods are bastards'..."

– Terry Pratchett, *The Colour of Magic*

Chapter V – Eccentrics Looking for a Story

Getting Something for Nothing

In modern humour, comedy lies in the situation. In ancient humour, it lay in the individual. Those who were funny were funny because of some eccentricity of their character that set them apart, usually by going against the conventions of society (and remember that one of the great social conventions was justice, or giving to each his due). The easiest way to do this was to try to get something for nothing.

When the ancients spoke of someone making himself ridiculous while violating the rule of justice by trying to get something for nothing, they were apt to think of eating, not only because eating is a physical necessity, but also because humour is a social phenomenon, and ancients preferred to dine in company, whether at banquets or in mess-halls. An obligation of the sacrificial meal was that it be a "well-balanced feast" (*Il.* 1.468), that is, one in which each person got their fair share, and Greeks regarded the one who eats alone (the *monophagos*) as somehow suspect.[1] One who tries to get food for free is a **parasite**[2] who sits beside you while you eat – the word comes from the Greek *para*, "beside" and *sitos*, "food." We often find the moocher, free-loader or sponge in our own comedy – think of Cosmo Cramer, Joey Tribbiani, Homer Simpson, or Garfield the cat – and we have many ancient descriptions of this type as well. Here is what Xenophon says in the *Symposium* (11-13), describing a dinner-party given by one Callias in honour of his boy-friend, Autolycus, who has just won the pancration contest[3] at the Panathenaic games. He writes:

> These people, therefore, were dining in silence, as though this had been ordered for them by some one more powerful. And Philip the Joker (*gelotopoios*) knocked on the door and told the slave to announce who he was, and that he wanted to be let in. He said he was prepared to provide everything he needed – to eat other people's food, and said that his slave was completely stressed from carrying – nothing, and not having had any breakfast.[4] When Callias heard this, he said, "But, gentlemen, it is shameful to begrudge a man one's roof; so let him come in." All the while he was looking at Autolycus, it was clear that he was checking out how the joke seemed to him. Philip, when he stood in the men's

---

[1] The *monophagos* is usually a glutton, who wants to stuff himself on sea-food (red-meat was available only at sacrifices and so could not be consumed alone). We will have more to say about him in Chapter VIII.

[2] See H.-G. Nesselrath, *Lucians Parasitendialog: Untersuchungen und Kommentar* (Berlin, 1985) and E. I. Tylawsky, *Saturio's Inheritance: The Greek Ancestry of the Roman Comic Parasite* (New York, 2002).

[3] Like our wrestling, but biting and eye-gouging were allowed.

[4] The slave Xanthias is similarly stressed at the beginning of Aristophanes' *Frogs*, and says so at considerable length.

quarters where the dinner was, said, "That I'm a joker, everyone among you knows. And I came willingly, thinking that a joker should come uninvited rather than invited to dinner."[5] "Lie down then,"[6] said Callias, "for those present are full of seriousness, as you can see, and perhaps rather lacking in laughter."[7]

Again, we read in Petronius' *Satyricon* 26 of a certain day on which Encolpius has the prospect of a free dinner at the home of Trimalchio (41-46 gives a portrait of the freedmen who habitually dine chez Trimalchio for free). Catullus offers an interesting inversion of this motif in his poem 13:

> You will dine well, my Fabullus, at my house
> in a few days, if the gods favour you,
> if you bring with you a good and mighty
> supper, not without a brilliant girlfriend,
> with wine and salt and all sorts of laughter....

Catullus isn't a total moocher, the poem goes on to show. He will supply a perfume, which the sex-goddess has given to his girlfriend. When Fabullus smells it, he'll ask the gods to make him all nose.[8]

While it was usually free food that the parasite was after, other things appealed to him as well. For example there was the clothes-thief (*lopodytes*). The theft of clothes was no small matter – unlike today, where you can just go out to the store and buy a new shirt or pair of pants, the Greeks and Romans had to make their own clothes, starting with the fabric. This work required any good Roman or Greek to have a number of women in his family working on it at any given time (after all, men wore the clothes – they didn't make them). In fact, the best epitaph that could appear on the tombstone of a Roman woman was "She made lots of wool."[9]

The first clothes-stealing episode in Greek literature is an odd scene in *Iliad* 6.232-36 in which the Greek Diomedes meets the Trojan Glaucus on the field of battle. You would naturally expect him to try and kill his enemy, but

---

[5] This is play on the proverb, "The good come unbidden to the banquets of the good", said to have been uttered by Heracles when he gate-crashed the wedding of Ceyx and Alcyone (Hes. fr. 264 Merkelbach-West and Bacch. *Paean* 4.23-25). A different twist on the same proverb is found in Pl. *Symp.* 174B.

[6] Greek and Roman men ate lying on sofas with t.v. dinner-tables in front of them. Our word 'cubit' is the length of the forearm with which one props up one's head while in bed (Latin *cubile*).

[7] For a good discussion of this passage, see J. Bremmer, "Jokes, Jokers and Jokebooks in Ancient Greek Culture," 11-28 in J. Bremmer and H. Roodenburg eds., *A Cultural History of Humour* (Cambridge, 1997).

[8] Could be a great idea for a short-story. What do you think, Gogol?

[9] R. Lattimore, *Themes in Greek and Latin Epitaphs = Illinois Studies in Language and Literature* (Urbana 1942) 297.

he has just wounded the goddess Aphrodite who was wandering round the field of battle (obviously a logical place for a goddess of love to take her morning walk), and he has been warned that the next time he hurts a god, he's toast. So he asks Glaucus, in effect, "Are you a god in disguise?" With the battle raging round them on all sides, Glaucus might have settled for a one word answer (which would have been "No"), but he chooses instead to get out the family photo-album, and make a long speech about his ancestors, which is naturally the sort of thing that any well-mannered person would do in the middle of a raging battle. From this Diomedes learns that their grandfathers used to be friends, and so proposes that they celebrate this ancestral connection by exchanging armour. (Remember that reciprocity, of which exchange is a species, is crucial to the ancient sense of justice and society.) So these two guys get naked in the thick of battle and put on each other's clothes. The thing of it is that Glaucus' armour is worth ten times as much as Diomedes' and, as Homer says, the gods took away his wits when he agreed to this exchange.[10]

Another example of rampant kleptomania regarding clothing appears in *Odyssey* 14.499-502. Odysseus, when camped out in the field on a cold winter's night without proper attire, sends one of his men on a trumped-up mission. The man leaves his cloak behind and Odysseus swipes it. As a further example, a poem of Sophocles survives (4 West *IEG* = Athen. 604d-f) that he wrote to his arch-rival Euripides. It seems that Sophocles had taken a boy out to the countryside for sex (remember that the ancient Greeks often had sex with young male children, and even the words "platonic relationship" are in reference to Plato being abnormal for *not* having sexual relations with his younger students). They each took off their clothes first, and when they were finished, the boy grabbed Sophocles' clothes and ran off leaving the famous poet to walk back into town in a kid's tunic. When Euripides heard this he said that he had had sex with the same boy, but never had to pay him for it, but that Sophocles had gotten what he deserved for his lechery, Sophocles wrote the following riposte (fr. 4 West, *IEG* = Athen. 604 d-f):

> It was the Sun, not the boy, Euripides, that made me
>> naked of my cloak. But while when you were having sex with him, poor
>>> thing,
> the North Wind joined you. You're not wise to call Love
>> a thief, who yourself sow someone else's field.

The whole poem refers to a fable of Babrius (18), according to which the North Wind and the Sun were arguing over who was more powerful. They decided to settle the question with a contest. Pointing to a certain farmer out tilling his fields, they agreed that whoever could force him to take off his coat would be the winner. The North Wind huffed and puffed, but the more he blew, the tighter the farmer wrapped himself up. Then the Sun came out and

---

[10] See R. Scodel, "The Wits of Glaucus," *TAPA* 122 (1992) 73-84, with bibliography.

began to shine, and eventually the man took off his coat and set it down. The moral: *you get more with honey than with vinegar.* The last line of Sophocles' poem hits especially below the belt, because it refers to Euripides' secretary Cephisophon. Rumour had it that he was Euripides' wife's real sex-partner, and that she just slept with Euripides whenever Cephisophon wasn't available, a bad experience that inspired the poet to create the ultra-misogynist title-character of his *Hippolytus* (*Vita Eur.* 6).

In Aristophanes' *Clouds* 177-79 one of Socrates' pupils explains to the country bumpkin Strepsiades how his master feeds them, proving that even the intellectual elite weren't beneath snatching the occasional piece of clothing:

> Having sprinkled fine ash over the table,
> and bent a souvlaki-skewer, he took the compass,
> and from the gym he stole the cloak.

This apparently means that Socrates began a geometry-lesson (the ash-covered table was the ancient answer to our chalk-board), using ash and a skewer that in happier times would have been employed in a barbecue, and then – in a contrary-to-expectation joke – he stole a cloak to sell for food-money.

As a final example of kleptomania and clothing, Petronius' *Satyricon* 12-15 describes the novel's anti-hero trying to trade a beautiful cloak that he has stolen for his own tattered rags, which someone else has found – the part of the novel that narrates those earlier events is sadly missing – because he has stitched his life-savings into the lining of the tattered old cloak.

Another thing that it would be really nice to get for free would be laid. Modern comedy has made a staple out of this with movies like *American Pie*, but sex and humour have been around long enough that the idea of combining them is nothing new. In Aristophanes' *Assembly Women* the women of Athens, who are always complaining about how badly their husbands run the government, conspire to meet early one morning, dress as men, and then go to the assembly and take it over. (This is quite a slapstick scene, because all the actors are male, dressed as women, now disguising themselves as men.)[11] The women's revolution is a communistic one and once they seize control of the city, they abolish private property, decreeing that everyone shall have all things in common, including their spouses. They foresee a problem with the arrangement, namely that everyone will want to have sex with the best-looking people, who will be quickly overwhelmed, so they decree that everyone can demand sex from everyone else, with the ugliest people taking the first turn. The play ends with a series of scenes showing how this arrangement might work – or not – in practice.

But then again, if you're going to try to get something for nothing, you may as well go for everything. A form of parasitism known in Rome but not in Greece was legacy-hunting (*captatio*) wherein a poor man would fawn all over a rich one – preferably an old, infirm rich one with no heirs of his own

---

[11] Shades of Viola from Shakespeare's *Twelfth Night*.

– inviting him out to dinner, giving him presents, and so forth, in the hopes of being written into his will. The final surviving scene of the *Satyricon* is a send-up, involving as it happens a very perverse banquet, of this custom.

Of course, managing to succeed requires a specialized group of skills. It wasn't easy to get something for nothing, despite the fact that it made you an object of comedy, and there was at least some entertainment value. It took skill.

How to be a Parasite

The parasite depends for his livelihood on keeping in the good graces of his host, and this usually entails flattery. So it is that the parasite is forced to become a smarmy, unctuous **flatterer**,[12] fawner, ass-kisser, brown-noser, and yes-man (Greek *kolax* [occasionally *aikalos, areskos,* or *thops*], Latin *assentator*), who kow-tows to his betters. This figure crops up many times in ancient literature. Indeed, Plutarch wrote a whole essay (*Moralia* 5) explaining how to tell a flatterer from a friend. The flatterer is usually uninvited to the party (Greek *akletos*, Latin *invocatus*), and either just sneaks in or has attached himself to an invited guest as his "shadow." Not having been invited, he has to make himself welcome in a hurry. This is how Theophrastus describes the flatterer, who is his *Character* number 2:

> One might understand flattery as a shameful kind of speaking, but one useful to the flatterer, and understand a flatterer as such a one who, as soon as he meets you, says, "Do you notice how people are staring at you? This happens to nobody else in the city but you." Or, "You were popular yesterday in the Stoa, for there were more than thirty people sitting there, and when the subject turned to who was best, starting from Himself, all people mentioned Himself's name." And as he says this, he takes a piece of lint from his cloak, and if some piece of chaff is blown by the wind into his hair, he gathers it, and laughing, says, "Do you see that since I haven't met you for two days, you have a beard full of grey – although you do have very black hair for one your age." And when Himself is saying something, he tells others to be quiet, and praises them as listeners. And when he's finished, he shouts, "Quite right!," and when he has made a cold joke,[13] he will stuff his cloak into his mouth as though unable to restrain his laughter. And he tells those whom they meet to stand back a bit until Himself has passed. Having bought apples and pears, he brings them to give to his children when Himself is looking, and, kissing them, says, "Chips off the old block!" And when buying boots with him at the cobbler's, he says that his foot is shapelier than the shoe. And when he is walking toward one of his friends, he will run ahead and say, "He's coming!" and, running back, "I've announced you." He thinks nothing of fetching something from the Women's Market without stopping for breath. Of the guests he will praise the wine first, and lying beside him say, "How temperately you're eating!" and, having picked

---

[12] On flatterers, see P. G. McC. Brown, "Menander's *Kolax* and Parasites and Flatterers in Greek Comedy," *ZPE* 92 (1992) 91-107, I. C. Storey, *Eupolis: Poet of Old Comedy* (Oxford, 2003)188-96.

[13] Or as we would rather say, a stale one.

up something from the table, say, "How good this is!" and ask if he's shivering, and if he wants to be wrapped up, and if he shouldn't bundle him up some more, and saying these things, he bends to his ear and whispers, and looks at that man even as he talks to others. And taking the pillows from the slave in the theatre, he arranges them himself. He will say that the house is well designed, the farm neatly planted, and the portrait a good likeness.

Homer's contemporary, Hesiod (*Op.* 372-73) warns his feckless brother "Let no woman with a shapely rear beguile your mind, / cajoling you with wheedling words. She really wants your barn," although this may suggest that she has a lack of ambition. The eponymous chorus of Eupolis' *Flatterers* describes its activities living by his wits and singing for his supper this way (fr. 172 *PCG*):

> But the way of life that we flatterers lead we'll
> tell to you – just listen. Since we are complete gentlemen,
> first of all we have a slave as our attendant –
> often someone else's, but a bit of him is mine.
> And I have two cloaks, pleasing to me.
> Always trading one for the other, I go out
> to market, and there whenever I see a man
> foolish and rich, I'm immediately onto him.
> And if Richy happens to speak, I praise him completely,
> and I'm astounded, seeming to delight in his words.
> And then we go to dinner, each of us to another's house,
> after foreign bread, where the flatterer must
> immediately say many pleasant things, or be carried out the door.
> I know a certain Acestor, who had undergone branding.[14]
> He told a dirty joke, and then the slave,
> led him out of doors and gave him over, wearing the stocks, to Oeneus.[15]

Menander also wrote a play called *The Flatterer* from which the following passage survives (C 190-199 Arnott):

> One man there is, one
> through whom all things have been ruined, Master,
> totally – I'm telling you. As many
> razed cities as you have seen, this alone has ruined
> them, as I have now discovered thanks to him.[16]
> As many tyrants as ever were, whoever as a great commander,
> satrap, leader of the guard, founder of a place,

---

[14] Runaway slaves were tattooed, so they could be identified more readily if they tried it again; see C. P. Jones, "Tatooing and Branding in Graeco-Roman Antiquity," *JRS* 77 (1987) 139-55.

[15] The stocks: handcuffs, but they fasten the neck as well as the wrists. Oeneus: the place where the bodies of condemned criminals were thrown into a pit.

[16] Pointing at Strouthias, the "flatterer" of the title.

general – for I'm talking about those completely
ruined – now this alone has ruined them:
flatterers. These men are wretched thanks to them.

The flatterer's preferred mode of action is **imitation**. Imitation is of
course, as Charles Colton put it, the sincerest form of flattery, although, in
the ancient context, that isn't saying a great deal. Athenaeus 249e-f has the
following anecdote about Dionysius the Younger of Syracuse:

> [He] also had many flatterers, whom ordinary folk called "Dionysokolakes."
> These people pretended not to see clearly at dinner, since Dionysius was near-
> sighted, and they groped for the food as though unable to see, until Dionysius
> guided their hands to the dishes. And when Dionysius spat, they would often
> offer their faces to be spat upon,[17] and, licking off his saliva, and even his vomit,
> they said it was sweeter than honey.

As we will see a bit later, flattery to this degree soon becomes parody, and
therefore impossible to take seriously – thus making it even more funny.

The same Philip the buffoon mentioned above resurfaces in Xenophon's
account of the banquet, asking the flute-girl to play more music so that he
can imitate a boy and a girl who have just danced (*Symp.* 22-23):

> And then he stood up and imitated the dancing of the boy and girl. First, since
> they had praised the way the boy appeared more handsome because of his
> gestures, he showed in rivalry with his whole body that whichever part he
> moved was uglier than nature had made it. And because the girl had bent
> backwards and imitated a wheel, so he tried to imitate one by bending forwards.
> Finally, because they praised the boy, since in his dance he had trained his
> whole body, he ordered the flute-player to strike up a faster beat, and threw out
> at once his legs and arms and head. And when he was overcome by exhaustion,
> he lay down and said, "This is proof, Gentlemen, that my dancing also is good
> training. For I'm thirsty. Let the slave pour me the big cup." "Yes, by Zeus," said
> Callias, "and for us too, since we also are thirsty from laughing at you."

If imitation involves making a likeness to the person flattered, then it was
natural for the flatterer to include in his repertoire the **comparison** or simile,
which is *drawing* a likeness. The comparison of someone to something,
especially to a plant or animal became a stock feature of the *makarismos* – the
pronouncing blessed that was called for at all sorts of banquets, especially
wedding feasts. This custom is not familiar to us, especially since most
grooms don't take kindly to being compared to a pear or a duck, but the
ancients lived close to the land,[18] and it was common in antiquity and may

---

[17] Do you need a footnote telling you that spitting in someone's face is
usually a sign of great contempt? If so, check out Soph. *Ant.* 1232.

[18] Italian *contadini* to this day use vegetables to describe people: an
artichoke is someone who has nothing left once you take him apart, a
sweet little girl is a "potato-let," a pea is someone of no account, and a
squash is, well, just a squash.

have come from the Near East, certainly we find it in the book of Psalms in the Hebrew Bible. Psalm 1 begins (verses 1-3):

> Blessed the man who does not walk in the counsel of the wicked.
> ....
> He is like a tree transplanted by a channel of water,
> whose fruit is given in its time, and its leaf will not wither,
> and all that he does shows prosperity.

An example of this occurs when Odysseus, waking naked and disoriented on Scheria after a shipwreck, chances to meet the Phaeacian princess Nausicaa. How to address her and get in her good books? He stands a good way off covering his privates with a shrub (one would imagine not a prickly one, as that would really be a cock-up) and says (*Od.* 6.162-65):

> Wonder holds me as I look at you.
> Such a thing on Delos once, beside Apollo's altar
> – the new shoot of a date-palm coming up – I saw,
> for I came there too, and many men followed me.

(Odysseus shows at once that, despite his present down-at-heels appearance, he is pious – why else would he go to the sacred island of Delos? – as well as rich and powerful; he is also inviting Nausicaa to think of him as a potential husband.) In this case, the comparison works – he's not only compared her to a tree (which is a good thing to be compared to, and certainly better than a monkey or a horse), but a tree at a sacred site. Furthermore, he has used the language of weddings, which if nothing else has injected an air of romance into the proceedings. Put together, it gets him very much on her good side.

The matter of comparison is a staple of Greek poetry, appearing far outside of the epic – Sappho says in one of her wedding-songs (115 Lobel-Page, Voigt):

> To whom, dear Bridegroom, should I well compare you?
> To a tender sapling most of all I compare you.

Flattery is a type of praise (*epAINos*), and it's amazing how often in ancient Greece praise involves comparison to plants or animals. There's always an aspect of the riddle (*AINigma*, enigma) to such praise. What does it really mean? Semonides said (fr. 8.1-2, 83-84 West):

> God made the mind of women separately
> in the beginning....
> ....
> One from a bee. Lucky he who gets her,
> for on her alone blame does not settle.

This passage is funny because of its context – Semonides spends most of his time comparing women to unfavorable animals, but while he is insulting the women, he is by extension also poking fun at the men in his audience unfortunate enough to have married them.[19] The comparison to a bee, although humorous to us, is not meant to be funny – it is a positive comparison that also appears in Xenophon, who states (*Oec.* 7.32) that a good woman should be like a queen bee. In fact, it is a fairly common positive comparison. The Pythia at the Oracle of Delphi was known as a bee (Pind. *Pyth.* 4.60), and everybody knew that bees were pious, hard-working laborers who never had sex (after all, it was common knowledge that they were born from flowers [Arist. *HA* 553a16-25, Verg. *G.* 4.197-209], and no flower child could ever have sex).

Semonides isn't the only Greek writer trafficking in riddles. Archilochus (fr. 201 West) says that the fox knows many things, but the hedgehog (Archilochus himself) only one – a big one, and Pindar (*Ol.* 2.87) compares himself favourably as the eagle of Zeus with the two crows (probably meaning his rivals Simonides and Bacchylides). Riddles of this type are all miniature beast-fables (*AINoi*) of the type made popular by Aesop. Of Aesop's many fables, let's recall the one about flattery (Babrius 77):

A crow stood having bitten with his mouth a cheese.
A fox, craving the cheese, with a crafty
word deceived the bird like this:
"Crow, beautiful are your wings and keen your eye,
marvelous your neck. You show the breast of an eagle.
You surpass all creatures with your talon.
Yet, though such a bird, you're mute and do not croak."
The crow was puffed up in his heart by the praise,
and casting the cheese from his mouth, he crowed.
The clever fox took it with greedy tongue.
"You were not mute," she said, "you do have a voice.
You have everything, crow. Just your mind has left you!"

It is obvious that the praise of the flatterer is far from always sincere: not only do ulterior motives lie behind it, but it is often subtly exaggerated. Through hyperbole, praise and its instrument, imitation start down the slippery slope of sarcasm.

When Flatterers turn Bad: the Clown

Greek shame-culture spawned poets who specialized in blame such as Archilochus and Hipponax, or praise such as Sappho and Pindar. In contrast to flatterers, real praise-poets were very much concerned with hitting the nick (*kairos*) or due measure of praise. Too little praise was as bad as too much. We see this with their use of correction or *epanorthosis*, as in Sappho fr. 105A Lobel-Page, Voigt:

Sweet apple reddens

---

[19] L. Shear, "Semonides Fr. 7: Wives and their Husbands," *EMC* N.S. 3 (1984) 39-49.

on the top bough, one farmers forgot
– no: couldn't get.

Of course, if somebody was receiving praise (or blame) that they never deserved in the first place, that required a response. For that they used retraction, as in Stesichorus' *Palinode* (192 *PMG*), in which he recants the story that Helen ran off with Paris and so started the Trojan War (a phantom-Helen did all this instead). The poem begins:

Not true the story:
neither did you go on the well-benched ships
nor come to the towers of Troy.

We see it again in the process of innovation we find in Pindar's *First Olympian* (line 36), which can possibly lead to the response "Thanks, I think":

Son of Tantalus, against my elders will I say...

Because the *kolax*'s praise has ulterior motives, it is potentially insincere and hence baseless. He is also vying for his host's attention amidst other flatterers. Therefore it tends to ignore the *kairos* and become excessive, as with Dionysius' flatterers, who told him that his vomit tasted like honey (and the fact that he believed this speaks volumes – not nice, or for that matter, tasteful volumes, but volumes). So it is that praise (*enKOMiazein* – a synonym for *epainos*) very quickly degenerates into ridicule (*KOMoidein*). It is a small step from insincere and excessive praise meant to please to sarcasm (*sarkasmos*), a Greek word still used today that literally means "tearing the flesh like dogs." This is a step especially likely to be taken by those, such as slaves, who are part of a great man's retinue whether he likes them or not.

The comparison with plants or animals in particular seems ripe for exploitation in sarcasm. The seventh-century poet Archilochus was engaged to marry Neobule when her father Lycambes, having apparently found a suitor with a bigger bride-price, called off the engagement. Archilochus then courted her younger sister with the following poem (S 478.24-41 Page, *SLG* = 196a.24-41 West, *Delectus*):

Neobule –
let another man have her. Yuck! She's overripe
and her virgin bloom has faded
with the grace she used to have.
For she seems...[20] Not moderately
... a mad woman.
To the curb!
May it not happen that...
I, having such a wife,
become a joy for my neighbours.

---

[20] The papyrus on which this poem is preserved is damaged here, and in several other places.

I want *you* much more,
for you aren't untrustworthy or two-faced,
but she's pretty sharp
and does lots of men.
I'm afraid that in my haste
I'd bear blind and untimely pups,
just like the bitch.[21]

In the same way, lover's nicknames like "Ducky" and "Little Dove" (Ar. *Plut.* 1011) could turn nasty. Contemporaries called Socrates' sidekick Chaerephon "the Bat," because he avoided the sun and was deathly pale (Ar. *Av.* 1564) and the politician Pericles was "Squill-head," because his head was shaped like this type of seaweed (Cratinus fr. 71 *PCG*). Several courtesans were called "Toad" because of their brown complexion (Ar. *Eccl.* 1101), in fact the Greek word for "toad" *phryne* is related to the English word "brown." By the way, the most famous "Toad" was tried for bilking her Johns, and her lawyer, Hyperides, exposed her bosom to the court so that the jury would be moved to pity – or some other favourable emotion – and so acquit her (Athen. 13 [590d-e]).

The poorest form, and ultimate parody of a parasite, and prototype of Charlie Chaplin's Little Tramp is the *bomolochus*, "one who waited about altars to beg or steal some meat offered thereon" (cf. Latin *bustirapus*). And from him comes the verb *bomolocheuesthai*, "to clown around, or lampoon." (Note that the clown, like the parasite, is defined in the first instance by his eating-habits.) This type is also called *sannas*, perhaps the origin (via Latin and Italian) of our word "zany."[22] His activity – mimicry and sarcasm – is that of the flatterer gone bad.

We have already examined the aggressive quality of laughter, and it should be noted that sarcasm, lampoons and parody could have potentially deadly effect. When Lycambes broke off Archilochus' engagement with Neobule, he satirized them in the marketplace with poems such as this (172 *IEG*):

Father Lycambes, what were you thinking?
    Who has stolen your wits
with which before you were well furnished? Now
    you seem to the townsfolk just a laugh.

---

[21] A saying had it that puppies are born blind, because their mothers are in too big a hurry to give birth. A human female who has had premarital sex is, obviously, just as impatient, so who knows how her kids will turn out?

[22] If that word does not, rather, come from the Venetian servants' name, Zanni (= Gianni). The "clown" was perhaps originally a "colonist," hence lacking in urbanity, the *pagliaccio* one so poor he slept on straw (*paglia*). The German words for "clown" are proper-names, *Kasper* and *Hans* as also perhaps is French *guignol*.

Dioscorides (*Anth. Pal.* 7.351) tells us that Lycambes and Neobule committed suicide to wipe away the shame of this abuse.[23] Apparently, beating the tar out of Archilochus never occurred to either of them.

The prologue of Aristophanes' *Clouds* of 423 contains the following scene in which an old farmer goes to study with the philosopher Socrates, thinking that if he's *that* much of a braniac, Socrates will teach him how to twist out of his debts (lines 218-27):

Strepsiades:	Come now, who is this man who's in the basket?
Pupil:	Himself.
ST	Who Himself?
P	Socrates.
ST	Oh Socrates!
Socrates:	[*no response*]
ST	Come, you there, call him for me – loudly.
P	Call him yourself; I'm busy. [*exits*]
ST	Oh Socrates!
	Oh Soccer-a-tease!
SO	Why do you call me, Earthling?
ST	First of all, I beg you, tell me what you're doing.
SO	I'm walking on air and overlooking the sun.
ST	...since from a basket you look down on the gods, but not from the ground – right?

Socrates was charged with impiety a quarter-century later in 399 and put on trial (it is a little known fact that this was in part due to a conspiracy of irritated basket-weavers who had noticed he continually stole from them). In the Platonic dialogue that purports to give his defence-speech he says (Pl. *Ap.* 19b-c):

> Let us take up, therefore, from the beginning what the accusation is out of which this slander has arisen, trusting in which, indeed, Meletus has brought this charge against me.[24] Well, what did those who slander me say in their slanders? As though it were the accusers' affidavit, we must read their words: "Socrates does wrong and is a busy-body, inquiring into the things beneath the earth and those in the sky and making the lesser argument greater and teaching others these same things." Some such thing it is. For you yourselves have seen these things in Aristophanes' comedy: a certain Socrates carried around there, claiming to walk on air and spouting much other nonsense, of which I know neither much nor little. And I speak not as one dishonouring such knowledge, if someone really is wise about such things – may I never have to defend myself against Meletus on such a charge! – but, gentlemen of Athens, I have nothing to do with these things.

---

[23] G. W. Bond, "Archilochus and the Lycambides: A New Literary Fragment," *Hermathena* 80 (1952) 3-11 at 10-11.

[24] Athens had no Crown Prosecutor. Private citizens were responsible both for launching law-suits and filing criminal charges. The incentive for the latter was seldom altruistic concern for the interest of the state.

Socrates was eventually convicted in this trial and sentenced to death by poison, proof, if any be needed, that if you don't know your audience, you die on stage.

If sarcasm can be deadly, flattery poses its own danger, in that it can easily produce... the quack!

Chapter VI – A Farmyard of Quacks

The Quack

A flatterer cannot ply his trade alone. He is of necessity someone else's side-kick (Latin *satelles*,[1] origin of our "satellite"). He is at once factotum, gofer, and shill. He is the toady who stands beside the snake-oil salesman's soapbox eating poisoned toads and quaffing Dr. Panacea's *Magic Cure-All Elixir* to demonstrate its restorative properties to the crowd, later dying in agony because the elixir was just as bad as the toad. And just who is this person the flatterer sidles up to, hoping for free stuff, and occasionally the chance to steal some clothes? It is the quack.

There is a danger that if you hear enough good things said about yourself, you may tend eventually to believe them. So it is that, as flatterer, the parasite will eventually push his host into the role of know-it-all, exacerbating any boastful qualities he might already have. This will be the case especially where the host really does have some field of competence, and can be led to think that his expertise extends into all areas of human endeavour. The shame-culture Greeks tolerated, indeed expected, boasting (Homer's phrase for "I am" is *euchomai einai*, "I boast myself to be") – as far as they were concerned, if you had your own horn, you should blow it. What they could *not* tolerate were people who boasted about skills that they did not themselves possess. Yet flattery begets vanity, and so is born the charlatan, crank, crackpot, mountebank or quack: the travelling Fuller Brush salesman hawking his wares, or the itinerant lecturer or other know-it-all, and his equivalent in the electronic-age, the infomercial televangelist talking-head sportscaster (soon to be part of the new series "Christian Xtreme Football!").[2] Such a person must be in perpetual motion, keeping one town ahead of the lynch-mob. His wandering (Latin *error*) is also as much mental as corporeal: he gets mixed up, though he will never admit it; don't believe a word that he says. From their term "to wander," *alaesthai*, Greeks coined a name for this fellow, the *alazon* (Romans called him *gloriosus*); this in turn begat a new verb, *alazoneuesthai*, "to be a quack, to quackify."[3] We say "fellow" and "him"

---

[1] Perhaps from the word in Etruscan – the Klingon-like language of ancient Tuscany – *zatlath*, "companion, bodyguard."

[2] The ancient Greek for "televangelist" – already found, and linked to wandering, in Aeschylus (*Ag.* 1273) – was *agyrtes*, the person who "passed the collection-plate" (*ageirein*) for the god.

[3] O. Ribbeck, *Alazon* (Leipzig 1882), D. M. MacDowell, "The Meaning of *Alazon*," 287-92 in E. M. Craig ed., *Owls to Athens* = Festschrift K. J. Dover (Oxford 1985). Stephanie West suggests that the term comes from the Akkadian *aluzinnu*, whom we met in Chapter IV; see M. L. West, "Some Oriental Motifs in Archilochus," *ZPE* 102 (1994) 1-5 at 2 n. 8. On wandering in ancient Greek culture, see the so-named book by S. Montiglio (Chicago and London, 2005).

advisedly, because there are no female *alazones* in ancient literature – women got to be laugh-worthy in entirely different ways.

If this person were a king, or otherwise powerful, his boastfulness would fall into the characteristic pattern in which satiety (*koros*) leads to wanton violence (*hubris*) resulting in ruin (*ate*) (Solon 6.3-4 West, Theogn. 153-54):[4] this, of course, is the stuff of tragedy. *Kolakeia* begets *alazoneia*, which is the *hubris* of a small man, who is not in a position to cause harm, and his story is a comic one.

Different writers had different definitions of the phenomenon. Aristotle, for example, defines an *alazon* thus (*Nic. Eth.* 4.7.10-13 [= 1127a])(A surgeon-general's warning: this work appears not to have been intended for publication; what we have seem to be Aristotle's own lecture-notes, which not surprisingly are nearly in point form. We have supplied in square brackets words essential to the meaning, but omitted in the text.):

> The person on the one hand who pretends [to have] more than exists for the sake of nothing seems trivial (for [otherwise] he would not delight in his lie), and he appears foolish rather than evil. If, on the other hand, [he pretends] for the sake of something – if for glory or honour, [he is] not too blameworthy, but if for money or as many things as [lead] to money, [he is] more shameful. (He is not a quack in power, but in choice, for according to him also having the ingrained habit, such a one is a quack).... Those, on the one hand who "quackify" for the sake of glory pretend [to have] such things from which praise or predication of happiness [come], those, on the other, for gain from which there is advantage to their neighbours and they can escape their notice not being [honest], like a prophet, sage, doctor. For this reason, most people pretend and "quackify" in respect to these things.

The two things to take away from this passage are that the quack operates out of "ingrained habit" like a mechanical character, and that certain people, such as physicians, use so much mumbo-jumbo jargon that no-one can tell whether they really know what they're talking about, or if they're faking it.

On the other hand, Theophrastus *Characters* 23 limits the *alazon* more or less to one who pretends to have more money than is actually the case:

> By all means quackery will seem to be some [arousal of] expectation of good things that do not exist, and the quack some such person as, standing on the canal-bridge, narrates to strangers that he has much money invested at sea, and will talk about the loan-business – how great it is, and how much he himself has earned and lost: and at he same time as he's running this hundred-metre dash of falsehood, he sends his young slave to the bank, since he has a drachma deposited there.[5] And he entertains a fellow traveler on the road eloquently

---

[4] D. H. Abel, "Genealogies of Ethical Concepts from Hesiod to Bacchylides," *TAPA* 74 (1943) 92-101.

[5] The Athenian monetary system used the drachma as its standard (it was a lawyer's daily fee; see Ar. *Vesp.* 691). A mina is 100 drachmas, a talent 60 minas.

saying that he served under Evander,[6] and how he made out, and how many drinking-cups studded with precious stones he brought back, and he argues about the craftsmen in Asia, that they're better than those in Europe. He will make this bombast, though he has never lived outside the city. And he says that he has three letters from Antipater[7] inviting him to come to him in Macedonia. Though lumber-export has been offered to him tax-free, he refuses, so that he won't be victimized by any "sycophant[8]." "The Macedonians really should have known better!" and that during the grain-shortage it happened that he gave expenses of more than five talents to the suffering among the citizens, for he just could not say no. And when strangers are sitting with him, he will ask one of them to work the pebbles [on his abacus], according to units of sixty drachmas, thirty drachmas, and minas, giving plausible names to each [of his supposed borrowers], and reckon the total as ten talents. He says he's contributed this much to them as *eranoi*,[9] and claims to be taking no account of triremes he's outfitted or other public benefactions he has performed.[10] Going to the horse-market, he pretends to the sellers that he wants to buy, and going to the stalls, he asks for a cloak worth two talents, and chews out his slave for having come along without his wallet. And though living in a rented house, he tells anyone who doesn't know him that it was his father's and that he's going to sell it, because it's too small for entertaining.

As for actual examples of the type, we find them in almost every play of Aristophanes. Examples of quacks in some of the plays of Aristophanes are Socrates in *Clouds* as a stand-in for all sophists, all the Athenian interlopers (priest, poet, prophet, surveyor, inspector and legislator) in *Birds*, the Commissioner of Public Safety in *Lysistrata* and Heracles, Euripides and Aeschylus in *Frogs*. In only two cases do the quacks have their own flatterers: Socrates has his students and Heracles has the slave-girls in Hades'; otherwise these figures come with their heads, as it were, pre-swollen. Among some Aristophanic plays that are also known as not-appearing-in-this-book, quacks surface as ambassadors in *Acharnians*, who are very well paid in return for claiming to know about affairs in foreign countries, Paphlagon in *Knights*, the old juror Philocleon in *Wasps*, Hierocles in *Peace*, the Euripides-loving Mnesilochus in *Thesmophoriazusae*, and Chremes in *Assembly Women*.

Here is the opening of Plautus' *Miles Gloriosus* (*The Braggart Soldier*) which shows a quackish soldier named Pyrgopolynices ("Tower of many victories") interacting with his flatterer, the slave Artotrogus ("Breadnibbler"):

---

[6] I.e. Alexander the Great.

[7] Alexander's successor as ruler of Macedonia.

[8] On this social pest, see further on in this chapter.

[9] Loans raised by contributions for the benefit of an individual, bearing no interest, but recoverable at law in instalments.

[10] *Litourgiai*, "liturgies," a kind of luxury-tax.

Pyrgopolynices: Take care that the gleam of my shield is brighter
     than the sun's rays are ever used to be, when it is cloudless,
     so that, whenever need arises, against a close-packed division
     it may blind with its keenness the keenness of my enemies' eyes.
     For I want to console this sword of mine,
     lest it lament or grow dispirited at heart,
     since a long time now I have been carrying it on holiday,
     though it longs, poor thing, to make stuffing out of the enemy.
     But where is Artotrogus?
Artotrogus: He stands beside the
     brave and lucky man with regal look,
     the warrior – why, Mars would scarcely dare to say
     that even his bravery matches yours.
P   Now, who was it I saved during the Battle of
     Bollweevil? Rumblefighter
     McFamousadvisorofinsubordination, Neptune's grandson.
A   I remember. Of course, you mean that man in golden armour
     whose legions you blew off with a breath
     as a wind does leaves or roof-shingles.

Not only is this fellow impressed by his own military might; he thinks he's quite the lady-killer as well. Of course, by the end of the play he's been exposed as both a coward and a turn-off to the opposite sex.

In Catullus poem 10 we see how flattery can bring on a fit of quackery, and also how the boaster can get his comeuppance:

My Varus took me to see his girlfriend
from the market, where I'd been hanging out:
a little slut, I could tell right away –
not, however, uncharming or unsexy.
When we got there, there came to us
various topics of conversation, among which, what
Bithynia was like now, how people were making out,
and how much money I'd cleared.
I told it like it was: nothing came
to the governors themselves, or their staff
whereby they could bring home their heads more richly oiled,
especially when one had a cock-sucker
governor who didn't treat his staff worth straw!
"But surely even so," they said, "you bought
what they say is native there:
men for your litter." So that in front of the girl
I might make myself out one of the luckier ones,
I said, "Things weren't so bad for me,
that, though the province has fallen on hard times,
I wasn't able to get eight men – sturdy ones."
(Though I had no-one either here or there
who could put onto his shoulder
the broken leg of a camp-cot.)
At this, like the little Sodomite she was,
she said, "I beg you, dear Catullus, loan these men

a while, for I want to be carried to
Serapis' temple." "Wait!" I said to the girl:
"That thing I said just now I have –
I wasn't thinking. My companion,
Cinna, I mean Gaius – he got them for himself.
But whether they're his or mine, what do I care?
I use them as often as if I'd bought them myself.
But you're really a pain and a nuisance,
if you won't let a guy day-dream!"

An example where the pretentious claim is not to money, but to expertise is found in Petronius *Satyricon* chapters 48 and 59 at the dinner of Trimalchio:

> When Agamemnon said, "A poor man and a rich man were enemies..."
> Trimalchio said, "What's a poor man?"
> "Very clever," said Agamemnon, and explained some *controversia* or other.[11]
> Immediately Trimalchio said, "If this really happened, it's not a *controversia*; if it didn't happen, it's nothing at all."
> We followed this and other jokes with most lavish praise.
> "I ask you," he said, "my dearest Agamemnon, whether you recall the twelve labours of Hercules, or the story about Ulysses, how the Cyclops pulled out his thumb with his fire-tongs? I myself used to read these things in Homer as a boy. And I myself with my own eyes saw the Sibyl of Cumae hanging in a jar, and when those boys used to say, "*Sibylle, qu'est-ce-que vous voulez?*," she used to reply, "*Je veux mourir!*"[12]
> ....
> A troupe entered and immediately banged their shields with their spears. Trimalchio himself sat on a cushion and, as the Homerists were declaiming in Greek verses, as they are pompously wont to do (*ut insolenter solent*), he read the script in Latin in a sing-song voice. Soon, when he'd gotten silence, he said, "Do you know what play they're doing? Diomedes and Ganymede were two brothers. Their sister was Helen. Agamemnon abducted her and substituted a hind for Diana. Now Homer is explaining how the Trojans and Parentines fought one another.[13] As you know, he won, and gave Iphigeneia, his daughter, to Achilles as a wife. That's why Ajax went insane, and right now he'll explain the rest of the plot."

Some Species of Quack: The Poseur, The Busybody and the Bully

The quack would cause you no trouble, if you could avoid him. This, however, is hard to do, and the quack is as addicted to symbiosis as the

---

[11] A *controversia* was a bogus legal-case used to train student-lawyers in debating-techniques.

[12] Here, as in Cicero's letter quoted in Chapter III, I translate the Greek words as French. (RDG)

[13] "Parentines" don't exist. Trimalchio is confusing Paris of Troy with the Tarentines – inhabitants of Taranto in Apulia.

flatterer. You cannot be a **poseur** (*phenax*) unless you have someone to pose in front of. He must ply his trade, talking nonsense (*phlyaria*) in front of an audience, in a public space if possible (captive audiences can be quite useful, but you have to take out the gag in order for them to congratulate you). Sophists are perhaps the archetypal example, but we also see this very clearly in Petronius' *Satyricon* 90 with the character of Eumolpus the poet giving spontaneous recitations of his work in an art-gallery:

> Some of those who were promenading in the colonnade threw stones at Eumolpus as he was reciting. But he, who recognized the applause for his genius, covered his head, and fled out of the temple. I was afraid that someone might call me a poet too. So having followed the fleeing man, I came to the shore and as soon as it was possible to stop out of weapons' reach, I said, "Tell me: what do you want for yourself with this disease? You've spent less than two hours with me, and you've spoken more often in poetic than in human speech. So I don't wonder if people chase you with stones. I too will weigh down the fold of my cloak with rocks so that as often as you begin to lose it, I may let blood for you from your head."
>
> He shook his head and said, "Alas, young man, not today for the first time have I read the signs. No, in fact as often as I enter a theatre in order to recite something, the crowd is wont to listen to me in this unexpected way. But so that you too may not have a quarrel with me, I will abstain from this food for the whole day."
>
> "Well then," said I, "if you swear off your bile for today, we'll have dinner together."

(Note that Eumolpus' behaviour is a "disease" caused by too much "bile," and that Encolpius proposes to cure it by the time-tested medical procedure of blood-letting, which in this case is stone-cold by any standards.)

It is a small step for the quack to move from the harmless poseur using you as an unwilling audience, to offering you unsolicited advice as a **busybody** or know-it-all (*periergos, polypragmon* or *philopragmon*).[14] One problem in this is that the busybody disturbs your peace of mind and tranquillity. Another is that the busybody isn't necessarily right about this advice, and for that matter, shouldn't be sticking his nose into the situation anyway. This is Theophrastus *Character* 13:

> Of course, busybodiness will seem to be a certain excess of words and deeds out of good intentions, and the busybody some such person as will stand up and promise of his own accord what he will not be able to give. And when a certain matter has been agreed to be just, he will enter into some one part of it, and be proved wrong. He will force his slave to mix more wine[15] than those present are

[14] V. Ehrenberg, "Polypragmosune: A Study in Greek Politics," *JHS* 67 (1947) 46-67; the opposite of the busybody is the quietist, *apragmon*, on which see L. B. Carter, *The Quiet Athenian* (Oxford 1986).

[15] The Greeks didn't drink their wine straight-up. They mixed it with water instead (cf. Chapter III note 39).

able to drink. He will separate in a fight even men whom he does not know. And having left the highway, he'll show you a short-cut, then not be able to find his way. He will go up to the general and ask when he intends to give battle and what orders he will give the day after tomorrow. He'll go up to his father and say, "Mom is already asleep in your room." And when the doctor has forbidden him to give wine to someone sick, saying that it's worth a try, he'll give it anyway, and the suffering one is sunk. When a woman has died, he will write on her tomb the names of her husband and of her father and of her mother and the woman's own name and where she was from, and in addition he'll write that these were all good people.[16] And when he is about to swear an oath, he will say to those present, "Before this too I've sworn many oaths."

The Spartans thought busybodiness was a particularly Athenian characteristic, if we can trust Thucydides (1.70):

> For [the Athenians] alone both have and hope alike for things that they intend through making their attempt on the things they plan swift. And they toil at all these things with labours and dangers all the time, and enjoy less than anyone what there is through always acquiring more, and consider a feast-day nothing else than doing what is necessary, and they consider peaceful idleness no less a misfortune than constant busyness. So that if anyone would say in a nutshell that they were born neither to have peace themselves nor to allow others to do so, he would speak the truth.

An early literary example of the busybody is Hephaestus interfering in a quarrel between his mother, Hera and Zeus in *Iliad* 1.568-600. This is a particularly innocent example, because he succeeds in putting an end to a quarrel they are having:

> So [Zeus] spoke, and the ox-eyed lady Hera was afraid,
> and sat down in silence, having bowed her heart,
> and the Olympian gods were upset throughout the house of Zeus.
> Then did Hephaestus, famous craftsman, begin to address
> his own mother bringing her comfort, white-armed Hera:
>   "Surely these will be pestilent deeds and unbearable,
> if you two quarrel like this for mortals' sake,
> and bring brawling among the gods. There'll be no
> pleasure in the good feast, since worse things will win out.
> To my mother I advise these things, even though she is very thoughtful,
> and to our Father, to bring comfort to Zeus, so that not again
> may the Father quarrel and disturb the feast for us.
> For if Zeus the lightener should wish
> to strike us out of our seats – for he's very much stronger...
> But you speak to him at least with soothing words,
> so that straightway Zeus will be propitious toward us."
> .....
>   So he spoke, and the goddess, white-armed Hera smiled,
> and, having smiled, she took the cup from her son's hand,

---

[16] So trying to bring her more glory, he winds up writing the inscription in size 10 font.

and he for the other gods starting from the right – for all of them –
poured sweet nectar, drawing it from the mixing-bowl.
Unquenchable laughter went up from the blessed gods,
as they saw Hephaestus bustling around the house.

But busybodies, of course, existed in real-life also. Euphiletus in Lysias
1.15-16 tells us how he was once approached on the street by a slave-woman,
who told him that his wife was cheating on him:

> After these things, gentlemen, when an interval of time had passed, during
> which I was very ignorant of my own misfortunes, there came to me a certain
> old slave-woman, sent by a lady with whom that man had committed adultery,
> as I learned later. This lady, being angry and considering herself wronged, since
> he no longer kept coming to her as before, kept watch until she found what was
> the cause. Coming up to me, therefore, the slave-woman, who had been
> watching my house, said, "Euphiletus, don't think I have come to you out of any
> busybodiness. For the man who is wronging you and your wife happens to be
> an enemy of ours. If you take your slave-girl, who goes to market and looks after
> you, and torture her, you will learn everything. It is," she said, "Eratosthenes
> from Oe who does these things, who has ruined not only your wife, but many
> others also. This is his specialty."

When Socrates was brought to trial on a charge of impiety by Meletus
and other accusers, he cross-examined them during his defence speech and
revealed that they had not devoted much thought to the subject on which
they had charged him. Socrates then said (Pl. *Ap.* 26e-27a):

> You're unbelievable, Meletus, and this even, as it seems to me, to yourself.
> For this man here seems to me, men of Athens, to be completely outrageous and
> unrestrained, and has simply brought this charge out of some outrage and want
> of restraint and youthfulness. For he seems like one who poses a riddle to test
> me: "Will Socrates the Wise know that I am joking and saying the opposite to
> myself, or will I deceive him and the other listeners?" For this man seems to me
> to say the opposite to himself in his indictment, as if he were to say, "Socrates
> is guilty of not believing in gods, but of believing in gods," and surely this is the
> charge of one playing games.

With the above passage we see how easy it is for the well-meaning
meddler (and more often the not-well-meaning meddler) to become the
greedy **bully** (*loidoros, pleonektes*), especially in legal contexts. One group of
legal bullies were the jurors, who were typically senior citizens with time on
their hands, earning a little extra spending money and getting a Geraldo
Rivera or Jerry Springer-style entertainment to boot by throwing their power
around. Aristophanes puts this account of the juror's life into the mouth of
the character Philocleon in *Wasps* 548-630 (speaking to his son):

> Indeed straightaway from the starting-line I will show concerning our power
> that it is less than no kingdom.
> For what creature is happier and more blessed than a juror,
> or more coddled or feared... and we're old men?

For when I first creep out of bed, big, six-foot tall men
spy me from the railings – as soon as I get close
they set in mine a hand that is soft, having stolen public funds.[17]
Lowering their voices, and pouring on the pity, they beg me,
"Pity me, Father, I beg you, if you yourself ever embezzled
when holding an office, or buying food for your mess-mates in the army."
He wouldn't even have known I were alive, but for his previous acquittal.
.....
Then, having been begged and having had my anger wiped away,
once I come inside I do none of all these things I promised,
but I listen to men hurling their whole voices after an acquittal.
Come then, what piece of flattery can a juror not hear there?
They bewail their own poverty and pile on false
misfortunes to those that exist, each as he comes in, until they equal mine.
They tell us myths and some joke from Aesop,
and they mock so that I might laugh and put aside my anger.
If we are not persuaded by these ploys, they immediately drag out their little
        children,
girls and boys, by the hand, and I hear them
cower together while they bleat, and then their father over the noise
begs me like a god, trembling to acquit him in his examination.
"If you like the sound of lamb, pity my children's voice!"
But what if I like piglets?[18] Persuade me with your daughter's.
Then we loosen a bit the guitar-peg of our anger against him.
Now isn't this great power and mockery of wealth?
.....
Now when boys are being registered, we can look at their genitals,
and if Oenagrus comes before us as a defendant, he doesn't get off til
he recites the most beautiful speech from *Niobe*.
And if a flute-player wins a case, as payment for it,
he straps on his flute and plays an exit-song for us jurors as we leave.
And if a father, dying and leaving his daughter as an heiress, gives her to
someone,
we tell him to get his head beaten along with his inheritance,
and from the shell that lies so solemnly over the seals
we give her to whomever begs and persuades us.
And we do these things without being accountable; no-one else does that.
.....
But the sweetest of all these things I had forgotten:
when I come home having my pay, then everyone comes at once as I approach,
congratulating me on the money, and first my daughter
washes and oils my feet and, bending over, kisses me,

---

[17] And therefore never having had to do manual labour.

[18] This is a double entendre – the Greek word for "piggy" is also slang for
female genitalia.

and calling me "Daddy-poo," fishes the three obols out of my mouth with her
    tongue.[19]
And the little woman, flattering me, brings out a steaming cake,
and then sitting next to me forces me: "Eat this;
nibble that!" I adore these things. And I don't need
to look to you and the cashier to see when he'll set breakfast out –
damned mumbler, for fear he may soon have to knead me another.
I get this pay as a shield against misfortunes; equipment that protects against
    missiles.

While bullies made for good stock figures in comedy, we also find real-
life instances of bullying in ancient literature. These can involve physical
abuse, as in the story of Conon in Demosthenes 54.3-9:

> I went out two years ago to Panactum, guard-duty having been assigned to
> us. Now the sons of this Conon here pitched tent near us, as we would not have
> preferred, for there was enmity from the beginning and sources of friction arose
> for us from this. About these please listen: these men used to drink every day all
> day as soon as they had had breakfast, and while we were on duty, they
> continued to do so. But we – as was our custom here – so we behaved abroad as
> well. When it happened to be the hour for other people to have dinner, these
> men were already far gone and abusive from wine often against the slaves who
> attended us, and finally against us ourselves. For, saying that our slaves had sent
> smoke toward them as they were cooking fish or had bad-mouthed them, or
> whatever, they hit them, and dumped their chamber-pots on them, and pissed
> on them, and left out nothing at all of licentiousness and violence. Seeing these
> things, and lamenting them, we first told them to leave, but when they kept
> scoffing at us, and did not desist, we told the matter to the general – all my
> mess-mates going together, not I apart from the rest. When he chewed them
> out, and punished them not only for their licentiousness toward us, but also for
> the things they were doing generally in the camp, they were so far from
> desisting or being ashamed that as soon as it got dark, immediately they leapt
> on us that very evening and at first were calling us names, but finally extended
> blows to me and made so much crowing and confusion around my tent that
> even the general and the taxiarchs came, and some of the other soldiers, who
> kept us either from suffering anything incurable or from doing anything, having
> been badly treated by these men....
>
> Now then, these are the things of which I thought it necessary to make no
> mention. Some time not long afterward as I was walking, as is my custom, in
> the evening in the market with Phanostratus, the son of Cephiseus, one of my
> chums, Ctesias, this man's son came upon us, drunk, at the Leocorion near
> Pythodorus' place. He saw us and croaked, and having said something to himself
> as drunks will so that we couldn't catch what he was saying, he went up to
> Melite, for there were drinking there (for we learned this afterwards) at
> Pamphilus, the launderer's shop this Conon here, a certain Diotimus,
> Archebiades, Smintheus, son of Eubulus, Theogenes, son of Andromenes, many
> more whom Ctesias got up and brought to the market. It happened that we were

---

[19] Yes, that really is where the Greeks kept their money. Those who wear
bed sheets don't have pockets (remember Encolpius putting stones into
the folds of his cloak?). At the very least, it can be said that the Greeks
truly did put their money where their mouth was.

turning back from Persephone's temple and walking again on the same street where the Leocorion is when we met them. When we met, one of them, I know not who, fell on Phanostratus, and held him while this Conon here and his son and the son of Andromenes fell on me and first stripped off my cloak and then tripped me and pushed me into the mud and with leaping on me and outraging me they put me into such a state that my lip was split open and my eyes swollen shut. They left me so badly off that I was able neither to stand up nor to speak. Lying there, I heard them say many and terrible things. Among other things there was some blasphemy, and I shrink to mention some of it to you. He, though, for this is a sign of his hubris and a proof that the whole matter was his idea – I will tell you this – he sang imitating victorious chickens, and he thought it right to beat himself on the ribs with his elbows instead of wings.[20]

As well as the physical bully, we also meet with his intellectual counterpart. A good example is Thrasymachus, who vigorously advocates a might-is-right philosophy in Plato's *Republic* 344d-e:

> Having said these things, Thrasymachus had it in mind to leave, like a bath-man having poured over our ears much and close-packed speech. But those present would not let him leave, but compelled him to stay and defend the argument that he had made. I myself was in great need and said, "Strange Thrasymachus, having thrown in such a speech, do you have it in mind to go away before teaching us sufficiently or before we learn whether it is truly like this or otherwise?" Or do you think it is a small matter to define the conduct of an entire life, by conducting which each of us will live the most profitable life? "Do I think," said Thrasymachus, "that it is otherwise?"
> "You seem to," I said...

Perhaps the greatest satisfaction comes when one of these bullies is defeated, restoring the social order. Indeed some humour can be found in the defeat of a bully like Thrasymachus, as it gives them their comeuppance. While these species of quack are related, there are other subsets, just as humorous.

More Species of Quack: The Sycophant, the Gossip, and the Babbler

The most important kind of bully at Athens bore the very odd name of **sycophant** (the Latin word is *delator*), which literally means "revealer of the figs." To understand this name we have to remember first of all that Attica, the territory of Athens, was not very fertile, and had few agricultural products. One of these, and a crucial source of revenue for the gross domestic product, was figs. The second thing to remember is that there was no police force or crown prosecutor; it was incumbent upon individual citizens to press charges against wrong-doers whenever they saw a crime being committed. One who saw a fellow citizen hoarding figs, failing to pay tax on the income made from them, or price-gouging in the marketplace could go and denounce

---

[20] A reference to the popular sport of cock-fighting.

him to the state officials, offering to reveal to them the whereabouts of the criminal's figs.[21]

It was a small step from this legitimate, if unpopular activity, to *threatening* someone with denouncing them to the officials in order to extort money or favours, or shake down and blackmail. When Peisthetaerus and Euelpides make a city in the clouds in Aristophanes *Birds* (1410-69) one of the Athenian interlopers is a sycophant, who wants to get wings from the birds to help him island-hopping as he goes from place to place perjuring himself, bringing malicious prosecutions and generally shit-disturbing.

It is very unfortunate that English-speakers have taken over the word "sycophant" without understanding its meaning. We use it as a synonym for "flatterer," whereas it is quite clear that the word really denotes a species of quack – a very malicious, underhanded species.

Another type of busybody, who is especially active in sexual matters is the **gossip** or tattle-tale, whom Greeks called the *psithyrizon* (literally, "the whisperer"). Not content merely to poke into other people's business, the gossip engages in what could be considered the ancient Greek version of tabloid journalism. Here are a few examples of his activity. We begin with Nausicaa, who after meeting Odysseus in *Odyssey* 6, offers to lead him home to her parents, the king and queen. But she says (lines 270-85):[22]

> For the bow and quiver do not matter to the Phaeacians,
> but masts and oars of ships and ships well balanced,
> delighting in which they travel over the grey sea.
> I shrink from an unpleasant reputation among them, lest someone later
> might blame me, for they are very arrogant throughout the town.
> Now some one of the worse sort might speak like this, once they have met us:
> "Who is this who follows Nausicaa, this handsome and tall
> stranger? Where did she find him? Now he'll be her husband.
> Or has she perhaps brought some wanderer from his ship,
> one of the outlanders, since there are no people nearby?
> Or what god much prayed-for in prayers has come
> climbing down from heaven, and will keep her all of his days?
> Better that she herself go and finds a husband
> from elsewhere, since she dishonours the Phaeacians
> in town who woo her – many and good ones too."
> So they will speak, and there would be reproaches for me...

We see similar people at work in Pindar's *Olympian* 1.41-51. The poet is addressing Pelops, who has been carried off to heaven by the love-struck Poseidon, contrary to the well known story where he is murdered by his father, cut up into a stew, and served to the gods as a taste test:

---

[21] R. Osborne, "Vexatious Litigation in Classical Athens: Sykophancy and the Sykophant," 83-102 in P. Cartledge et al. eds., *Nomos* (Cambridge 1990) and D. Harvey, "The Sykophant and Sykophancy: Vexatious Redefinition?" 103-121 (Ibid.).

[22] See also Lysias 7.18.

> When you were missed, and never to mother the searchers brought you home,
>   soon in secret one of the jealous neighbours said
>   that into rolling fire-boiling
>   water they cut you limb-meal
>   with a knife, and about the tables last
>   of all your flesh they broke and ate.

So, the jealous neighbour who is making up stories is to blame.

Catullus is well aware of their existence when he advises his girlfriend in poem 5 to kiss him so much that they won't be able to gossip about it, on the fairly specious grounds that the more kisses there are, the harder they will be to count, and the less the likelihood of anyone giving them the evil eye (for which statistical accuracy is apparently a prerequisite):

> Let us live, my Lesbia, and let us love,
> and the rumours of rather severe old men
> let us count all as one penny!
> Suns can set and come again;
> for us when once brief light has set,
> night is one perpetual time of sleeping.
> Give me kisses – a thousand, then a hundred,
> then another thousand, then a second hundred,
> then up to another thousand, then a hundred.
> Then – when we will have made many thousands –
> let's jumble them, so we can't tell,
> or any bad man hex us,
> when he knows how many there are of kisses.

(Vergil in *Aeneid* 4.173-97 has a description of gossip, *Fama* that is quite extensive, but is a personification of Rumour as an evil winged woman, rather than an account of her human agents, the gossips themselves.)

Another type of quack is the **babbler** (*lalos*), who says things autistically to himself without caring whether anyone is listening – rather as cell-phone users seem to be nowadays. In Chapter III we met Archimedes, who ran down the street naked shouting *eureka!*, "I've found it!" When we last saw him, we pointed out the most obvious problem with his behaviour (he's naked in public), but it bears mentioning also that he is also talking to himself. After all, what will passers-by say? "Found *what*? Obviously not your clothes. Your inner-streaker, perhaps?"

In the last section we met the mumbling slave in Aristophanes' *Wasps*, which was apparently a stock-character (cf. Ar. *Ran.* 747, Herod. 6.7) and the mumbling drunk in Demosthenes' speech against Conon. Another example of someone talking to himself is the great Attic orator, Demosthenes. When he was young, he suffered from a lisp (not the interchange of "th" for "s" that sometimes plagues English-speakers, but a tendency to pronounce all "r"s as "l"). Plutarch (*Dem*. 11.1-2) tells us that Demosthenes strove to correct this problem by using voice exercises. His favourite was to go to the sea-side, fill his mouth with pebbles, and shout over the sound of the waves.

Great. So, first he lisps and now he's shouting with pebbles in his mouth. How helpful is that?

Yet another person who winds up talking to himself is the foreigner. Greeks called foreigners "barbarians."[23] We have inherited this word from them, but added to it a notion of Viking bravado that it originally lacked. For Greeks, barbarians were simply people who did not speak Greek, and so everything they said sounded (to Greeks) the same, rather like "bar bar bar...."[24] Most barbarians whom the Greeks encountered were Asiatics, who struck them as not at all "barbaric" in our sense, but far too refined and effeminate, with their Persian slippers, tiaras, and ear-rings. Euripides in his *Orestes* has a messenger run out of the house to reveal the goings-on within. Messengers from within are a constant of the Attic theatre, because convention forbade playwrights to show people actually being killed on stage, the audience could only hear, via messenger-speech, about atrocities already committed within. For some reason, in this particular play, Euripides chose to make the messenger a Phrygian (i.e. someone from present-day Turkey), who is so cowardly that he rushes out to report a murder, BEFORE it has actually happened (in the event, in fact, it never will), and does so, moreover, in pidgin Greek (lines 1369-75):

> I have fled the Argive sword from death
> in barbaric slippers
> over cedarwood house of porches
> and Doric triglyphs
> (Gone! Gone! Earth! Earth!)
> In barbaric fleeings –
>   argh!

We do not know for sure how comic Euripides intends this slave to be. We are without doubt correct, however, in believing that the foreign Rubber God at the end of Aristophanes' *Birds* is intentionally hilarious. In that play two Athenians team up with a bunch of birds and found a city in the clouds. This blocks the air-rights of the gods, and smoke from sacrifices, instead of reaching Olympus, just hits Cloudcuckooland and bounces off. The gods, soon starving, like the post-deluvian gods in the *Epic of Gilgamesh*, sue for peace and to this end send an embassy to Cloudcuckooland. This embassy consists of three gods: the stern and noble Poseidon, lord of the sea and brother of Zeus, Heracles, who was once a human but has been apotheosized (i.e. transformed into a god) and whom comedy always portrays as a moronic glutton, and – perhaps for politically correct inclusiveness – a god of the

---

[23] Cf. E. Hall, *Inventing the Barbarian: Greek Self-Definition through Tragedy* (Oxford 1989).

[24] Or, to say it with a lisp, *blah, blah, blah*....

foreign, barbaric Triballi tribe, a certain Rubber God,[25] who cannot, of course, speak Greek. When the embassy arrives, they find that our Athenian hero has found some of his fellow-citizen birds guilty of treason, condemned them to death, and is just now barbecuing them (a form of comic behavior we will examine further in chapter VIII). Poseidon advocates a hard-line, pro-god policy, but once Heracles has caught a whiff of the barbecue, he's all for making a deal. They then turn to the Rubber God, and ask his opinion. He replies (1628-29):

Saunaka baktarinkrousa.

Heracles immediately steps in to translate: "He says I've spoken very well," and so by a vote of two to one, the gods accept the Cloudcuckoolanders' terms, and settle down to feast.

Wanting to end this Chapter on a slightly more edifying note, let us point out that any piece of writing is also a kind of autistic babbling, that talks *at* rather than *to* its audience. In Plato's *Phaedrus* (274c-275b) Socrates tells the story of the Egyptian, Theuth[26], who invented hieroglyphs, the first kind of writing. So proud of himself was he at having invented this "cure for forgetfulness," as he fancied it, that he rushed to see the pharaoh, assuming that he would appoint him vizier or something equally prestigious. Imagine his disappointment when the pharaoh, having listened carefully as he explained his new invention, replied as follows:

> When [men] have learned this, it will offer forgetfulness to their mind through not caring for their memory, so that through trust in external writing using foreign signs, they will not remember by themselves. You have found an elixir not of memory but of reminder. You bring your pupils the appearance of wisdom, not the truth, for having been made by you very learned without education, they will seem to be very wise, while being ignorant for the most part and hard to be with, having become seeming-wise instead of wise.[27]

To put this into the context of our present discussion, Theuth and his invention will wind up, according to the pharaoh, turning everyone into a quack.

Socrates concludes his tale by saying (275d):

> For perhaps, Phaedrus, writing has this strange aspect, and how truly similar to painting it is! For its offspring too stand there as though living, but if

---

[25] Greek *tribein* means "to rub," hence to pass one's time like a Parisian *flâneur*. "To rub one's peg," of course, means "to jerk off" (Automedon, *Anth. Pal.* 5.128).

[26] Perhaps the inspiration for the story of Corinthian glass – a kind of early plastic – mentioned in Pet. *Sat.* 50.

[27] See the comments on this passage in J. Derrida (B. Johnson trans.), Dissemination (Chicago, 1981) 75-84.

you should ask something, it haughtily keeps total silence. The same also are words: you would think that sentient beings were saying something, but if you ask what has been said, wanting to learn more, it always means the same one thing.

Interestingly, many of the quacks have specific gender roles, most of them male. Only a few, such as the gossip, appear as both men and women. Indeed, it is possible to say that the male and female worlds were in many ways separate, and the comic roles differed for each sex.[28] But, before we can look at that, we need to examine the poor characters who have the quack inflicted upon them.

---

[28] We will explore women's roles more fully in Chapter IX.

Chapter VII – A Sucker for Every Occasion

The Unwilling Victim

Unfortunately, the quack cannot exist for long in a social vacuum, or even in the presence of the moocher alone. Inspired by the attentions – and convinced by the lies – of the flattering moocher, the quack will draw his light out from under its bushel and shine it on any unsuspecting person he meets, whether they want it or not. Thus we encounter the sucker (*koroibos*) – the poor fool who finds himself *unable* or, through a misplaced sense of tact, *unwilling* to escape the attentions of the quack, and so becomes his captive audience. The word *koroibos* – still found in Modern Greek in the form *koroïdo* – derives from a man's name, a legendary idiot who tried, among other things, to measure waves (Lucian *Philops.* 3 with Schol., *Suda* s.v.).[1]

The most archetypal captive audience occurs not in comedy at all, but in tragedy in the title-character of Aeschylus' *Prometheus Bound*, who spends lines 561-912 of the play nailed to a rock listening to the whining ramblings of Io, the talking cow. Call us heartless, but we find this pretty funny.

Comedy does, however, also provide a good view of the sucker, e.g. in the parodos (that is, the chorus' entry-song) in Aristophanes' *Frogs* 209-267. In that play the god Dionysus is on his way to the underworld to rescue Euripides and has to row the ferry-boat of the dead all by himself. In an effort to keep his rowing in time, he begins to sing. No sooner has he begun, however, than he is interrupted by the frogs (ghost-frogs, actually) who inhabit the infernal lake. They sing their customary song (*brekekekex koax, koax*) over top of his, destroying his own song, and mucking up his rowing-rhythm in the process, yet trapped as he is in the middle of the lake of Hell, Dionysus has no choice but to listen, and eventually to start croaking himself – there is something intrinsically quackish about frogs (think of the title-character in A. A. Milne's play, *Toad of Toad Hall*):

Chorus of Frogs:
    Brekekekex koax koax
    brekekekex koax koax.
    Marshy children of the fountains,
    let us sing the flute-accompanied
    cry of hymns – my fair-throated song
    koax koax,
    which about the Nysaean son
    of Zeus, Dionysus in the marshes we used to shout,
    when the hung-over pub-crawling
    crowd of folks came down to my sanctuary
    on the feast of Pots.
    Brekekekex koax koax.

Dionysus:

---

[1] R. G. Austin, *P. Vergili Maronis Aeneidos Liber Secundus.* (Oxford 1964) 150-151. See the next chapter.

I at least am beginning to ache
on my tail-bone koax koax.

C   Brekekekex koax koax.

D   Perhaps to you it's of no concern.

C   Brekekekex koax koax.

D   Just drop dead, koax and all!
For there's nothing but koax.

C   Rightly too, you meddling man,
for the fair-lyred Muses love me
and hoof-footed Pan who plays voiced by the reed,
and guitarist Apollo delights in the reed
that I tend for his frets
in the water of my marshes.
Brekekekex koax koax.

D   But I have blisters
and my rump started to sweat long ago.
Soon it will bend over and say...

C   Brekekekex koax koax.

D   But you song-loving tribe,
desist!

C   We'd rather sing
if ever on sunny
days we hopped through the galingale
and the reed, delighting in
the often-diving tunes of songs,
or fleeing Zeus's rain
we sang a watery, nimble chorus-song
in the depths
with bubble-blusterings.

D   Brekekekex koax koax.
I'm catching this from you.

C   We'll suffer dreadfully, then.

D   More dreadfully will I, if I
explode from rowing.

C   Brekekekex koax koax.

D   Damn you! I don't care!

C   We will have croaked

> as much as our throats
> can open all day long.
>
> D   Brekekekex koax koax.
>   You will not win with this.
>
> C   Nor will you beat us at all.
>
> D   Nor will you beat me
>   ever, for I will have croaked
>   all day long until I will beat you with koax.
>   Brekekekex koax koax.

Dionysus becomes the sucker, but unwillingly. He's surrounded by the frogs, cannot reach them, cannot escape, and is therefore forced to deal with them on their own terms. For a brief time, he truly becomes their "toady."

The sucker may try to evade the quack, but seldom with success. Consider this story that Cicero tells about Publius Cornelius Scipio Nasica, who was consul in 191 B.C. (*De Oratore* 2.68 [276]):

> Just so was that saying of Nasica. When he had come to the poet Ennius and his slave-girl told him, when he asked at the front door, that Ennius wasn't at home, Nasica felt that she said this on her master's orders and that he really was inside. A few days later, when Ennius came to Nasica's and asked for him at the door, Nasica shouted out that he wasn't home. Then Ennius said, "What? Don't I recognize your voice?" Here Nasica said, "You're a shameless man! When I asked for you, I believed your slave-girl that you weren't home, and you don't believe me myself?"

It's important to note that in this case the sucker, Ennius, really has no defense against the quacky Nasica, just as in the previous example Dionysus has no defense against the frogs. Nasica catches him unawares, and by the time Ennius realizes what is happening, it's too late for him to duck out of it. Likewise, Encolpius, Ascyltus and Giton (who gradually morph from moochers into suckers as their bellies are filled in the dinner-party episode of Petronius' *Satyricon*) don't have much luck in trying to get away from their overbearing host, Trimalchio (72):

> Trimalchio said, "Therefore, since we know that we are destined to die, why not let's live? So that I can see you all happy, let's take ourselves to the bath. On my life, you won't regret it: it's hot as a furnace!"
>
> "True, true," said Habinnas. "Making two days out of one – nothing I like better!" He leapt up in bare feet and began following the clapping Trimalchio.
>
> I looked at Ascyltus and asked, "What do you think? As for me, if I see a bath, I'll die on the spot."
>
> "We're agreed," he said: "While they're heading for the bath, we'll escape in the crowd."
>
> When we had decided this, Giton led the way through the colonnade and we came to the front door, where the chained dog greeted us with such a ruckus that Ascyltus even fell into the pool. Not only that, but, drunk myself also, who

had been scared even of a painted dog, as I was helping the swimmer, I too was dragged into the same abyss. However, the porter saved us, who by his intervention both calmed the dog and pulled us trembling onto dry land. As for Giton, meanwhile, he saved himself from the dog by a very cunning plan:[2] whatever we had given him at dinner, he scattered before the barking animal, and it, distracted by the food, forgot its fury. For the rest, when shivering and wet we asked the porter to let us out the door, he said, "You're wrong if you think you can go out the same way you came in. No-one of the guests is ever let out by the same door: they come in through one and go out through another."[3]

(This group is really quackish enough that they cannot ultimately be victimized. In the end they are saved by the bell – well, by a false fire-alarm, actually – and escape in the confusion that ensues.)

The suckers that we have been considering so far are robbed only of their time and peace of mind, but why stop there? A true sucker can be fleeced of just about anything. A most interesting case is an early example of identity theft. A certain Athenian named Mantias had two sons, one by his wife and one by his mistress. As was the custom, he named his legitimate son Mantitheus, after his own father. The illegitimate son he named after that boy's maternal uncle, Boeotus. Mantias died while the boys were both young, and Boeotus began to pass himself off as Mantitheus, and the real (or at least the original) Mantitheus took him to court to try and get back exclusive rights to the use of the name "Mantitheus, son of Mantias." He hired the speech-writer Demosthenes to craft a prosecution-speech for him. The speech (39) contains the following *reductio ad absurdum* (34-36):

> But, oh most difficult Boeotus, definitely stop all the things you are doing. But, if you don't want to, be persuaded by this at least, by Zeus. Stop causing problems for yourself and blackmailing me. Be satisfied that you have a city, a living, a father. No-one is driving you from these things – certainly not me. But since you say you are my brother, if you also act in a brotherly way, you will seem to be a relative, but if you plot, go to court, envy, badmouth, you will seem to have fallen into another person's property and to treat it as though it doesn't belong to you. I have not done any wrong at all even when my father had not yet acknowledged you as his son. For it isn't my job to know who that man's sons are, but his job to point out whom I ought to consider as a brother. Therefore, throughout the time that he did not acknowledge you, I did not consider you as a relative, but since he has acknowledged you, I also think that you are. What is the sign of this? You got a share of your patrimony after our father's death. You have a share in the sacred and the profane things of the house. No-one is depriving you of these. What more do you want?

---

[2] The narrator Encolpius, of course, wouldn't – to quote Blackadder – "recognize a cunning plan if it stripped itself naked, dyed itself purple, jumped on top of a harpsichord and started singing, 'Cunning plans are here again.'"

[3] A nouveau-riche pretension. So Tevye in *Fiddler on the Roof* would, if he were rich, have three staircases: one going up, one coming down, and one leading nowhere just for show.

(*To the jury*) If he says he is suffering terribly, and weeps, and laments, and accuses me, whatever he says, don't believe him (it would not be right, for the discourse is not now about these things), but consider that it is possible for him to get no less justice while called Boeotus.

(*To Boeotus*) Why do you love quarrels so? No longer! Don't be such a willing enemy to us, for I am not to you, since even now – so that this may not escape your notice – I am rather speaking on your behalf, thinking it right that we not have the same name, if for no other reason than that it is necessary for the listener to ask, "Which one?" if there are two Mantitheuses sons of Mantias.

He will reply, "The one whom Mantias was forced to acknowledge," if he means you. Now how can you want that?

While this is an unusual case, the sucker may lose all manner of things: clothing, furniture, and jewelry to name but a few. In some cases, this is simply because he is too weak, old or feeble to defend himself. For example, in chapter V we considered the case of Sophocles, who went outside the walls of Athens to have sex with a boy, and once they were finished, the boy leapt up, grabbed Sophocles' cloak and ran back home, leaving the great poet to walk the streets in a cloak ten or twelve sizes too small for him (Athen. 604d-f).

The Egghead

American movies often celebrate stupidity as a virtue in itself (*Forrest Gump, Waterboy,* and *K-Pax*) as well as being a source of comedy (*Dumb and Dumber*, or any other movie starring Jim Carrey). Greeks and Romans did not usually have this problem. The Greeks coined the word "moron," but it describes for them a condition more contemptible than ridiculous; the Fool who is at once village-idiot and court-jester, like Yorick from Shakespeare's *Hamlet*, seems to be a product of the nordic imagination.

There are rare examples of Greeks finding nitwits funny – often in sexual contexts. Consider the beginning of Aristophanes' *Clouds* (416-52):

> Would that the matchmaker had died badly
> who convinced me to marry your mother,
> for the rustic life was the sweetest one for me,
> moldy, unswept, lying down anywhere,
> full of bees, and sheep and olive-cakes.
> Then I married Megacles',[4] Megacles' son's
> niece from the city, rustic though I am –
> haughty, luxurious, Coesyrified.[5]
> When I married her, I lay down with her
> stinking of wine-lees, crates, wool, leftovers,
> but she instead of myrrh, saffron, French kisses,

---

[4] Megacles: a prominent Athenian politician, and grandfather of Pericles.

[5] Coesyra was a famously elegant woman, about whom we know nothing else.

expense, gluttony, Aphrodite Colias and Genetyllis.[6]

This passage does not merely paint an amusing picture of an Eddie Albert and Eva Gabor match not made in heaven; it leads us to wonder how it happens, in this society that so carefully sheltered its women, that Strepsiades' wife had such great sexual sophistication on her wedding-night. Megacles' family has used a matchmaker deliberately to seek Strepsiades out as a husband for this girl. Can it be that she has violated the strong social taboo and slept around, and that the family has had to marry her off below her station to a man who is well off, but lower class, and naive enough not to realize that he is being used? If so, we can congratulate ourselves at seeing a misfortune of which its victim himself is unaware.[7] We will reserve further discussion of specifically sexual naivety for Chapter IX.

Often it is not physical, but mental impairment that creates the sucker's great vulnerability. There is a Byzantine collection of jokes called *Philogelos*, "the Lover of Laughter," which may reasonably be thought to preserve a number of ancient specimens (in fact the story about Nasica and Ennius figures in the collection as number 193). These jokes typically feature the *scholastikos*, "pedant" or – as we prefer – "egghead," the scholarly type with his head so far up in the clouds that he has no idea how to run his day-to-day life, and so often winds up a loser – literally being too smart in all the wrong ways for his own good. Already in Chapter III we considered Thales falling down a well while looking up at the stars. He is the granddaddy, so to speak, of all eggheads. It would perhaps be apt to call eggheads the ancient equivalent of the dumb blonde joke or in Italy of the *carabinieri* (policeman)-joke, but with smart people – indeed, it is perhaps the only case where a character is laughed at for acting stupid, as opposed to outsmarting himself, and even there it stays close to that line. Here are some examples:

An egghead, wanting to teach his donkey to go without food, stopped feeding him. When the donkey starved to death, the egghead exclaimed: "Just my luck! No sooner does he learn to go without food, than he up and dies." (*Philogelos* 9).

An egghead wanted to go to bed, but had no pillow, so he ordered his slave to bring him a jar instead. When the slave asked if a jar wouldn't be too hard, the egghead replied, "Good point! Better stuff it with feathers first." (*Philogelos* 21).

An egghead, trying to sell his house, carried one of its bricks around in his pocket as a sample. (*Philogelos* 41).

An egghead, a barber and a bald man went on a journey. One night they found themselves between cities and had to camp out in the open. They agreed to take turns staying awake to watch over the baggage. The barber drew the first watch, and for a lark spent his time shaving the egghead. When his watch was over, he

---

[6] Two goddesses of sex.

[7] C. G. Brown, "Strepsiades' Wife: Aristophanes, *Clouds* 41 ff," *Prometheus* 17 (1991) 29-33.

woke up the egghead to take his turn. While standing watch, the egghead happened to scratch his head, and not feeling his hair, exclaimed, "What an idiot that barber is! He's woken up the bald man instead of me!" (*Philogelos* 56).

An egghead bought some antiques in Corinth and shipped them back home. As they were being loaded onto the ship, the egghead told the captain, "Be careful: if you damage these, you'll have to buy me new ones." (*Philogelos* 78).

Two eggheads were on the lam. One hid in a well, the other in a marsh full of reeds. Some soldiers headed out in search of the men, and coming upon the well, they let down a helmet as a bucket to fetch some drinking water. Hearing the helmet, and thinking that a soldier was coming down the well, the first egghead begged for mercy and was captured. No sooner had the soldiers told him that if he'd only stayed quiet they wouldn't have noticed him, than the second egghead shouted, "Don't notice me, then – I'm not saying anything!" (*Philogelos* 96).[8]

And:

An egghead's friends came to congratulate him on the birth of his new baby. The egghead replied, "I owe it all to you, my friends!" (*Philogelos* 98).

The egghead is consistently – one might almost say "terminally" – stupid in a funny way, but of course even normally bright people can have their dumb moments, especially when under the influence of alcohol. Three examples of this may suffice. The first is the story of the Trojan horse. Vergil (*Aen*. 2.238-39) describes how the Trojans broke open their own city-walls to drag the monster in:

Boys around it, and unwed girls
sing hymns, and rejoice to touch the rope with their hands.

They are, of course, so eager to party that they innocently aid and abet the destruction of their own city.

Another is the story that Herodotus (6.129) tells about the tyrant Clisthenes of Sicyon choosing a suitor for his daughter. He gathered together the most eligible bachelors in all of Greece and interviewed them. He decided to extend the honour to Hippoclides of Athens, and threw a great banquet, at the end of which he planned to announce his choice. This is how things turn out in Herodotus' own words:

---

[8] This joke survives til our own time: Three escaped convicts were on the lam, ran into a barn and hid in three potato-sacks. The cops searched the barn, and finding the first sack, kicked it. The convict inside said, "Miaow," and the cops said, "It's just a bag of cats." They found the second sack and kicked it, and the convict inside said, "Bow-wow," and the cops said, "It's just a bag of puppies." Then the cops found the third sack and kicked it, and the convict inside said, "Potato."

When it was after dinner, the suitors had a contest in music and public-speaking. As the drinking continued, Hippoclides, far surpassing the others, ordered the flute-player to play a pavane for him, and when the flute-player obeyed, he danced. And while he seemed to himself to be dancing pleasingly, Clisthenes, seeing the whole affair, grew nervous. After resting awhile, Hippoclides ordered someone to bring in a table, and when the table came in, first of all he danced on it some Spartan steps, then other Athenian ones, finally propping his head on the table, he gesticulated with his legs.[9] Clisthenes, hating due to the first and second of his dances that Hippoclides should still become his son-in-law, given his dancing and lack of shame, restrained himself, not wanting to start screaming at him. But when he saw him gesticulating with his legs, he could no longer hold himself back, and said, "Oh son of Tisander, you have danced away your marriage." Hippoclides replied, "No worries for Hippoclides!"

Or recall the anecdote about the trireme-house at Agrigento that we considered in Chapter III.

The Willing Victim

Perhaps the greatest sucker is someone who *actively wants* to lose something very valuable. Philosophers often behave in this way. Jesus advised (Matthew 6.38-42) you to turn the other cheek; if a man asks you for your cloak give him your shirt also; and if he asks you to walk a mile with him walk with him two. Pagan Greek philosophers had a similar ethic, being willing, like Socrates, to sacrifice their very lives in aid of a noble cause. To the extent that when they boasted that they regarded death with equanimity, normal people typically responded "Of course you're not afraid of death; you philosophers are half dead already" (Pl. *Phaedo* 64), proving that even in the ancient world philosophy was putting people to sleep.

The historian Herodotus in particular liked stories of this type. We will consider three here. The first concerns Candaules, king of Lydia, who lost his throne to a certain Gyges, proverbial for his wealth. One Charon the carpenter says of him (Archil. fr. 19 West):

I don't care about the affairs of Gyges, rich in gold.
Not yet has jealousy seized me, nor do I envy
the works of the gods, nor do I desire great tyranny.
These things are far from my eyes.

Plato tells a story about how Gyges' family came to power (*Resp*. Book II, 359d-360a):

The abuse of power that I mean would certainly be such if it happened to them to have the power that they say came to Gyges, ancestor of the Lydian king. For he was a shepherd serving the man who ruled Lydia at that time. A great rain and earthquake happened, and some of the ground was ruptured, and

---

[9] Those who wear bed sheets don't have pockets (see Chapter VI, n.19). Neither do they wear underwear.

a cavern opened up under the spot where he watched his sheep. Seeing this, and marveling, he went down into it. And he saw many marvelous things that the mythographers relate, including a horse bronze, hollow and fitted with windows. Bending down, he saw through them a corpse inside, which appeared to be bigger than a man. There was nothing else, except upon his hand a golden ring, which having taken, he left. When the usual gathering of shepherds took place at which every month they brought word to the king about his flocks, he too came wearing the ring. As he was sitting with the others, he happened to turn the stone of his ring toward himself on the inside of his hand. When this happened, he became invisible to those sitting with him, and they spoke of him as absent. He wondered, and feeling for his ring, turned the stone outward and became visible once more. Noting this, he tested the ring to see if it had this power, and so it happened for him that turning the stone inward he became invisible, and outward visible. Having perceived this, he immediately arranged to become one of the messengers to the king. He went and committed adultery with his wife. Persuaded by her, he killed the king and so took his throne.

Now if there were two such rings, and the just man put on one and the unjust the other, there is no one, as it seems, so steadfast that he could remain in a state of justice and dare to abstain from other people's things and not touch them, it being possible for him to take whatever he wanted from the market without fear, and going into houses sleep with whomever he wanted, and kill and free from prison whomever he wanted, and do all other things among men as if he were a god.

Now this story, in which invisibility and voyeurism play such a role, does not seem to have been the original one. Herodotus preserves a less fantastic explanation for Gyges' wealth (Hdt. 1.8-12):[10]

Now Candaules was in love with his own wife, and, loving her, he thought he had by far the most beautiful wife of all. Thinking these things – for there was among his bodyguard a certain Gyges, son of Dascylus who pleased him most of all, and Candaules put before this Gyges the most serious of his affairs – he also praised to him the beauty of his wife. When not much time had passed – for things were fated to turn out badly for Candaules – he said this to Gyges, "Gyges, I don't think you are persuaded by me speaking about the beauty of my wife (for it happens with people that the ear is less trustworthy than the eye). Arrange that you may see her naked."

Having shouted aloud, he said, "Lord, what unhealthy speech have you spoken, ordering me to see my mistress naked? At once with putting off her dress, a woman puts off her modesty..." Saying these things he resisted, fearing lest some bad thing might come to him from these things.

But the other answered thus, "Be bold, Gyges, and do not fear either me, that I have spoken this speech as a test for you, nor my wife, lest any harm should come to you from her. For above all I will contrive that she not know that she has been seen by you. For I will place you inside the room in which we sleep behind the open door. After I have come in, my wife will come to bed. There stands near the door a throne. On this she will place her garments one by one, and you can see her with great tranquillity. When she walks away from the

---

[10] For an interesting take on this story, see R. Davies, *Fifth Business* (Toronto, 1970) 172-83.

throne toward the bed, you will be behind her back. Let it be a care to you then that she not see you going out through the doors."

Since he was not able to escape, he was ready. Candaules, when he decided it was time for bed, led Gyges into the room, and immediately after this his wife arrived. As she came in and set down her clothes, Gyges was watching. When he was behind her back as the woman was going to bed, he slipped out and left. And the woman saw him go. Realizing what had been done by her husband, she did not shout out for shame, nor appear to have realized, having it in her mind to punish Candaules, for among the Lydians, and among nearly all barbarians, even for a man to be seen naked brings him into great shame.

Then therefore showing no sign, she kept her peace. But as soon as it was day, making ready those of her servants whom she saw to be most faithful to her, she called for Gyges. He, not suspecting that she knew any of the things that had been done, came when called, for before also he was accustomed, whenever the queen called, to come. When Gyges arrived, the woman said, "Now, Gyges, I give you a choice. There are two roads present. Turn down whichever you wish. Either kill Candaules and take me and the kingdom of the Lydians, or you yourself must immediately die, so that totally obeying Candaules you may not in the future see what you ought not. But either he who counseled these things must die, or you who saw me naked and did what is not our custom."....

So the plan was arranged, and when night came (for Gyges was not let off the hook, nor did he have any escape, but was compelled that either himself or Candaules must die) he followed the woman into the bedroom. She gave him a dagger and hid him behind the door. Afterward, while Candaules slept, Gyges came out and killed him and took both his wife and his kingdom.

An anonymous fifth-century playwright turned this story into a tragedy, of which one brief fragment, a speech by Candaules' wife, survives (fr. adespoton 664 *TrGF*)lines 18-33:

For as I saw Gyges, and not just a likeness of him,
I feared lest there was some ambush of murder within,
which is the price of monarchy.
But when I saw that Candaules was still awake,
I recognized what had been done, and who had done it,
and as though not comprehending, though with heart in turmoil,
I locked in silence [unexpressed?] my cry of shame.
For me as I tossed on the mattress in thought
the night was interminable from sleeplessness,
but when the all-shining Morning Star arose,
messenger of day's first light,
him I woke from bed and sent away
to give laws to the people; persuasion's word
was ready for me [which does not allow?
A king to sleep all night [   ]
But Gyges a summoner [is now calling to me...

Although this was considered fit subject-matter for a tragedy of choice, it strikes us as being rather a comedy of errors from the very first line, "now Candaules was in love with his own wife" (as though this were the most unusual thing in the world for him to be). Normal men guarded their wives with great jealousy, keeping them behind locked doors in the harem. Candaules has this great prize, his wife's body, which he is free to enjoy in private, but instead he wants to give this privilege away, while other men would hide it. In the process of giving this away, he loses also his kingdom, and indeed, his life; he thinks he is skillfully manipulating events, yet both he and Gyges are mere puppets in the hands of the queen.

Our second story concerns the Athenian law-giver, Solon and his visit to Gyges' successor as king of Lydia, the equally wealthy Croesus (Hdt. 1.30-33):

For these reasons, and for tourism, Solon left home and came to Egypt to the home of Amasis, and also to Sardis to that of Croesus. When he arrived, he was hosted in the palace by Croesus, and afterward on the third or fourth day, on Croesus' orders his servants led Solon around the treasuries and showed him how great and wealthy everything was. When he had seen and examined everything that was proper for him, Croesus asked, "Athenian guest – for great report has come to us about you and your wisdom, that as a philosopher you have come to many lands for the sake of tourism – now desire has come to me to ask you if, of any people you have seen, someone is the most happy?"

He asked this, expecting to be the happiest of men, yet Solon didn't flatter him, but using reality, said: "King, Tellus the Athenian."

Croesus, shocked at what had been said, asked earnestly, "Why do you judge Tellus to be the happiest?"

He said, "On the one hand, in a flourishing city he had noble sons and he saw sons born to all of them and all surviving, and on the other, when he had done well in life, as things go with us, the end of his life was most glorious. For when battle happened for the Athenians aiding our neighbours in Eleusis, and when we had made a rout of the enemy, he died most beautifully, and the Athenians both buried him at public expense where he fell and honoured him greatly."

So did Solon encourage Croesus, having said many and wealthy things about Tellus. Then he asked him a second time whom he had seen after that man who seemed altogether to have won second place at least.

He said, "Cleobis and Biton. To them, who where Argive by race, life was good, and as well as that, the strength of their bodies was great: for both were prize-winners, and moreover this tale was told. There was a feast of Hera among the Argives, and their mother had to be drawn by a team to the temple, but her oxen weren't back from the fields in time. And constrained by the time, the young men put on the yoke themselves, and drew the car, and their mother rode on the car, and drawing her five and forty stades, they led her to the temple. When they had done these things, and been seen by the crowd, the best end of life happened... For after they had sacrificed and feasted, falling asleep in the temple, the young men never got up again, but were held by this end. And the Argives made images of them and set them up in Delphi as being the best of men."[11]

---

[11] They're still there, and have their own room in the Delphi museum: see Alan Walker, *Delphi*. Athens, 1977: 110.

Solon gave second prize for happiness to them, and Croesus, growing angry, said, "Athenian guest, is our happiness so cast by you as nothing that it doesn't even make us equal to private citizens?"

And he said, "Croesus,... one who is not maimed, not sick, inexperienced in misfortunes, fair in children, fair in form, and in addition to these things, if he will end his life well – this man is he whom you seek, for he is worthy to be called happy. But until someone has died, you must call him not 'happy,' but 'lucky.'"

Saying these things to Croesus, he did not much please him, and taking no account of his speech, he sent him away thinking him to be very ignorant who dismissed present good and told him to look to the end of every matter.

If only Solon had been willing to play the role of flatterer, he would have come away wealthy, but he deliberately snubbed Croesus' wealth by giving him answers to his questions that, however philosophically interesting, were guaranteed to tick him off.

The third story that Herodotus (3.40-43) tells is particularly interesting: about the tyrant Polycrates of Samos, who wanted to throw away his most precious possession:

Polycrates did not escape the notice of Amasis being so lucky, but this was a concern for him. When his luck became yet more by much, he wrote these things in a little book and sent it to Samos: "Amasis to Polycrates says this. Sweet it is to learn that a dear and friendly man is doing well, but your great fortunes do not please me, since I know that God is jealous. And I wish both for myself and those for whom I care that some of their business should be lucky and some stumble, and so to do alternately differently over time, rather than to be always good. For I know of no one I have heard of in a story who lived his life to the end from the root with no badness, faring well in all things. So be persuaded by me, and do this for your fortune: think what you can find worth most to you, and at which, if you lost it, you would grieve your heart the most, and cast this thing where it will never come back again among men...."

Having read these things, and considering in his heart that Amasis had put it well, Polycrates sought which of his possessions he would be most vexed in his heart if he lost, and seeking, he found this: he had a ring that he wore made of gold, having an emerald stone, the work of Theodorus, son of Telecles of Samos. When he decided to throw this away, he did as follows. He filled a penteconter with men, boarded it, and ordered them to row into the sea. When they were far from the island, taking off the ring with all of his fellow sailors watching, he threw it into the sea. Having done this, he sailed away, and came home regarding it a misfortune.

On the fifth or sixth day after this misfortune happened, a fisherman caught a big and handsome fish, and thought it right to make a gift of it to Polycrates. Bringing it to the door, he said that he wanted to come into Polycrates' presence. When he was brought before him, he said, giving him the fish, "King, having caught this, I did not think it right to take it to market, even though I live by the work of my hands, but it seemed to me to be worthy of you and your kingship. So bringing it, I give it to you."

He, pleased at these words, replied, "Surely you have done well, and our pleasure is twofold – at your words and the gift. So we invite you to dinner."

The fisherman, holding these things a great honour, went home, and the slaves, cutting open the fish, found that there was in its belly Polycrates' ring. When they saw it, they took it quickly, rejoicing, brought it to Polycrates, and, giving him the ring, told him how they had found it. But seeing that God had entered into the matter, he wrote everything that he had done and how it had turned out in a little book and, having written, sent it to Egypt. When Amasis had read the little book that came from Polycrates, he learned that it is impossible for man to save man from something that is coming, and because he considered Polycrates destined not to end well, since he was lucky in everything, who even found what he had thrown away, he sent a herald to Samos to break off their friendship. He did so for this reason: so that when great and dreadful misfortune finally overtook Polycrates, he would not be saddened in his heart over the loss of a friend.

Amasis' prediction was prescient: Polycrates was eventually captured by a Persian satrap and crucified. So it is that Polycrates cannot even succeed at *losing*, and is such a dud that he loses his friend into the bargain.

The character who becomes a sucker willingly and without reservation is a relatively rare phenomenon. It is important to note, though, that none of this happens through stupidity. For that matter, the only stupidity that we see in the sucker at all appears in the egghead, and even there it is a stupidity created out of distraction. The egghead is so brilliant that he cannot be concerned about smaller things, and it is in those smaller things, like loudly congratulating himself for being smart enough to keep quiet while being hunted by soldiers, that he is caught.

Another thing of note is the sex of these suckers – all of our examples have been men. Indeed, the ancient world was one where all people had their place in society, as did both genders. The quack was almost exclusively male. The sucker was also male – and, as we shall see, so was the character who would step in to save him.

Chapter VIII – Bursting the Bubble and Other Oddities

The Ironist

To every action, there is an equal and opposite reaction. Some people are so afraid of becoming quacks, or being mistaken for quacks, that they adopt the exact opposite rhetorical strategy from *hyperbole*, namely *meiosis*, and become ironists.

In his 1934 book, *The Origin of Attic Comedy* Francis Cornford rightly says:

> In tragedy, the hero's enemy is his own *Hubris*; the conflict between the disastrous passion and its opposite, *Sophrosyne*,[1] is fought out in his own breast... Here is a point of difference from Comedy. The *Sophrosyne* of Comedy is the spirit of genial sanity, in all its range from the flicker of lightning reason and the flash of wit, through the large humour of common sense, down to the antics of the fool, marking ironical play with every form of absurdity... The adversaries here are incompatible and must remain distinct. The duel of comedy is everlastingly fought out between them.[2]

The character tending toward hubris is the quack whom we met in Chapter VI. We must now consider the character who tends toward temperance, using *meiosis*, or understatement, instead of *hyperbole*. It is owing to the fact that quackery and its antidote are distributed among two separate characters that Old Comedy, the genre represented for us by Aristophanes, always contains as part of its structure a contest (*agon* – the origin of our word "agony," the feeling of muscle-pain you get while wrestling). In its purest form this is the contest in which the quack meets the anti-quack, the quack defeats him in argument, which is the quack's specialty after all, and then the quack is driven off the stage, and out of society by force.

The quack's nemesis who gives him his comeuppance is a fellow the Greeks called *eiron*, a word that seems to come from their verb for asking a question, *eresthai*. This is the down-to-earth right-thinking everyman who asks common sense questions, which the quack can't answer. He bursts the quack's balloon, unmasking him for the phony and fraud he is.[3] We have not taken over this word into English, but we have borrowed the related abstract noun as our "irony." Irony for us includes sarcasm, when you say one thing and mean the opposite (*"That's* a nice dress") and tragic irony as in Sophocles *Oedipus Rex* where the audience knows, as the hero himself does

---

[1] Literally "a safe diaphragm," which is perfectly logical since every informed Greek knew that conscious thought occurred in the diaphragm, and the brain was only good for making semen.

[2] F. M. Cornford, *The Origin of Attic Comedy* (Cambridge 1934) 182-84.

[3] O. Ribbeck, "Ueber den Begriff des *eiron*," *Rh. Mus.* 21 (1876) 339-58, W. Büchner, "Über den Begriff der Eironeia," *Hermes* 76 (1941) 340, L. Bergson, "Eiron und Eironeia," *Hermes* 99 (1971) 409-22, and F. Amory, "Eiron and Eironeia," *C&M* 33 (1981-82) 49-80.

not, that he's ruling Thebes on borrowed time.[4] Note that both as sarcasm and as tragic irony, the concept has to do with unequal levels of knowledge, and especially of self-knowledge.

This is how Aristotle describes this character whom we will call, for want of a better English term, the "ironist" in the *Nicomachean Ethics* 1127a:

> Ironists, speaking on the side of the lesser, seem to be more pleasing in character [than quacks], for they seem to speak not for the sake of gain, but in order to avoid pomposity. And most of all, these people reject what is honoured, as Socrates especially used to do. But those who prefer small and obvious things are called "prudes capable of anything"[5] and are more easily looked down upon. And sometimes it seems to be quackery, like the dress of the Spartans, for excess and extreme negligence are both "quackisms."[6] Those who use irony moderately and about things not too readily apparent are pleasing.

Aristotle's disciple Theophrastus, who treats the *eiron* as his very first character, agrees with Aristotle in the essential definition, but finds the type much more offensive than his master does. He describes the ironist as follows (*Char.* 1):

> Indeed, irony would seem to be – to take it as a type – affectation toward the worse in deeds and words, and the ironist some such person as, coming upon his enemies, wants to chitchat and not hate them; and to praise those present, whom he has set upon in secret; and to those whom he has fought in court, even to sympathize with them when they lose, since they are suffering badly; and to forgive those who bad-mouth him; and to laugh at things that are said about him; and to those who are wronged and feel it, to speak mildly; and to those who want to meet him urgently, to tell them to go back home; and to admit nothing of the things he does, but to say that he's still planning them; and to make excuses: "I'm here just now," "I'm late among them," and "I'm feeling weak;" and to those who are borrowing and taking up a collection, to say that he isn't rich; and, when selling, that he will not sell; and, when not selling, to say that he *will* sell; and, having heard something, to pretend not; and, having seen, to claim not to have seen; and, having agreed, [to claim] not to remember; and to say that he will inquire into this, doesn't know that, and marvels at the other – why, once he himself reached the same conclusion about it. All the time he's clever at using such a manner of speech: "I don't believe it!" "I don't understand," "I'm shocked!" "You mean he's become other than himself"?"

---

[4] To limit ourselves to book-length studies, consider J. A. K. Thomson, *Irony: An Historical Introduction* (Cambridge 1927), G. G. Sedgewick, *Of Irony: Especially in Drama* 2nd ed. (Toronto 1948), B. L. States, *Irony and Drama: A Poetics* (Ithaca 1971), and P. Vellacott, *Ironic Drama: A Study in Euripides' Method and Meaning* (Cambridge 1975).

[5] This is a literal translation of the parts of this word, which occurs only here. The big Greek dictionary glosses this as "humbugs," but what are they? I might suggest the translation "nit-pickers" (RDG).

[6] Less is sometimes more, a point of view we've tried – but failed – to have our accountant adopt.

"These things weren't reported to *me*," "Seems like a paradox," "Go tell someone else," "I don't know whether to disbelieve you or to convict him," and "Don't believe everything you're told."

By asking his simple, down-to-earth questions, the ironist opens up a gap in the knowledge, and ultimately in the self-knowledge of the quack. He casts him into the role of "answerer," and the Greek for "answerer" – and later "actor" – is *hypokrites* – origin of our word "hypocrite." A perfect example of this sort of ironist is Lysistrata, the title character of the play by Aristophanes. While the men of Athens are busy debating strategic withdrawals, Lysistrata reduces the entire argument to a single, simple question: do the men want to make war, or have sex?[7]

Perhaps the clearest example of the confrontation between quack and ironist that we WILL quote is the opening of Aristophanes' *Clouds* in which the country-bumpkin Strepsiades meets for the first time his neighbour the arch-sophist and super-quack Socrates, who is hanging in a basket "walking on air and looking down upon the sun." Here is their conversation together with the chorus of Clouds (358-73):

Chorus: Hail, oh elder, born long ago, hunter of Muse-loving words!
        And you, priest of finest nonsense! Tell us what you seek,
        for we would not listen to another at least of today's upper-air experts
        (except for Prodicus: to him for his wisdom and thought, but to you,
        because you both swagger in the streets and cast to one side your two eyes
        and shamelessly bear many hardships, and on our account always look grim).

Strepsiades:
        Oh Earth, what a voice! How holy, and solemn, and awe-inspiring!
Socrates: Yes, for – you know – these alone are gods, and
        The others are all ridiculousness.
St   But our Zeus (come on!), by the Earth, isn't *he* the Olympian god?
So   What Zeus? Don't babble. Zeus doesn't exist.
St   What are you saying?
        But who rains? For tell me this-here first of all.
So   These ones, of course. And I will teach you this with great signs.
        Come, for wherever have you watched it raining without clouds?
        Yet it ought to rain from a clear blue sky, and these ones should be absent.
St   Yes, by Apollo, this at least you've proved well by your speech just now.
        ...and to think that before I really thought it was Zeus pissing through a sieve!

---

[7] But we're not going to give you a passage from this, partly because we want to play around with Socrates instead, and partly because we're sadists. Deal with it.

So it is that Socrates' talk of theology is reduced first to meteorology and then finally to bathroom matters.[8] While this may make for piss-poor philosophy, there is something odd about this picture of Socrates as the perfect quack.

Socrates

There is a passage from Aristophanes' *Clouds* in which the country bumpkin Strepsiades, who has been driven into debt by his son Pheidippides' passion for horse-racing, goes to Socrates' school next door to his house to learn debating techniques that will help him wriggle (*strephein*) out of paying his debts. In that play we have a model disposition of the four main character-types: the flatterer Chaerephon (he doesn't appear on stage in the surviving, revised version of the play, wherein his role is taken by an anonymous pupil), the quack Socrates, the sucker-creditors, Pasias and Amynias, the ironist Strepsiades and the buffoon Pheidippides.

There's a serious problem, however. Socrates was famous in his lifetime not for quackery, but for his irony. Why, then, has Aristophanes cast him in the role of quack? Perhaps he doesn't care about such niceties; he is, after all, a comic poet trying to raise a laugh, and there is something similar between quackery and irony (not connected with a squashed duck, which is obviously flattery); Aristotle, remember, classes them both as types of self-misrepresentation. Perhaps Aristophanes wants to ridicule the sophists like Protagoras and, finding Socrates to have a more ridiculous external form than any of them, casts him as the model sophist. In the same festival in March 423 in which Aristophanes produced *Clouds*, Ameipsias staged the now lost *Connus*, which also ridiculed Socrates by name (Connus was Socrates' music teacher, Test. 5 *PCG*). Fairly obviously, then, the philosopher had done something in that year that brought him to the attention of the public in an unflattering way.

It is quite possible, though, that Aristophanes was not just using Socrates without caring at all about who he really was and what he stood for. The two men were on friendly terms, after all, if we can trust the portrait of them painted in Plato's *Symposium*. We like to think that he was taking a secret delight in casting Socrates in the opposite role to the one he had chosen for himself, as if to say "your famous irony is no better than quackery." Indeed, before Strepsiades goes to Socrates' school he tries in vain to persuade Pheidippides to go in his place,[9] and the young man refuses with these words (102-104):

---

[8] L. E. Woodbury, "Strepsiades' Understanding: Five Notes on the *Clouds*," *Phoenix* 34 (1980) 108-27 = *Collected Writings* (Atlanta 1991) 335-54.

[9] Which, for a Greek, is the appropriate thing to do. The ancient Greeks didn't believe in lifelong learning. In fact, the word for education, *paideia*, comes from the word *pais*, meaning "child."

Oh no! They're villains, I know. You mean
those quacks, those pale-faces, those barefoot men,
such as that poor devil Socrates and Chaerephon.

Later in the play, Strepsiades seems to equate the two terms as he girds his
loins to enter Socrates' school (lines 443-51):

If I can get out of debt,
I will seem to men to be
bold, eloquent, daring, reckless,
loathsome, a gluer together of lies,
fluent, polished with lawsuits,
a law-book, castanet, fox, gimlet,
thong, **ironist,** oil, a **quack,**
whip-scarred, stained, twisty, troublesome,
meatloaf-licker.

What then was Socrates' famous irony? In his speech in his self-defence
on the charge of impiety in 348 he describes a conversation he had with one
Callias (Plato *Apology* 20a-c):

Then there is another man also, from Paros, here – a wise man, whom I
have found out is in town. For I happened to come to a man who has paid more
money to sophists than all others, Callias the son of Hipponicus. So I asked him,
for he has two sons, "Callias," I said, "if your two sons were two colts or calves,
we would have to get a trainer for them, and hire someone who would make
them noble in respect of their appropriate virtue, and this man would be one of
those horse-trainers or farmers. But now, since they're two human beings,
whom do you have in mind to get as their trainer? Who is knowledgeable about
such virtue, the human and civic one?[10] For I imagine you have considered this,
since you have acquired sons. Is there anyone," I said, "or not?"
    "Certainly," he said.
    "Who?" I said, "and where from, and how much does he charge to teach?"
    "Evenus," he said, "dear Socrates, from Paros, five minas."
    And I pronounced Evenus blessed, if he truly had this skill and taught for
so reasonable a price. I myself at least would primp and plume myself if I knew
these things. But I do not know them, gentlemen of Athens.

This perfectly encapsulates Socrates' ironic mode. He has found a man
willing to declare himself an expert and questions him, in the course of
which questioning the mask slips and the man's apparent expertise is
revealed as a sham. Socrates' questions bring a lofty philosophical question
("What is the best education for our youth?") down to earth ("What if they
were horses?") in a practical commonsense way. It also, quite possibly, takes
a side-swipe at Aristophanes' play, in which horse-raising was the initial
source of all the difficulty.

---

[10] "Civic" (*politikos*), because, remember, humans are the animals who
live in societies (*poleis*).

One of the most beautiful examples of Socratic irony is his relationship with Alcibiades the handsome and unprincipled young aristocrat, who fell in love with Socrates and hoped to trade sex for wisdom.[11] In understanding this situation it is important to remember that Socrates was famous for also being hideous in a break-the-mirror-by-looking-at-it style. In fact, in Xenophon's *Symposium* 5.6 Socrates says (ironically!) that his snub nose is supremely beautiful, because the purpose of nostrils is to aid in breathing, and who could breathe better than he, equipped as he is with such big blow-holes on each side of his face. This is how Alcibiades' describes his love-affair with Socrates once he has burst as an uninvited guest into a party thrown by the tragic poet, Agathon (Plato's *Symposium* 217a-219b):

> But considering that [Socrates] took my good looks seriously, I thought it was a windfall and my marvelous luck, since I would be able, by giving favours to Socrates, to hear everything that he knew. For I thought a great deal of my looks. Having thought about these things, though before then I was not accustomed to be with him alone without a servant, then I sent the servant away, I got together with him alone – for I have to tell you the whole truth; but all of you pay attention, and, Socrates, if I lie, cross-examine me – when we used to be together, I alone with him alone, I thought he would immediately say to me the sorts of things that a lover says to his sweetie in private, and I was glad. But actually none of those things happened, but having spoken with me just as he was wont to do, and having spent the day with me, he left and went home. After that, I invited him to work out with me, and I worked out with him, in order to accomplish something there. He worked out with me, and wrestled often with no one around, and – what do I have to tell you? – I got no further. When I accomplished nothing in this way, it seemed to me that I had to set on the man harder, and not let him go, since I had put my hand to the task, but I had to know what was the matter. So I invited him to dine with me, literally like a lover plotting to seduce his sweetie. And he did not immediately listen to me, but nevertheless in time he was persuaded. And when he came the first time, having eaten, he wanted to leave. That time, feeling ashamed, I let him go. But the next time I plotted to seduce him, once we had dined, I kept talking continuously into the night, and when he wanted to leave, saying as an excuse that it was late, I forced him to stay. So he spent the night on the couch he shared with me, on which we had dined, and no one else was sleeping in the room but us.
>
> Up to this point, my speech has been fine to say to anyone, but from here on you wouldn't have heard my speech unless firstly, as the saying goes, wine (with or without children) speaks the truth,[12] and secondly it seems wrong to me, having entered into my praise, to hide Socrates' arrogant deed... and the suffering of the viper's bite infects me still. For they say that perhaps someone who suffers this doesn't want to say what it's like except to those who have been bitten, since they alone know and understand if he dares to do and say anything because of the pain. And I have been bitten and struck by a more painful thing,

---

[11] This is not the place to discuss at length Athenian attitudes toward homosexual love. If you're interested, the best place to look is K.J. Dover's *Greek Homosexuality* (Cambridge, Mass. 1978).

[12] The saying is "Wine and children speak the truth."

and in the most painful of places one can be bitten – in the heart, or soul, or whatever I ought to call it – and bitten by the words of philosophy, which are fiercer than an adder and, whenever they seize a young and not untalented soul, make it do and say whatever. And looking again at the Phaedruses, Agathons, Eryximachuses, Pausaniases, Aristodemuses and Aristophaneses – do I need to mention Socrates himself? – all of you share the madness and bacchic frenzy of philosophy. So all of you listen, for you will understand what I did then, and what I'm saying now, but as for the slaves and, if there is anyone else profane and rustic, let them place great gates upon their ears.

Well, gentlemen, when the light was put out and waiters gone, it seemed good to me not to beat about the bush, but to say freely what I thought. So, nudging him, I said, "Socrates, are you asleep?"

"No, I'm not," he said.

"Know what I think?"

"No. What?" he said.

"You seem to me," I said, "to be the only lover worthy of me, but you appear to me to be shy about mentioning it to me. That's what I think. I think it to be completely senseless not to do you this favour any more than if you needed anything else of my property or my friends.' For nothing is more important to me than that I might become a better person, and I think no one is more likely to help me with this than you. I would be more ashamed in front of thinking men if I had not given such a man my favours than before the many and the thoughtless if I had."

And he, having listened, said very ironically in exactly his typical way, "Dear Alcibiades, you surely must be no fool, if what you say about me happens to be true, and there is some power in me through which you might become better. You would see in me a beauty extraordinary and altogether different from your good looks. If, then, looking down on it, you're trying to share it with me, and exchange beauty for beauty, you seem to me to be not a little greedy, but in exchange for appearance you want to acquire the truth of beautiful things, and you intend really to exchange "bronze for gold."[13] But, good sir, think harder, lest you fail to notice that I'm nothing. For the sight of the mind begins to see clearly when that of the eyes tries to give up its sharpness, and you are still far from this."

Having listened, I said, "That's how things are. I've spoken about them not otherwise than how I think. Now you must plan what you think will be best both for you and for me."

"Well said!" he replied. "Some time down the road we'll think it over, and do what seems best to both of us about this and about everything else."

This is irony not in the low-brow form of sarcasm, which is plain lying, for Socrates says nothing to Alcibiades that he doesn't believe. This is how the famous student of Greek philosophy Gregory Vlastos describes Socrates' attitude in this scene:

We can see how Socrates could have deceived without intending to deceive. If you are young Alcibiades courted by Socrates you are left to your own devices to decide what to make of his riddling ironies. If you go wrong and he sees you have gone wrong, he may not lift a finger to dispel your error, far less feel the obligation to knock it out of your head. If this were happening over trivia no

---

[13] We discussed this passage of the *Iliad* in Chapter V.

great harm would be done. But what if it concerned the most important matters – whether or not he loves you? He says he does in that riddling way which leaves you free to take it one way though you are meant to take it in another, and when he sees you have gone wrong he lets it go. What would you say? Not, surely, that he does not care that you should know the truth, but that he care more for something else: that if you are to come to the truth, it must be by yourself for yourself.[14]

The Loner, the Glutton, the Cannibal and the Cook

We have focussed so far on the characters that come into being through the violation of the rule of justice that separates humans from animals as it is manifested in the social context of the "evenly divided feast," to use Homer's phrase (*Iliad* 1.468, etc.). Through trying to get something for nothing, and thereby preventing everyone from getting his due, a man becomes a flatterer, causing a chain-reaction that brings into being the buffoon, the quack and the ironist. These are the four main types of character that arise in relation to eating (among other things – keep in mind that just about anything that can be obtained can be compared with food in this metaphor; money is food that you can spend for goods and services, and sex is food that makes you feel good while tending to be awkward when you're drunk), but they are not the only ones. Now we will bid farewell to this theme of violating justice (as fun as it was) by considering, by way of example, four other lesser types.

The feast is, of course, a social occasion, and a great perversion of it is to avoid it altogether as a **loner** (*monophagos* – one who eats alone, specifically eating fish, which as a non-sacred animal, could be eaten alone outside of a sacrificial feast, even though it would make the eater rather fishy at best).[15] It is characteristic of Greek, socially-based humour, that the loner is usually depicted in relation to food rather than, say, to sex. While wanker-jokes were not unknown,[16] they never achieved the popularity they have among us. In Aristophanes' *Wasps* when the young man Contracleon has managed to lock his dad, Procleon, up and keep him from going out to serve on juries, he decides to provide him with a court in his own front yard to give him something to do. The first case he hears is that of a dog Labes, proving, if any doubted, that every dog gets his day in court. Labes is ostensibly charged with theft of a cheese, but the real problem is that he did not share any with his accuser, but ate it alone. Here is how the scene (lines 893-998) begins:

---

[14] G. Vlastos, *Socrates: Ironist and Moral Philosopher* (Cambridge 1991) 44.

[15] See J. Davidson, *Courtesans and Fishcakes: The Consuming Passions of Classical Athens* (Hammersmith and London, 1997) 3-35 and S.D. Olson and A. Sens, *Archestratos of Gela: Greek Culture and Cuisine in the Fourth Century B.C.E.* (Oxford, 2000).

[16] K. J. Dover, *Greek Homosexuality* (New York 1980) 97, to which add Eubulus fr. 120 *PCG*.

Philocleon:
> Who is this defendant? How he'll be convicted!

Bdelycleon:
> Now hear the charge. "The Cydathenaean Dog
> has indicted Labes of Aexone
> for wrongdoing in respect of cheese, in that by himself he ate
> the Sicilian one. Penalty: figwood collar."[17]

P   A dog's death, once he's convicted!

B   And this defendant here, Labes, is present.

P   You villain! How thievish he looks!
> How, having grinned, he thinks he will deceive me!
> Where is the prosecutor, the Cydathenaean Dog?

Dog: Bow wow.

B   Present, sir.

P   Now this one is another Labes,
> good at least at barking and licking pots.

B   Silence! Sit down! You, there: stand up and speak for the prosecution.

P   (Well then, meanwhile I'll pour and drink this soup.)

D   You have heard the indictment I have brought,
> gentlemen of the jury, against this dog here. For he has done
> the most horrible of deeds to me and to the yo-ho-ho.[18]
> Having run off into the corner, he "sicilized"
> a lot of cheese, and filled himself up in the dark.

P   (By Zeus, that's clear. This wretch
> just now gave me a most horrible
> belch of cheese!)

D   And he didn't give me any when I asked.
> Now which of you will be able to do well,
> if no one gives anything to me your (watch) dog?

P   (Yes, he gave nothing to the public, that is to me,
> for the man's no less hot [headed] than my soup!)

We see this character-type again in Cnemon the cranky old man who gives his name to Menander's *Dyscolus (the Curmudgeon)*. He lives next to a cave of the Nymphs to which pilgrims are always coming to offer sacrifice. Here's a scene (lines 442-87) in which one of the pilgrims makes the mistake of trying to borrow a stew-pot:

Cnemon:
> Villains! May you die badly! They make me
> idle. For I'm not able to leave
> my house alone. These Nymphs are my
> misfortune. They live nearby, so that it seems to me

---

[17] The stocks are meant (cf. Chapter V note 15), though dogs, of course, often wear collars. Fig-wood makes us think of sycophants (*lit. fig-revealers*) and suggests that this prosecution is a malicious shake-down.

[18] This, the cry of the rowers in the navy, is here used as a collective noun to mean "crew," which in turn serves as a metaphor for the ordinary citizenry.

that I should move, having knocked down my house
here. How these house-breakers sacrifice!
They bring picnic baskets, wine-jars – not for the goddesses,
but for themselves. Holy frankincense
and offering-cake: the god gets this all placed
upon the fire, and the tip of the loin
and the gall-bladder, because they are inedible. Giving
these to the gods, they themselves swallow everything else.
Old woman, quickly open the door, for we must
work inside, it seems to me.

Geta: The little cauldron – you say – you've forgotten it?
You're completely hung over. What shall we do now?
We must disturb the neighbours of the god,
it seems. Slave! By the gods,
I don't think more wretched little slave-girls
are reared anywhere. Slaves! They know nothing else but
how to screw – Noble slaves! –
and how to shift the blame if anyone should see. Slave!
What Hell is this? Slaves! There isn't one
inside. Aha! Someone seems to be running up.

C   Why are you burning down the door, thrice-wretched one?
Tell me, buddy.

G   Don't bite.

C   I will, by Zeus,
and I'll eat you alive.

G   Don't, by the gods.

C   Is there any contract, unholy one,
between you and me?

G   No contract. That's why
I have come not asking back a debt from you
or holding summonses, but to ask for a little cauldron.

C   Little cauldron?

G   Little cauldron.

C   Whipping-post,
do you think I sacrifice cattle and do the things
that you do?

G   I don't think you'd sacrifice a snail.
But farewell, good sir. The women
told me to knock on your door and ask.
I've done so. There isn't one. I'll go back
and tell them. Oh most honoured gods,
this fellow here is a grey-haired viper.

There are various possible reasons why someone might want to eat alone, but perhaps the most obvious is so that he could have all the food for himself, and so it is that the loner tends to merge with the **glutton** (*gastris, laphyktes, margos*). It is a prejudice of Greek thought that because gluttons spend so much of their time thinking about their stomachs, they have no time left to think about anything else, and therefore are morons (cf. Hes. *Theog.* 26). This leads us to the oddest poem in the Greek language, the *Margites*, allegedly composed by Homer in a blend of dactylic and iambic metres that broke the "grammar" of Greek verse composition. This was a case of form following function, because the poem describes the misadventures on his honeymoon of the idiot who gave it its name – such an idiot was Margites, in fact, that he did not know whether it was his mother or his father who gave birth to him and who declined on his wedding-night to sleep with his bride lest she give a bad report of him to her mother (Phot. *Lex.* I 406 Naber = *Suda* iii 323.12 Adler). Margites finally relented, and consummated his marriage, when (on her mother's advice) his bride told him that a scorpion had bitten her vulva, and the ointment would only work if applied by a man's prick (Eust. *In Hom.* P. 1669.48). Unfortunately only a handful of fragments of this poem survive. Here they are (frs. 1-7 West *IEG*):

1   There came to Colophon a certain old and inspired bard,
     servant of the Muses and far-shooting Apollo
        holding in his own hands a fair-voiced lyre.

2   The gods did not make him a digger or a ploughman
     or skilled in any other way, for he failed at every job.

3   He knew many works, but knew them all badly.

5   The fox knows many things, but the hedgehog one – big one.

7   ...bladder (?) and with his hand outstretched
     (he brought his penis to) the pot, and pushed it
     right in. Then in two] troubles he was held:
     (his penis was in his hand,) and in the chamber-pot
     his hand was firmly stuck,] and he couldn't get it out.
     (He really had to go,) and he pissed in it right away.
                Then he thought of a new plan.
     Immediately he leapt up,] and leaving his mattress [warm,
     opened the closely-jointed] doors and ran outside.
                    through the black night.
                    and trying to free his hands
                    through the black night
                    he ran] and did not have a torch.
     (He found   's) wretched head
                    and it seemed to him to be a rock
                    and with stout hand
                    he turned it into little pieces.

We don't know the hapless victim of Margites' attempt to escape the clutches of the chamber-pot, but he must have been bald. The bald head mistaken for a rock occurs in the ancient *Life of Aeschylus*, according to which an eagle, having caught a tortoise in its talons and wanting to crack its shell, mistook Aeschylus' bald pate for a rock, and dropped the animal on it, so killing both reptile and poet (*Vita Aesch.* 2.17-21 = T 32 Wil.).[19]

---

[19] M. R. Lefkowitz, *The Lives of the Greek Poets* (London 1981) 72.

It's true that there's no actual gluttony in this poem, so far as we can see. There may be some implication of it, however, since the second fragment makes one wonder what Margites actually is capable of doing, since just about everything else, including sex, he seems to fail at. The greatest confirmed glutton in Greek is Heracles (who was at once uniquely and paradoxically a hero – meaning that he is dead and can intercede with the gods when sacrificed to – and god, and at once a tragic figure in Sophocles' *Women of Trachis* and Euripides' *Heracles*, and the perfect comic glutton as in Euripides' *Alcestis*). At the end of Aristophanes' *Birds* (1565-1629) the gods discover that the city of Cloudcuckooland built by Peisthetaerus and the birds in mid-air is cutting off the smoke rising from sacrifices on earth. The gods send an embassy of Poseidon, Heracles and a Triballian god (whom we met in Chapter VI) to Peisthetaerus to work out a solution to this problem. They arrive to find Peisthetaerus barbecuing some of his fellow citizens whom he has tried and convicted of treason and at the smell of the barbecue Heracles forgets his mission and can think only of agreeing with Peisthetaerus in order to get some food. He then offers to "translate" for the incomprehensible Triballian. By claiming that he agrees with him he wins over the embassy by a vote of two to one in favour of Peisthetaerus. Here is the episode (Note that the name "Triballian" happens to sound like the Greek for "rub" and this "Rubber God" spends most of the scene self-absorbed, rubbing himself):

Poseidon
> It's possible to see this city now
> of Cloudcuckooland, to which we are ambassadors.
> Hey you: what are you doing? Are you wearing your cloak to the left like that?
> Why don't you put your cloak on right?
> Oh you wretch! You're a real Laespodias![20]
> Oh democracy, wherever will you take us,
> if the gods vote for this god here?

Triballos
> Will you keep still?

Po   Drop dead! I have seen
> that you're the most barbarian of gods.
> Come, what will we do, Heracles?

Heracles   You've heard me say
> that I want to hang the man
> whoever it is who walled off the gods.

Po   But, good sir, we have been chosen as
> ambassadors of peace.

H   Then it seems to me doubly better to hang him.

Peisthetaerus

---

[20] The ancient commentators say that Laespodias was a man who wore his cloak crooked to conceal a rash on his ankle. If you believe this explanation, I have a nice bridge I'd like to sell you...

Somebody pass me the cheese-grater. Now the silphium.[21]
Somebody bring me the cheese. Fan the coals!

Po   We, being three gods, greet
      you, man!
Pei   But I'm grating silphium.
H   What kind of meat is this?
Pei   Some birds
      have been found to have done wrong in rising up
      against the democratic birds.
H   Then you grate silphium
      over them first?
Pei   Hello, Heracles
      What is it?
Po   We have come as ambassadors
      from the gods for an end to the war.
Slave   There's no oil in the flask.
H   And yet fowl should be well basted.
Po   For we get no benefit from fighting,
      and you, by being friends to us gods,
      would have rainwater in your ponds
      and would always have halcyon days.
      In authority over all these things we have come.
Pei   But never before did we start
      a war against you. Now we'd like, if it seems good,
      if you have come to do the right thing now,
      to make a truce. The right thing is this.
      Zeus must give to us birds
      his sceptre, and if we change enmity to friendship
      on these terms, I invite the ambassadors to breakfast.
H   That's good enough for me! I vote...
Po   What, you wretch! You're a fool and a glutton.
      Would you deprive your father of his power?
Pei   Really? Will not you gods be more
      strong, if birds rule below?
      Now, crouching under the clouds,
      bent-over mortals perjure themselves by you.
      But if you had the birds as allies,
      whenever someone swears by crow and by Zeus,
      the crow will come down and, flying at the
      oath-breaker unseen, will poke out his eye with his pecks.
Po   By Poseidon, you've said that well!
H   I think so too.
Pei   What, then, do you say?
T   Nabaisatreu.
Pei   You see? This one approves. Now further
      listen to how much more good we can do.
      If someone of men, having vowed a victim to one of the gods,
      then talks his way out of it, saying,

---

[21] A spice reminiscent of garlic-powder in flavour. Available
wherever fine Indian foods are sold.

"The mills of God grind slow," and reneges for greed,
we'll do these things...

Po   Come, let me see what!

Pei   ...when he happens to be counting his money,
this fellow, or is sitting in his bath,
a kite, having flown down and snatched up in secret
two sheep, will bring this price to the gods.

H   I vote we give the sceptre back
to them, I do.

P   Now ask the Triballian.

H   Triballian!

T   (*rubs himself.*)

H   Do you want a beating?

T   Saunaka baktarikrousa.

H   He says I've spoken very well.

Now, the glutton is not just someone who wants to eat a lot, but who wants to eat *everything* – including things that are forbidden. And the most forbidden food of all is human flesh. So it is that the perfect glutton is the **cannibal** (*omositos*). You might think that cannibalism is no laughing matter, but the Greeks and Romans found it endlessly funny. Indeed one of the earliest jokes in Greek literary history is spoken by the Cyclops. Here is *Odyssey* 9.353-70:

> So I spoke, and he took it and drank it down. He was terribly delighted,
> drinking the sweet drink, and he asked once again a second time:
> "Give me more willingly, and tell me your name
> now, so that I can give you a guest-gift in which you will delight,
> for the life-giving plough-land bears for the Cyclopes
> wine of fine grapes, and the rain of Zeus increases it,
> but *this* is a distillation of nectar and ambrosia!"
> So he spoke. Yet again I gave him flame-faced wine.
> Three times I brought and gave it, and three times he drank in folly.
> Yet when the wine had come to the Cyclops round his heart,
> then indeed I addressed him with honeyed words:
> "Cyclops, you ask my famous name. I will tell
> you. But you give me a guest-gift, as you have promised.
> Nobody is my name. My mother and father
> call me Nobody, and all my companions."
> So I spoke, and he immediately replied to me with pitiless heart:
> "I'm eating Nobody last after his companions,
> and the others first: this will be your guest-gift."

Another case of comedic (to the Romans) cannibalism appears near the end of the surviving portion of Petronius' *Satyricon*. The novel's antihero Encolpius and his accomplice Eumolpus have moved to Croton in southern Italy. As far as we can make out from the fragments Eumolpus poses as a sick old man, rich but childless with Encolpius pretending to be his slave. They get all manner of invitations to dinner in exchange for promising to write their hosts into Eumolpus' will. In the end Eumolpus dies (or pretends to die) and the will is read. Of course Eumolpus in fact has no money at all and so had to devise some way of preventing his erstwhile hosts from trying to cash in. Here is the will as given in chapter 141:

> All those who have legacies in my will, except for my freedmen, will inherit on this condition, which I have laid down: they must cut my body into pieces, and eat it in front of witnesses...

With all this eating going on, there has to be a **cook** (*mageiros*) in the neighbourhood.[22] In Greek and Roman comedy the cook provides a kind of food-porn, describing delicious meals for the vicarious pleasure of the audience. He also sometimes morphs into a quack boasting of skills he does not possess, inflicting the truth behind his skills on the unsuspecting diners. When the cook makes his entrance into literature it is in Euripides' *Cyclops*, which retells Homer's story. In that play Odysseus runs out of the cave as a messenger describing what is happening inside and characterizing the Cyclops as the *mageiros* from Hell (lines 387-404):

> He filled a ten-bottle mixing-bowl
> by milking his calves and pouring in the white milk,
> and he set out a wooden cup three cubits
> wide, and – it seemed – four deep,
> and sharp spits burnt with fire on the ends
> and smoothed with a sickle on the shafts, a branch of thorn,
> and bowls as big as Etna for catching blood from axes' jaws.
> And when everything was ready for the god-hated
> cook from Hell, he snatched up two men
> from my companions, slaughtered them, and with one stroke
> <   >
> one of them into the bronze-nailed hollow of the cauldron,
> and the other again, having snatched by the tendon at the tip of his foot,
> striking on the sharp point of a rocky stone,
> he splattered his brains. Having butchered
> his flesh with a fearsome knife, he roasted it on the fire,
> and the limbs he put into the cauldron to boil.

Although it is a horrifying scene, there is some humour in it, at least to the Greek mind. Remember, the cannibal is the ultimate glutton, and in this case, the food being prepared is human flesh. If it isn't funny, it's being done by somebody who is. Cooking by itself could be funny on its own, however. Here is a fragment of Antiphanes' *Philotis* (fr. 221 [222] *PCG*):

> A   So then, I say, boil the little grey-fish,
>   as at other times, in brine.
> B   The little bass?
> A   Roast whole.
> B   The shark?

---

[22] J. C. B. Lowe, "Cooks in Plautus," *CA* 4 (1985) 72-102 and John Wilkins, *The Boastful Chef* (Oxford 2000).

A	Boil it in gravy.
B	The little eel?
A	Salt, oregano, water.
B	The conger?
A	The same.
B	The ray?
A	With herbs.
B	There's also a slice of tuna.
A	You'll roast it.
B	Meat of a kid?
A	Roast.
B	The other?
A	The opposite.
B	The spleen?
A	Let it be stuffed.
B	The "fasting" fish?
A	This man here is killing me!

Our last example is the opening of Plautus' *Ghost* (*Mostellaria*), where we see the results of cooking and gluttony. In this play a man has gone out of town on business leaving his son in charge. The younger man is a real party animal and has trashed the house, when news comes that the father is returning sooner than expected. Unable to clean up the mess in time and needing an excuse to keep the older man out of the house, the boy and his slave concoct the story that the house is haunted. In the opening scene the farmhand Grumio arrives with news of the father's imminent return, which he imparts to the cook Tranio. The two slaves are contrasted on the country-mouse and city-mouse model (1-14):

Grumio:
    Come here and get out of the kitchen, whipping-post,
    who show me your genius among the frying-pans.
    Come out of the house, our master's ruin.
    By Pollux, I'll take proper vengeance on you in the country, sure as I live!
    Come here, I say, you stench, out of the kitchen! Why are you hiding?
Tranio:
    What, damn you, is this shouting of yours here in front of the house?
    Do you think you're still in the country? Move away from the house!
    Go off to the country! Get crucified! Move away from the door!
    (*Hits him.*)
    Well, is this here what you wanted?
G   I'm done for! Why are you beating me?
T   Because you're alive.
G   I'll put up with it. ...But just let the old man come home.
    Just let him come home safely, whom in his absence you devour.
T   You neither say something like the truth, nor the truth, Blockhead!
    How can anyone devour anyone else in his absence?

(Note the hint of yet another cannibalism-joke in the last line.)

The comic cook survives as far as the late Latin schoolboy joke, "The Piglet's Will," which we shall consider in Chapter XII. These were almost entirely male comedic figures – there are virtually no women filling these roles. However, women did have a role in comedy, one that was at times considerably different from the male one.

Chapter IX – The Sexual Dimension

The Slut

Almost all of our character examples have been men – men who are quacks, buffoons, gluttons, and other types of comedic archetype. But women also had their role to play in comedy, and it was a role defined by their gender. We have spoken so far about characters that seek to violate the boundary between animals and humans that is constituted by justice, all male. While justice is public, outdoor, male and involves as its essential symbol food, modesty is private, indoor, female and involves sex.

We see this first of all with the purpose of marriage as laid out in the ancient betrothal formula: "I betroth to you this my daughter, young man, for the ploughing of legitimate sons" (Menander' *Dyscolus* 842-43, cf. fr. 682 Koerte) – the ploughing-image, which seems vulgar to us, was part of the language of high culture as evidenced by Creon's taunt to Ismene when she points out that if Creon goes through with his plan to execute Antigone, his own son will lose his fiancée in Sophocles' *Antigone* (569): "Others too have fields for him to plough!" The problem of legitimacy was paramount in the eyes of Greek males. We see this from *Odyssey* 1.206-16 in which Athena disguised as Mentes asks Telemachus about his father:

> But come tell me this, and say it truly,
> if indeed you are such a son from Odysseus himself.
> It's scary how you resemble the head and beautiful eyes
> of him, since so often we spent much time together,
> that is before he went to Troy, where others too,
> the best of the Achaeans went in hollow ships.
> But from that time on neither have I seen Odysseus, nor he me."
>   Her then Telemachus thoughtfully answered,
> "Well then, stranger, I will answer you very truthfully:
> my mother says that I am his, yet I for my part
> don't know, for no-one yet has himself known
> his descent."

Women, of course, might commit adultery, a constant threat in the Greek male imagination, but they might also acquire children by other means, since baby-making was the purpose of marriage, and they could endanger their status as wives if they didn't "deliver." This fear of so-called supposititious children stands behind one of the central works of western literature, *Oedipus Rex*. Here are lines 775-88, Oedipus speaking:

>   I was considered the man
> greatest among the citizens there, before a certain
> fate befell me – worthy to wonder at,
> yet not at least worth the attention I gave it.
> For a man at a dinner-party, overcome with liquor,
> shouted in his cups that I had been foisted off on my father.
> I barely kept it together throughout the present day,
> but on the next, going to my mother and my father,

I questioned them. And they
bore the shameful story ill from him who let it slip.
I was pleased by both their responses, and yet
this always chaffed me, for it spread about a lot.
So in secret from my mother and father I went to Delphi...

Aristophanes, as you might expect, makes much of this fear. He has Mnesilochus, Euripides' cousin, disguise himself as a woman to infiltrate the women-only festival of the Thesmophoria (dedicated to Demeter and Kore) to spread pro-Euripides propaganda among the women, who naturally hate the poet. The fact that he apparently could pass as a woman among other women is beside the fact. He says (Ar. *Thesm.* 502-516):

I know another woman who said she was in labour
for ten days, until she could buy a baby.
And her husband kept going round trying to buy oxytocin
and an old woman brought a baby in in a pot,
stuffed – so it wouldn't cry – with a honeycomb.
When the one who brought it in nodded, immediately the woman screamed,
"It's coming! It's coming! Husband, now I'm about to
give birth!" (for she had kicked the inside of the pot).
He, rejoicing, runs in, and she yanks the comb out of
the baby's mouth, and it cries.
Then the creepy old woman who brought the baby
runs smiling to the husband, and says,
"A lion, a lion is born to you! Your spitting image
in every way – why, even his little dick
is just like yours: all shrivelled like a honeycomb!"

This fear that one might be raising at one's own expense someone else's sons accounts for two odd features of Greek custom: the fact that they thought adultery a worse crime than rape (because you usually know when a rape occurred and can expose any baby born as a result) and that men often reared their sister's children in preference to their wives' (because they had at least some genetic connection to the former, whereas with the latter, who knows?).[1]

This fear left its mark on domestic society in the virtual house-arrest under which Athenian males kept their womenfolk. We'll call this state of affairs *purdah*, which is an Urdu rather than a Greek word. Consider these few passages of Greek literature. First we find the purdah turned against the husband in Lysias 1.9-10:

First of all, therefore, Gentlemen (for I must tell you these things), my little

---

[1] Adultery and rape: see E. M. Harris, "Did the Athenians Regard Seduction as a Worse Crime than Rape?" *CQ* 40 (1990) 370-77, and R. Omitowoju, *Rape and the Politics of Consent in Classical Athens* (Cambridge 2002); on the avunculate (uncles raising nephews), see J. Bremmer, "Fosterage, Kinship and Circulation of Children in Ancient Greece," *Dialogos: Hellenic Studies Review* 6 (1999) 1-20, with bibliography.

house has two storeys: the upper and lower, equal as women's quarters and men's. Now, when we had our baby, its mother breast-fed it, and, so that, if she had to wash it, she shouldn't run any risk climbing down the stairs, I moved upstairs, and the women moved below. And so it had become our custom that often my wife went downstairs to sleep with the baby, so that she could give it the teat so that it wouldn't cry. And things happened like this for a long time, and I never suspected anything, but I was so naive that I thought my wife was the most chaste of all the wives in the city.

Again here is Lysias 3.6-7a, in which we can see what happens when men break the purdah:

For, having learned that the young man was at my house, he came to my house at night, drunk, having knocked on the doors, he came into the women's quarters while my sister and female cousins were inside, who had lived in so orderly a way, that they were ashamed even to be seen by members of their household. Now this man came to this point of violence that he didn't want to leave until, thinking that he had done the most dreadful thing, those who were present, and those who were with him, seeing him entering among young and orphaned girls, drove him off by force.

And, finally, consider Plato's *Symposium* 176e:

Having heard these things, everyone agreed not to make the party on the present occasion one of drinking, but rather to drink only for pleasure.
"Well, then," said Eryximachus, "Now that this is decided, to drink as each one wishes and that there be no compulsion, I make the following motion: that we say 'ciao' to the flute-girl who has just now come in, and let her play to herself or, if she wishes, to the women within, but that we spend time together today making speeches, and which speeches, if you wish, I am willing to propose to you."

This segregation was so thorough that a woman going berserk with joy, as at Hieron's intervention in 477 B.C. in a dispute between Rhegium and Locri in southern Italy, might make a public spectacle of herself – by just standing in the doorway.[2] Consider Pindar's *Pythian* 2.18-20:

You, oh son of Deinomenes, the Western
Locrian maiden praises before her house
after war's intractable toils,
having, thanks to your power, a safe look in her eye.

This physical segregation had a verbal component. Women were not only not to be seen; they were not to be spoken of. For all intents and purposes, they were un-people, objects to be privately possessed and never shared. This is how Pericles concluded his funeral oration for the Athenian soldiers who

---

[2] L. E. Woodbury, "The Gratitude of the Locrian Maiden: Pindar *Pyth.* 2.18-20," *TAPA* 108 (1978) 285-99 at 297 = *Collected Writings* (Chico, CA, 1991) 282.

died in the first year of the Peloponnesian War (Thuc. 2.45b):[3]

> And, if I must make mention of womanly virtue to as many as are now in widowhood, I will reveal all my advice in brief. The greatest glory for you is not to be worse than your in-dwelling nature, and of whom there is least discussion among men either of virtue or of blame.

The title character of Aristophanes' *Lysistrata* is perhaps very unusual, because she may represent a real woman, the priestess of Athena, Lysimache.[4] Usually when a woman is spoken of, it is in matters of sex, and a right-thinking woman does not discuss such things (the same with boys, who were as much sexual objects as the women; cf. Pl. *Lys.* 204b-c). This is how Nausicaa reacts to the mention of marriage, when she asks her dad to borrow the car to take her clothes to the Laundromat, so they'll be clean in case one of her brothers decides to go dancing tonight, in *Odyssey* 6.63-70:

> "...and they always want to have newly-laundered clothes
> to go to the dance, and all these things have been on my mind,"
> So she spoke, for she was ashamed to name blooming marriage
> to her dear father. But he intuited all, and replied with a word:
> "I don't begrudge you the mules [to drive the car], or anything else.
> Go: for the servants will harness for you
> the well-wheeled lofty surrey with the fringe on top."

Again in Vergil's *Aeneid* 12.64-69 when Amata mentions her daughter, Lavinia's impending marriage...

> Lavinia received her mother's words with tears
> aplenty pouring down her cheeks, into which much redness
> injected fire that ran through her warm face,
> as when someone will have dyed Indian ivory
> with *murex*, or where many white lilies, mixed,
> blush with the rose, such colours the girl showed on her cheek.

In a related story, at least to our subject, Harmodius and Aristogeiton became the famous tyrannicides of Athens when they slew the tyrant Hippias. The dictator, Hipparchus, Hippias' brother, was in love with Harmodius, who rejected him in favour of a commoner, Aristogeiton. Irked by this rejection, Hipparchus refused to allow Harmodius' unmarried sister to carry a basket in the Panathenaic procession, ...so of course he had to kill him (Thuc. 6.l.54-59). He had to kill him, because by this refusal Hipparchus

---

[3] Compare D. Schaps, "The Woman Least Mentioned: Etiquette and Women's Names," *CQ* 27 (1977) 323-30.

[4] See J. Henderson, *Aristophanes: Lysistrata* (Oxford 1978) xxxviii-xl.

was implying that Harmodius' sister was no longer a virgin.[5]

Against this backdrop, one can see the necessity for sexual virtue among women. Remember what Archilochus said about Neobule in Chapter V:

> but she's pretty sharp
> and does lots of men.
> I'm afraid that in my haste
> I'd bear blind and untimely pups,
> just like the bitch.

Bear this in mind in considering the "outlook from the wall" episode in the *Iliad* 3.146-80 in which in the ninth year of the war Priam asks Helen to identify the Greek chieftains whom he's been fighting for nearly a decade (his intelligence-gathering is on a par with CSIS'):

> Those about Priam, and Panthous and Thymoetes,
> Lampus and Clytus and Hicetaon, scion of Ares,
> Oucalegon and Antenor – both wise –
> sat, leaders of the people, by the Scaean gates,
> having retired from war through old age, but still good
> speakers, like cicadas, who throughout the wood,
> sitting on the trees, give off their lily-like voice.
> Such leaders of the Trojans were upon the tower.
> As they saw Helen coming to the tower,
> softly they spoke to each other these winged words:
> "No wonder that Trojans and well-greaved Achaeans
> suffer griefs so long for such a woman:
> terribly like the immortal goddesses she seems in appearance,
> but even so, although she is such a one, let her return to the ships,
> lest she be left behind to us and our children a punishment."
> So they spoke, and Priam called Helen with his voice:
> "Come here before me, dear child. Sit by me,
> so that you may see before you your husband and your kinsmen by marriage and your friends.
> You are not to blame for me, but the gods, you see, are to blame,
> who brought upon me the dreadful war of the Achaeans.
> May you name out for me this giant?
> Who is this Achaean man so good and big?
> Indeed, all others are bigger by a head,
> yet I have not yet seen with my eyes a man so handsome
> nor so reverend. He seems like a kingly man."
> Helen answered him, shining among women,
> "You are venerable to me, dear father-in-law, and terrible.
> Would that evil death had pleased me when I came here
> following your son, and left my marriage-chamber and relatives
> and newborn son and lovely companions.
> But would that these things did not happen, and I melt with weeping.
> I will tell you this, about which you question and inquire:

---

[5] B. M. Lavelle, "The Nature of Hipparchos' Insult to Harmodius," *AJP* 107 (1986) 318-31.

he is Atreus' son, wide-ruling Agamemnon,
both a good king and a strong spear-man...
But he was brother-in-law to me (dog-face!), if ever that really was!"-

The word Helen uses is *kunopis*, literally "dog-face."[6] Helen is hardly a
"dog" in our colloquial sense – hers is the face that launched a thousand
ships[7] (and that only means that it might be somewhat flat now). Neither is
she a "bitch" – if anything she is *too* friendly to men. She is like a dog in that
she does not know the boundary between what should be done inside and
what outside, for her matings are public knowledge, and of a concern for two
whole armies of men.

The Scoffer, the Shrew, and the Tease

While the slut breaks the bonds of modesty and so draws laughter upon
herself inadvertently, and most often unknowingly, the **scoffer** (*skoptria*)
does so deliberately. In some ways, the scoffer is like a form of self-knowing
quack, drawing attention to herself and knowing exactly how to do it. The
most important example of this is from the *Homeric Hymn to Demeter* lines
191-205:[8]

> And [Metaneira] yielded her seat to her, and told her to be seated.
> But Demeter, who brings the fruits in their seasons and gives good gifts,
> did not want to be seated on the shining chair,
> but remained unwilling, casting down her beautiful eyes,
> at least until Iambe, who knows clever things, set before her
> a well-made seat, and cast over it a silver fleece.
> Then, sitting down, she held before herself her veil with her hands
> and sat a long while, not speaking, grieved, on the throne,
> nor did she greet anyone with a word or in any way with a deed,
> but without laughing, unfed on food or drink,
> she sat wasting away with desire for her deep-girdled daughter,
> until with jests Iambe, who knows clever things,
> joking much, turned aside the holy Lady
> to smile and laugh and have a propitious heart.
> She indeed also thereafter pleased her in her moods.

This passage is similar to the scene we considered in chapter VI in which
Hephaestus defuses the tension on Olympus arising from the quarrel
between Hera and Zeus by pouring nectar and making himself a figure of
ridicule. Here too there is an emotional crisis, in this case the mourning of
Demeter, that is defused by Iambe's jests. Thanks to her Demeter "snaps out

---

[6] Cf. M. Graver, "Dog-Helen and Homeric Insult," *CA* 14 (1995) 41-61.

[7] C. Marlowe, *Doctor Faustus* V.i.97.

[8] See N. J. Richardson, *The Homeric Hymn to Demeter* (Oxford 1974) 213-
17, and L. O'Higgins, *Women and Humour in Classical Greece* (Cambridge
2003) esp. 37-57.

of it" long enough to continue, this time successfully, in her quest for her daughter. These two passages together illustrate an important point, namely that laughter and strong emotion cannot coexist, and laughter can be used by the intellect to reassert its control over the emotions.

Apollodorus' *Library* 1.5.1 tells this same story, but adds one detail when he says, "A certain old woman, Iambe, by mocking made the goddess laugh. For this reason, they say that the women at the Thesmophoria perform jests." This makes Iambe the eponymous inventor of the iambic metre and the poems composed in it which are lampoons, such as those of Archilochus that drove Lycambes and Neobule to suicide. (The word "iambic" probably really comes from the verb *iaptein*, "to send, drive on [of missiles]").

But we still don't know how Iambe made Demeter laugh. We can be pretty sure that it was by saying or doing something obscene. This is because the Scholiast (ancient commentator) to Lucian, *Dialogues of the Courtesans* 7.4 (page 280.12-20 Rabe) describes the Haloa festival – which like the Thesmophoria was a women's only festival in honour of Demeter – this way:

> In this [feast] a certain women's rite is also conducted at Eleusis, and many childish things and mockeries are spoken. Only the women go in, and they have the licence to say whatever they want, and in fact at that time they say the most shameful things to one another, and the priestesses, approaching the women in secret, counsel in their ear illicit love as though it were some esoteric thing, and all the women carry and lift up before one another shameful and improper genital-images of bodies, both male and female.

The ancient encyclopaedist Hesychius has an entry under the word *gephyris* in which he says that during the procession from Athens to Eleusis in celebration of the mysteries of Demeter a woman sat with veiled head on the bridge over the Cephisus river making jokes against those passing by and against prominent citizens. The word for "joke" (*skomma*) perhaps comes from the word *skops*, the name of the little horned owl, which was famous in Greece, as the magpie is with us, for mimicking, and therefore apparently mocking other birds (compare Theocritus 1.136, with Gow's note).

In the Orphic version of Demeter's story Iambe is replaced by a figure named Baubo. Fragment 52 Kern of the Orphic hymns reads:

> So saying, she hoisted up her skirts and showed all of her body,
> and the unfitting spot.[9] The boy Iacchus was there.
> He laughed and kept throwing it with his hand under Baubo's crotch.
> The goddess laughed aloud and laughed in her heart
> and she took the gleaming jar into which the barley-drink was put.

We know from the story of Hippoclides in Chapter VII that Greeks didn't wear underwear, so when Baubo flashed (*anasurein*) Demeter, the god saw all there was to see – and happily, for the sanity of the readers, this was not described in detail. No-one knows for sure the origin of the name Baubo, but

---

[9] The reading of the text is uncertain; see M. Marcovich, "Demeter, Baubo, Iacchus, and a Redactor," *Vigiliae Christianae* 40 (1986) 294-301.

it may come from the Greek for "bow-wow," since as we saw in the last section dogs are the symbol of shamelessness.

The name, now a common noun, has a different meaning in the Mimes of Hero(n)das written in Alexandria in the 260s BC. Here is an excerpt from *Mime* 6 (lines 12-19 and 58-78). Metro has come to Coritto's house to find her shouting at her maids:

Metro: Dear Coritto, you are worn down by
      the same yoke as I (i.e. lazy slaves).
      I too gnash my teeth day and night
      and bark like a dog at these nobodies.
      But the reason I came to see you –
Coritto: Out from under our feet,
      damn you, snoops! Nothing but ears and tongues,
      and otherwise all holiday!
M   I beg you, don't lie,
      dear Coritto. Whoever was it who stitched for you
      the scarlet dildo (*baubo*)?
....
C   He's someone from – I don't know – Chios or Erythrae,
      bald and short. You'd say he's the very
      Prexinus. You wouldn't be able so to compare
      fig to fig. But when he talks, you'll know
      he's Cerdon, not Prexinus.
      He works at home, and sells in secret,
      for now every door bristles with tax-men.
      But his work is genuine Coan. You'll think
      you see the handiwork of Athena, not Cerdon.
      I – because he came bringing me two, Metro –
      when I saw them, at first glance my eyes bugged out:
      erections that firm real men don't make
      (for we're by ourselves). Not only that,
      but their softness was a dream, and the little laces
      were wool, not laces. Another cobbler kinder
      to a woman you won't find for looking!
M   How, then, did you pass up the other one?
C   Why didn't I buy it, Metro?
      I wasn't able in any way to persuade him.
      I kissed, I stroked his bald-spot,
      I poured him something sweet to drink, called him "Honey-pie."
      Only my body I didn't give him to use.

It is perhaps worth noting that the sacrificial animal offered to Demeter is a piglet, because it was the cheapest animal, ideally suited to this most democratic of cults.[10] Now it happens that "piggy" (*choiros*) is the commonest

---

[10] W. Burkert (P. Bing trans.), *Homo Necans* (Berkeley, Los Angeles and London, 1983) 256-64.

Greek slang for the female genitals.[11] This meaning is richly exploited in Aristophanes' *Acharnians* 729-50, 764-96 and 817-19 at the height of the Peloponnesian War in which the Acharnian farmer Dicaeopolis declares his own private peace with Sparta, opens a market, and invites all comers to trade. Here is a Megarian come to sell his daughters disguised as pigs (the humour of the original is greatly increased by the newcomer's hick-like West Greek Doric accent):

Megarian: Hello, market in Athens, friend to Megarians.
        I've been longing for you, by Zeus of Friendship, like a mother.
        But, pitiable little daughters of a wretched father,
        come up to the crackers, to see if you'll find any here.
        Listen up! Lend me your – stomachs:
        do you prefer to be sold, or to starve to death in a bad way?
Girls: To be sold! To be sold!
M: I agree. But who is so foolish
        that he would buy you at a clear loss?
        But I have a Megarian trick:
        I've prepared to say that I'm bringing you for sale as pigs.
        Put on these pig-feet
        so that you might seem to be from a good sow.
        For, by Hermes, if you come home
        unsold, you'll feel starvation in a bad way!
        Put on these snouts, too,
        then get into this here sack.
        Now grunt and oink
        and speak the words of the pigs from the Mysteries.[12]
        I'll call to Dicaeopolis, wherever he is:
        Dicaeopolis! Would you like to buy some pigs?
Dicaeopolis: What! A Megarian?
M: We've come to sell...
....
D: What have you brought?
M: I've got pigs for the Mysteries.
D: Well said! Show me.
M: They're very beautiful.
        Stretch out your hand, if you like. See how fat and beautiful they are?
D: What's this thing here?
M: A pig, by Zeus!
D: What are you saying? Where in the world did this pig come from?
M: A Megarian.
        Isn't this a pig?
D: It doesn't look like one to me.
M: (*aside*) Isn't it terrible! You see the man's scepticism?

---

[11] For more than you ever wanted to know about this subject, see J. Henderson, *The Maculate Muse* 2nd ed. (New York and Oxford, 1991) 131-32 (see note 9 above).

[12] A piglet was the standard sacrifice to Demeter at the beginning of the Eleusinian Mysteries.

He doesn't agree that this is a pig. (*To Dicaeopolis*) But, in fact,
if you wish, bet me thyme-flavoured salt
that this isn't a pig, as the Greeks use the term.

D: But it's a human being's!

M: Yes, by Diocles,
it's mine: don't you see she's *someone*'s?
Do you want to hear her speak?

D: Yes, by the gods, I do.

M: Speak quickly, piggy.
Won't you? Are you silent? You're going to die the worst death!
I'll bring you back home, by Hermes!

G: Oink! Oink!

M: Is this a pig?

D: Now at least it seems a pig.
Yet if it grew up, it would be a cunt.

M: Know well that within five years
it will look like its mother.

D: But can this other one be sacrificed?

M: Of course.
How could it not be sacrificed?

D: It has no tail.[13]

M: It's young. But when it becomes a sow,
it'll have a big, fat, red one.
If you want to rear it, this is the pig for you!

D: How her cunt resembles the other one's!

M: Well, they have one mother and are from the same father.
If it were fattened, and were downy with fur,
it would be the most beautiful pig to sacrifice to Aphrodite.

D: But a pig isn't sacrificed to *Aphrodite*!

M: Not a pig to Aphrodite? Yes – to her alone of the gods.
Indeed, the meat of these pigs
is the sweetest thing, when it's pierced on a spit!

....

Sycophant: Hey, you: where are you from?

M: A pig-dealer from Megara.

S: Then I denounce these pigs
as enemy goods. You too!

The joke, of course, works because of a play on words. The Megarian, strictly speaking, is describing his goods. In modern English, however, some of the meaning is lost. Imagine for a moment, though, if the Megarian was talking about selling "pussies."

Could the women themselves have jested about their genitals, comparing them variously to owls, dogs, pigs and other animals? Here we see a violation of modesty – deliberate this time – as a breaking of the boundary between human and animal.

We have seen how women bring laughter upon themselves accidentally and then deliberately. Now we will see how they direct laughter toward

---

[13] Only animals that were physically perfect could be sacrificed to the gods. "Tail" is slang for "penis".

others, especially men (which is only fair, as the men seem to be the ones laughing so far). These are women in the role of **shrew**. The archetypal nagging wife is Hera, perennial bane of Zeus' existence. She is not alone, however. Let's return to the diners in Xenophon's *Symposium*, whom we met in chapter V. Here is section 2.8-10:

> At this, the other one began to play the flute for her, and someone standing beside the dancer gave her hoops – up to twelve. She, taking them all, kept dancing and then threw them up spinning, judging how high she had to throw them so that she could catch them in turn.
>
> And Socrates said, "Gentlemen, it is clear from many things, and from what this girl is doing, that the female nature happens to be no worse than the male, though it lacks knowledge and strength.[14] So that if each of you has a wife, let him pluck up his courage and teach her whatever he wants to have her know."
>
> And Antisthenes said, "How, then, Socrates, believing this, do you too not educate Xanthippe, but you want the wife who of all – I think – who are, and have been, and ever will be, is the most difficult?"
>
> "Because," he replied, "I see that those who wish to become equestrians don't buy the most docile, but the most spirited horses. For they think that, if they are able to control such horses, they will easily manage others. So I, too, wanting to deal and converse with humans, have acquired this wife, knowing well that if I can submit to her, I will easily pass time with all other people."

The source of laughter is, of course, from Xanthippe being used as an example – by the way Socrates deals with her, the other guests at the banquet are made to look humorous.[15] We have also already noted Socrates' addiction to ironically comparing humans to horses; in this case there is a special point, because the name Xanthippe means "tawny horse." Xenophon of course, as well as all the guests at his imagined banquet are male, so this anecdote gives us a patriarchal perspective. When we turn to the scant surviving examples of female voices, however, we see that the image of women criticizing men under the guise of humour is well substantiated. This is where we have the shrew – so difficult that she makes Socrates look like a saint for even being associated with her.

---

[14] Socrates (rare for a Greek) is not sexist. Women lacked knowledge and strength, because they were forbidden, in Athens at least, from going to school or performing athletics.

[15] "– A shrew, John Eglinton said shrewdly, is not a useful portal of discovery, one should imagine. What useful discovery did Socrates learn from Xanthippe?
"– Dialectic, Stephen answered."
J. Joyce *Ulysses* 1922 (Harmondsworth 1968) 190.

Whenever Xanthippe
wasn't feeling too chippy,
she would bawl at Socrates:
'Why aren't you Hippocrates?'
W. H. Auden, *Academic Graffiti* (London, 1971) 60.

The **tease** works in a different way, similar to the scoffer, but where the scoffer draws attention to herself, the tease draws attention to the foibles of others. Here again, back from Chapter III, is a woman's work-song from the island of Lesbos (*Carm. Pop.* 869 Page):

> Grind, mill, grind,
> for Pittacus always grinds
> as he rules over great Mytilene.

David Campbell notes that this song "may be metaphorical, either with the meaning 'oppress' or with obscene reference."[16] Again, here is a wedding-song of Sappho, which gave J. D. Salinger the title for his *Raise High the Roof Beam, Carpenters* of 1963 (fr. 111 Lobel-Page, Voigt):

> Up with the roof-tree,
>   Hymenaeus!
> Raise it, carpenters,
>   Hymenaeus!
> The bridegroom is coming, like Ares,
> much bigger than a big man!

Now Ares was big. REALLY big. And we're not just talking about his head. He gets knocked over on the plain of Troy during the theomachy (battle of the gods) in the *Iliad* 21.407 and Homer tells us that he covers seven acres when he falls, no doubt inconveniencing a number of farmers by knocking over their barns. Sappho's praise of the bridegroom is clearly "over the top," and several scholars have argued that there is one particular part of his anatomy relevant to the wedding-night that won't fit through the door without some renovations.[17]

Here is another example. One of Pindar's earliest poetic efforts was fr. 29 Machler:

> Ismenus, or Melias of the golden distaff,
> or Cadmus, or the holy race of Spartan men,
> or Thebe with her frontlet of lapis lazuli,
> or the all-daring strength of Heracles,
> or the much-rejoicing honour of Dionysus,
> or the wedding of white-armed Harmonia –
> about which thing should we sing?

When he showed these lines to the poetess Corinna, his older

---

[16] D. Campbell, *Greek Lyric Poetry* (Glasgow 1967) 449.

[17] G. S. Kirk, "A Fragment of Sappho Reinterpreted," *CQ* 13 (1963) 51-52, H. Lloyd-Jones, "Sappho Fr. 111," *CQ* 17 (1967) 168, and J. F. Killeen, "Sappho Fr. 111," *CQ* 23 (1973) 198. Not everyone accepts the obscene reading; see M. Marcovich, "On Sappho fr. 111 L.-P.," *Humanitades* 5-6 (1963-64) 223-27.

contemporary in Thebes, she is said (Plut. *de glor. Athen.* 4) to have replied that "he should sow with the hand, not with the whole sack." In all of these examples, we see the tendency to use metaphor in a mildly riddling, teasing way.

Turning now to Rome, we find the first poem (number 51 in his collection, lines 1-12) that Catullus composed for his girl-friend Clodia (a.k.a. Lesbia), wife of Metellus Celer. The poem describes Catullus' jealousy as he sees his beloved sitting next to her husband:

> He seems to me to be like a god.
> He – if possible – surpasses the gods,
> who, sitting opposite you, repeatedly watches
>   and hears you,
> sweetly laughing, which destroys all
> my senses: for the minute,
> Lesbia, I look at you, no power is left,
>   Lesbia, over my voice,
> but my tongue grows sluggish, under my limbs
> a light flame runs, with their own sound
> my ears ring, my lights are covered
>   with twin night...

These lines are an almost verbatim translation of Sappho fr. 31 (Lobel-Page, Voigt). Long ago Ulrich von Wilamowitz-Moellendorff pointed out that on Lesbos (unlike in Rome) women and men would not so easily be found sitting in each other's company, and argued that Sappho's original poem was a wedding song. The man in her poem – the groom – was not like the gods because he was so lucky; he was like them because he was strong enough to tolerate the beauty of the addressee – the bride – that provoked all the symptoms in Sappho.[18] (This is a really nice interpretation, because it means that Catullus has completely changed the meaning of the poem without changing any of its actual words.) But what are Sappho's symptoms symptomatic *of*? George Devereux argued that she was having an anxiety attack, but Laura O'Higgins has recently claimed instead that what Sappho experiences as she looks at the bride is an orgasm.[19] If so, her poem is as over the top in its own way as fr. 111, and clearly teases both bride and groom by praising them *too far*. This is the technique of flattery pushed in the direction of mockery.

This type of humour is not confined to adult women. Little girls played a game of tag in which they sang a tortoise-song. One girl would sit in the middle of a circle being the tortoise while the others ran round her. At the

---

[18] See R. D. Griffith, "In Praise of the Bride: Sappho FR. 105(A) LP, Voigt," *TAPA* 125 (1995) 55-61 at 55 n. 5.

[19] G. Devereux, "The Nature of Sappho's Seizure in FR. 31 LP as Evidence of her Inversion," *CQ* 20 (1970) 17-31 (this was critiqued by M. Marcovich, "Sappho fr. 31: Anxiety Attack or Love Declaration?" *CQ* 22 [1972] 19-32); and O'Higgins op. cit. 97.

appropriate moment in the song she jumped up and tagged one of them, who became the tortoise in her turn. The song goes like this (*Carm. Pop.* 876 Page):

A: Turtle-turtle, what are you doing in the middle?
B: I'm weaving wool and Milesian thread.
A: What was your son doing when he died?
B: He leapt from white horses into the sea.

Leaping from white-horses into the sea is a comically exaggerated metaphor for ejaculation; the girls do not really need to know or understand this in order to play the game, any more than modern children need to know that the May-pole around which they dance is a phallic symbol.[20] We end with one last children's song (though not one confined this time to girls) – it is the swallow-song with which children on the island of Rhodes welcomed back the swallow that marked the return of spring by going trick-or-treating (*Carm. Pop.* 848 Page):

Come, come, Swallow,
bringing the fair weather,
the fair anniversary,
with your white belly
and your black back.
Roll a fruitcake out of your rich house,
a cup of wine
and a basket of cheese.
The Swallow does not
spurn wheat-bread and
egg-bread. Shall we go away or shall we take it?
If you will give something, do so, but if not, we will not let you go.
Either we will carry off your door or your lintel
or your wife sitting inside.
She is small. We'll carry her off easily.
If you bring us something, may you bring a big thing.
Open, open your door to the Swallow.
We aren't old men, just kids.

The justly most famous example of teasing in ancient literature comes from Aristophanes' *Lysistrata*. Women all over Athens are on a sex-strike, trying to force their husbands to vote for peace. Aristophanes gives us, exempli gratia, a glimpse of how this affects the life of one couple, Cinesias ("Banger") and his wife, Myrrhina ("Octopussy"). All male characters in Old Comedy were costumed with enormous phalluses, which could be ignored when not needed, or used in a variety of ways as props – in one scene (*Wasps* 1341-44) an old man and a slave girl are climbing up some steps, and he invites her to use his phallus as a rope or hand-rail – but their most obvious use is to show sexual arousal. Such is the case in this scene (lines 845-958):

---

[20] R. D. Griffith and G. D'Ambrosio-Griffith, "Il gioco della chelichelone," *Maia* 43 (1991) 83-87.

Cinesias: Woe is me! What a spasm holds me,
        and a cramp as if I were stretched on the rack!
Lysistrata: Who is this who stands within the guard-posts?
C: It's me.
L: A man!
C: Of course, a man. (*points to the evidence.*)
L: Won't you get lost!
C: Who are you to throw me out?
L: The day-watch.
C: By the gods, go and call out Myrrhina for me.
L: Why should I call out Myrrhina for you. Who are you?
C: Her husband, Cinesias of Paonidae.
L: Well, hello there! Your name is not
        without fame or unknown among us.
        For always your wife has you in her mouth.
        If ever she eats an egg or an apple,
        "This is for Cinesias," she says.
C: Oh, for the love of God!
L: By Aphrodite, if ever the conversation
        turns to men, immediately your wife says
        that any other man is trash next to Cinesias.
C: Go now and call her!
L: Why? Will you give me something?
C: Yes, by Zeus, whatever you want.
        I've got this. I'll give you what I've got.
L: O.k. I'll go and call her for you.
C: Go quickly,
        for I no longer have joy in life,
        since she left my house.
        I suffer when I come home, and everything
        seems empty to me, and I know no joy
        in food when I eat, for I'm *hard*!
Myrrhina: I love, I love him! But he doesn't want
        to be loved by me. Don't call me to him.
C: Oh, sweetest Myrrhina, why are you
        doing this? Come down here!
M: By Zeus, I won't!
C: Won't you come down, when I'm calling, Myrrhina?
M: You're not begging. You're just calling me.
C: I'm not begging? I'm worn out!
M: I'm leaving.
C: Don't go! Listen at least to our little
        baby! You: won't you call Mommy?
Baby: Mommy! Mommy! Mommy!
C: Hey, what's wrong with you? Don't you
        pity your baby – not washed, not breast-fed for five days?
M: I do pity it. But it's the father who's being careless.
C: Come down, strange one, to your baby!
M: ...Whom I bore. I must go down! What's wrong with me?
C: She seems to me much younger, and sweeter to look at.
        Yet she's peevish toward me, and stuck up.
        This is what wears me down with desire!

M: Oh you sweetest baby of a bad father,
   come let me kiss you, sweetest thing to your Mommy!
C: Why, oh villain, do you do these things to me, persuaded by those
   other women? You make me suffer –
   and you yourself are pained.
M: Don't touch me!
C: And the money at home – mine and yours –
   you're letting dwindle.
M: Fat lot I care!
C: You don't care that your woof-threads
   are being pecked at by chickens?
M: I don't, by Zeus!
C: And the rites of Aphrodite are unobserved by you
   for so long! Won't you come back?
M: By Zeus, not I, unless you desist and
   stop the war.
C: Well, if you wish,
   we'll even do these things.
M: Well, if you wish,
   I'll even leave here – but now I've sworn an oath [to stay].
C: Climb down to me after all this time!
M: No...But I won't say that I don't want you.
C: You want me? Why won't you lie down, little Myrrhina?
M: Don't be ridiculous: in front of the baby?
C: By Zeus! Manes, take this baby home!
   There: the kid's out of the way.
   Won't you lie down?
M: Where could anyone even do it, dear?
C: Where? Pan's place is good.
M: And how could I go back pure again to the Acropolis?
C: That's easy: washed in Clepsydra.
M: Since I've sworn, could I break my oath, dear?
C: On my head be it. Think no more of your oath.
M: Come now, let me get a little cot for us both.
C: No way: the ground is good enough for us.
M: No, by Apollo! I won't lie down with you
   on the ground.
C: (*aside*) The woman want's me... it's plain enough!
M: There! Lie down quickly, and I'll undress.
   But that thingummybob – the mattress – should be fetched.
C: What sort of mattress? Not for me, at least.
M: Yes, by Artemis!
   It's nasty on the bed-springs.
C: Well, give me a kiss.
M: There!
C: Aye yae yae! Now, come right back!
M: Here's the mattress. Lie down, and I'll undress.
   ...And the what's it? – pillow. You don't have one.
C: But I don't *need* one!
M: But, by Zeus, I do.

C: This penis of mine's getting wined and dined like Heracles![21]
M: Stand up! Hop up! Now, I have everything.
C: I can believe it. Come here now, little precious.
M: I'm already undoing my bra. Remember now:
    don't trick me about the treaty.
C: By Zeus, may I die if I do!
M: You don't have a blanket.
C: By Zeus! I don't need one. I want to fuck!
M: Don't worry. You will: I'm coming right back.
C: The woman will wear me away with the bedding!
M: Get up!
C: I'm already *up*!
M: Do you want me to rub you with myrrh?
C: No, by Apollo, I don't!
M: Yes, by Aphrodite, whether you want to or not.
C: Would that the myrrh were spilled, by Fart!
M: Stretch out your hand, take, and anoint yourself.
C: This here myrrh is useless, by Apollo,
    except for wasting time and *not* smelling of sex.
M: What a fool I am! I brought the myrrh from Rhodes!
C: It's good! Leave it, silly!
M: You keep babbling.
C: May the first man who ever distilled myrrh die most horribly!
M: Take this flask.
C: I'm already holding *this* one.
    You wretch, like down, and don't bring me
    anything else!
M: I'll do it, by Artemis.
    See: I'm taking off my shoes. But, dearest,
    do vote for peace.
C: I'll take it under advisement.
(*exit Myrrhina*)
    The woman has destroyed and worn me away:
    having peeled back my skin, she's gone!

        (*Sings*) Oh, how do I suffer? Whom will I fuck,
        Now I'm cheated of the fairest of all?
        How to care for this little babe?[22]
        Where is Dogfox, the Pimp?
        HIRE ME A NANNY!

And so in the end, with the whole house turned inside out, and all the furniture on the front lawn, Cinesias is left singing a quasi-tragic aria lamenting his erection.

---

[21] Comic poets for some reason often show Heracles kept waiting for his dinner, compare Aristophanes' *Wasps* 60.

[22] Holding his phallus.

The Adulterer and the Cuckold

Men had their own ways of making a nuisance of themselves in the domestic sphere, though. One of the most destructive ways of sticking yourself, so to speak, in someone else's business is sleeping with his wife, and the **adulterer** (*moicheus*) becomes a major pest, and an object of ridicule. The stories of both Agamemnon and Odysseus involve adultery; in Agamemnon's case the actual infidelity of his wife Clytaemnestra with Aegisthus, in Odysseus' case the potential infidelity of his wife Penelope with the young men of Ithaca who are her suitors. In *Odyssey* 8.266-367 the blind bard Demodocus sings the following story about adultery on Olympus:[23]

> Yet he, playing the lyre, began to sing a beautiful song
> about the love of Ares and fair-crowned Aphrodite,
> how first they mingled in Hephaestus' home
> in secret. He gave her many things, and shamed the bed and couch
> of Hephaestus, the lord. Yet to him as messenger came
> the Sun, who had seen them mingling in love.
> When Hephaestus heard the heart-aching tale,
> he stepped to go into his smithy, brewing evils in the depths of his mind,
> and he placed a great anvil on its stand, and cut fetters
> unbreakable, unloosable, so that they might stay right where they were.
> Yet when he had made a trap, angry at Ares,
> he stepped to go into his bedroom, where his own mattress lay,
> and about the bedposts he poured fetters round in a circle,
> and many too had poured forth from above, off the roof-beam,
> like fine cobwebs, that no-one at all could see,
> not even of the blessed gods. For he had contrived them trickily.
> Yet when the whole trick over the mattress he'd poured,
> he set out to go to Lemnos, well-built city,
> that to him of lands is much the dearest of all.
> Nor was it a vain watch that golden-reined Ares kept.
> When he saw Hephaestus, famous smith, going away,
> he stepped to go to the home of very famous Hephaestus,
> craving the love of Cythera's fair-crowned girl.
> And she recently from her father, the very strong son of Cronus
> having come, was there. He came into the house,
> and put his hand in hers, and spoke a word, and named her:
> "Come here, Dear. Let us turn bed-ward to the couch,
> for Hephaestus is no longer in town. Perhaps, indeed,
> he is going off to Lemnos among the Sintians, rustic of voice."
> So he spoke. And it seemed pleasing to her to sleep.
> So the two of them ran and got onto the mattress, and about them the fetters
> poured, fashioned by much-thinking Hephaestus,
> nor to move any of their limbs was it possible, nor to get up.
> And then indeed they knew that they were no longer going to flee.
> Soon, coming then, there returned to them the very famous doubly lame one,
> having turned back before he reached the Lemnian land,

---

[23] C. G. Brown, "Ares, Aphrodite and the Laughter of the Gods," *Phoenix* 43 (1989) 283-93.

for the Sun kept watch for him and was a tattletale.
And he stepped to go toward his house, sad in his own heart,
and he stood in the entrance, and anger seized him wild,
and he shouted shockingly, and called to all the gods:
    "Zeus, father, and all blessed gods, who are forever,
come here! So that laughable deeds, and not tolerable, may you see:
how me, being lame, Zeus's daughter, Aphrodite
has always dishonoured, but loves destructive Ares,
since he is handsome, and sound of foot, while I at least
was born feeble. Yet no-one else is at all to blame for me,
but my two parents, who ought not to have borne me.
But, look! How the two of them lie in love,
having gone onto my mattress. But I, as I look, am sad.
I don't expect they will lie like this any more not for a minute,
even though they love each other lots. They will not soon want
to sleep. But a trick and a trap will hold them back,
until to me her father gives back really all the bride-price
that I placed in his hand for his dog-faced daughter,
because, beautiful she is, but she can't control herself."
    So he spoke, and the gods gathered to the bronze-built house.
There came Poseidon, earth-holder, then came helpful
Hermes, and there came lord far-working Apollo.
But the more female goddesses stayed for shame each at home.
The gods stood in the entrance, givers of good things,
and unquenchable laughter indeed arose from the blessed gods,
seeing the craftsmanship of much-thinking Hephaestus.
And thus would one say, looking to another nearby,
    "Crime doesn't pay. For the slow one catches the swift.
So even now Hephaestus, being slow, has caught Ares,
though he is swiftest of gods who inhabit Olympus
(being mad) with his handiwork. So he owes the adulterer's fee."
    So they to one another were saying such things,
but to Hermes did speak the lord, Zeus's son, Apollo:
    "Hermes, Zeus's son, minister, giver of good things,
indeed would you like, even with heavy fetters laden,
to sleep in bed beside golden Aphrodite?"
    To him replied then the minister, slayer of Argus,
    "If only this could happen, Lord far-shooting Apollo!
Fetters three times as many, boundless might hold me
and all you gods be looking – and all the goddesses! –
Still would I sleep beside golden Aphrodite."
    So he spoke, and laughter arose among the immortal gods.
But laughter did not hold Poseidon, but always he kept begging
Hephaestus the famous worker that he might free Ares,
and having spoken to him, he addressed him in winged words:
    "Set him free, and I promise to you as you wish:
to pay all that is fitting among the immortal gods."
    Him then did the very famous doubly-lame one answer:
    "Do not, Poseidon earth-shaker, ask me this.
For worthless to receive are the pledges of the worthless.
How could I bind you with immortal gods,
if Ares left, having fled from his debt and fetters?"

Him then immediately answered Poseidon, shaker of earth,
"Hephaestus, if ever Ares should flee out from under his debt,
and go escaping, I myself will pay it to you."
Then, did the very famous doubly lame one answer:
"It is not seemly to decline your word."
So speaking, the strength of Hephaestus undid the fetters
and the two of them, when they had been released from the fetters,
strong though they were, immediately left. He went to Thrace,
and she came to Cyprus did laughter-loving Aphrodite,
and Paphos, where is her sanctuary and smoking altar.
But when her the Graces had washed and anointed with oil
immortal, which preserves the gods who are forever,
they put on her lovely garments, a wonder to see.
These things the very famous singer sang.

This may seem like an odd move for Hephaestus, particularly since he has just taken his wife's shameful acts and displayed them for the entire community, but it is actually a just recourse. Since Ares is a god, he is immortal, and therefore cannot be killed when caught *in flagrante delicto*. However, as seen earlier in our example of his pouring nectar for the other gods from the *Iliad*, Hephaestus does act for the sake of correction through the manipulation of laughter. Where in the *Iliad* he manipulates laughter to fall upon himself, thus defusing a situation, here he is manipulating laughter to fall upon the adulterers, shaming them into correct action.

The one god who does not laugh is Poseidon, and his lack of laughter itself is best seen as a flattering thing. As demonstrated in earlier chapters, he who laughs runs the risk of becoming part of what he laughs at, and Poseidon attempts to negotiate a settlement to the situation, rather than becoming implicated in it. This places him on a firm moral high ground, above even Hephaestus, who is the one who has corrected the situation.

The Greeks were convinced that women were always committing adultery. After all, they were women, and they had to do SOMETHING with their spare time (sex being more interesting than knitting, of course). As we saw earlier in this chapter, the male relative of Euripides, Mnesilochus has infiltrated the women's festival of the Thesmophoria disguised as a woman in Aristophanes' *Thesmophoriazusae*. This is his account in lines 466-501 of the behaviour of women:

Firstly, Ladies, to be so very angry
at Euripides, having had such bad things said about us
is not remarkable, nor to boil over with anger.
Why, I myself also at least – may I live to enjoy my children! –
hate that man, unless I've lost my mind.
Nevertheless, among each other, we must give an account,
for we are alone and there's no-one to carry abroad our speech.
Why, being in this situation, should we blame him
and take it hard if two or three of our bad deeds
he has learned and tells, when we've done ten thousand?
I myself first, so as not to mention anyone else,
was my own accomplice in many dreadful things. This is just

the worst: when I had been married three days,
my husband was sleeping with me, and I had a boy-friend
who'd deflowered me when I was seven.
This fellow, desiring me, came and scratched at the door,
and immediately I recognized him, and went down in secret.
My husband asks, "Where are you going?" "Where?
A twisting's seized my bowels, Husband, a real pain:
I'm going to the latrine." "O.k. Go."
Then he ground juniper-berries, anise and sage.[24]
Meanwhile I, pouring water on the hinge,[25]
went out to the adulterer. Then I leaned
by Apollo of the Street, prone, holding onto the bay-tree...
These things, you see, Euripides never said.
Nor that by the slaves and mule-drivers
we get screwed, if we can't find anyone else. That too he doesn't say.
Nor that whenever we have been "oiled" by someone
at night, at dawn we chew garlic
so that our husband, smelling us, may leave the house
without suspecting we've done anything wrong. These things, you see,
he's never said. And if he rebukes Phaedra,
what is that to us? Nor has he ever said
that a wife showing her husband her new top –
how it looks in the light – sent away her hidden
adulterer, he's never said.

We have mentioned in the previous section the case of Eratosthenes, whom Euphiletus killed when he caught him in bed with his wife in *Lysias* 1.[26] Normally the punishment for adultery was less severe, and apparently to the Greeks quite amusing.[27] We hear about it in Aristophanes' *Clouds* 1083-84:

(Greater Argument speaking)
What if, persuaded by you, he gets "radished" and singed with ash?
What argument will he have to say in order not to have his asshole widened?

---

[24] Ancient Milk of Magnesia

[25] To lubricate it, so it won't squeak.

[26] In Athens, a man caught in adultery with another man's wife could be killed with impunity. This was slightly drastic (or more sexist, depending on your viewpoint) than ancient Jewish law, under which *both* parties were to be stoned (Leviticus 20.10, John 8.5).

[27] D. Cohen, "A note on Aristophanes and the punishment of adultery in Athenian law," *Zeitschrift der Savigny-Stiftung fur Rechtsgeschichte, Romanistische Abteilung* 102 (1985) 385-87 and J. Roy, "Traditional jokes about the punishment of adulterers in ancient Greek literature," *LCM* 16 (1991) 73-76.

How the radish felt about it is another matter, and considering where it was going, there were probably ill feelings on both sides. The idea of being sexually used by something that is not sexual is a recurring theme, however, when it comes to humour.

In a lost comedy by Plato (the comic playwright, not to be confused with the famous philosopher) one character is reading a cookbook that explains what sea-food is good for your sex-life, when he is interrupted by his friend who is irritated with the recitation (fr. 189.20-22 *PCG*):

A   The red mullet doesn't want to give tension to the sinews,[28]
     for it is by nature of the virgin Artemis, and hates erections.
     Now, as for the mussel...
B   ...May it strike you, creeping under your anus!

As a further example, Catullus 15 reads as follows:
I commend to you myself and my beloved,
Aurelius. I ask a modest indulgence,
if in your heart you've ever wanted to ask anyone
to be chaste and more or less intact:
may you keep a boy pure for me –
I don't mean from people in general – I don't fear
those at all who in the marketplace now here, now there
go about intent upon their business;
I fear you and your penis,
a threat to boys, good and bad.
May it court wherever it wants, as it wants, anyone
you wish who's ready, when you're abroad.
I ask for this boy, as I think, modestly.
But if your bad mind and heartless madness
drive you, Sinner!, to such a crime
that you provoke my head with monkey-business,
woe is you, and your evil fate,
by which, feet together and back door wide,
radishes and mullets[29] will run!

When it comes down to it, the adulterer, like so many other active (as opposed to passive; the adulterer actually does something to somebody rather than having something done to him, at least until the radish gets involved) comic figures, is a species of quack. If the adulterer is a quack in so far as he interferes with another man's business, the **cuckold**, the passive element of the adulterous equation, is also a quack in so far as he does not know himself – he thinks he is a good husband fulfilling his wife's needs, while in fact he is not. Oddly, Latin doesn't have a word for "cuckold," but Greek, which has a word for just about everything, has an obscure one – *kerasphoros*.

---

[28] i.e. the penis.

[29] The mullet is a kind of spiny fish. It is also a hair-style favoured by hockey-players. Having a hockey-player's head inserted rather than a fish could also be an effective deterrent.

Kerasphoros literally means "horned," but how could men whose wives cheat on them be said to have horns? They were certainly not "horny," an expression that can be traced no further back than 1785. After all, if the women were getting enough at home, they wouldn't need lovers, would they? You might think that the cuckold is like someone being given "bunny-ears," who looks foolish to everyone else without knowing it himself, but the true explanation is more complicated – and a lot weirder. It has to do with capons. To make a capon, you take a baby boy chicken and put it on your kitchen table. Then you give it a glass of your Uncle Adolf's schnaps. When the chicken has drunk enough schnaps to get quite wobbly, you fish around inside its rear with your finger, pull out its testicles, and cut them off with a razor, hence the word "capon" (from Greek *koptein*, "to cut off"). It will then grow up to be plumper, tastier, and a whole lot quieter than the rooster it would otherwise have become. Now it may not be true that if you've seen one chicken, you've seen them all, yet they *do* look a lot alike. So to tell a capon from a rooster-in-waiting, and either from a hen, someone decided that while the little guy was anesthetized, why not cut off his spurs (i.e. toes) and graft them onto the comb on top of his head. They will take root and grow there, and the bird will be instantly recognizable as a capon by these "horns." The cuckold is "horned" in that he is metaphorically, as the capon is literally, emasculated, having had his sexual prowess called into question. (Interestingly, the English word *cuckold* also has an avian source. It alludes to the cuckoo's habit of laying its eggs in other birds' nests... one of the things you should probably consider, when you learn about the birds and the bees.) Here is how Catullus describes a cuckold in poem 17:

> Oh Colony, who wants to play on your long bridge,
> and are prepared to leap, but fear the ill-made
> legs of your little bridge standing on renovated pilings,
> lest they collapse and lie in the hollow mud –
> may a good bridge be yours for your pleasure,
> on which even the Salisubsali[30] could undertake their rites!
> Give me this gift of greatest laughter, Colony.
> A certain fellow-citizen of mine I want from your bridge
> to go headfirst into the muck, head over heels,
> wherever in the whole lake and stinking bog
> the depth is deepest.
> How stupid is the man! He knows less than a boy
> of two, sleeping on his father's trembling elbow!
> To whom, when there is married a girl in greenest flower,
> a girl more delicate than a tender little kid,
> to be watched more carefully than ripest grapes,
> he lets her play as she wants. Neither does he count it a straw,
> nor does he even get up, but like a birch tree

---

[30] A comically expanded nonce-word (the real name is Salii) for a college of priests dedicated by Numas to the service of Mars, who performed ritual dances in archaic military garb; see J. B. Rives, *Religion in the Roman Empire* (Oxford, 2007) 83.

lies in a ditch chopped by a Ligurian axe,
wholly senseless, as if nothing ever happened,
this idiot of mine sees nothing, hears nothing:
whether he himself is or isn't – even that he doesn't know!
Now, I want to throw him headfirst from your bridge,
in case perhaps he might suddenly shake of his dull lethargy
and stupid mind, and leave them behind in deep mud,
like a mule its iron shoe in the muck that sucks.

Notice how Catullus uses the comparison to plants and animals familiar from wedding songs to describe this dysfunctional union. Note also that, although they are mortal enemies of one another, the adulterer and the cuckold are both species of quack. It is important to remember that being a quack yourself does not protect you from being irritated by other quacks.

Part III
The Classical Way

All the enlisted men and officers on combat duty had to sign a loyalty oath to get their map cases from the intelligence tent, a second loyalty oath to receive their flak suits and parachutes from the parachute tent, a third loyalty oath for Lieutenant Balkington, the motor vehicle officer, to be allowed to ride from the squadron to the airfield in one of the trucks. Every time they turned around there was another loyalty oath to be signed.

– Joseph Heller, *Catch-22*

Chapter X – Epic Proportions

Humour and the Iliad

Having made this synchronic survey of the way that humour works, perhaps at all times, certainly throughout the Classical period, we turn now to see how humour developed over the course of that time.

In many ways, we prefer today to think of the epic as something solemn and serious – the idea of a funny epic just doesn't quite seem right. However, in almost all of the great Greek epics, humour has played a very large part (hardly surprising, as if Greeks bards knew how to do anything, it was play to an audience).

We'll start our examination of the humorous in Greek Epic by considering four passages in the *Iliad* that involve humour. The first is the scene in Book One in which Hephaestus puts an end to the quarrel of Zeus and Hera by pouring nectar to the gods. This passage is quoted in full in chapter VI. There are a couple of extra things to note, outside of what we have already examined.

Note that the laughter of the gods is unquenchable (*asbestos*). Greek never says what the gods are or have, but only what they are not or do not have. They are *im*-mortal and age-*less*; they are *an*-emic, having ichor instead of blood, and their matings are *never* without issue (whether all of Zeus' children have to wear name tags at family gatherings due to sheer numbers is also not mentioned). This way of talking about gods is called "negative theology" and it is continued in their discussion of their *un*-quenchable laughter. Animals, by contrast, do not laugh, or to put it in Aristotelian terms (*Part. An.* 3.10 = 673a) "man is the only animal that laughs." Thus the god/human/animal division of the universe on which we have long since commented manifests itself in terms of laughter as well as in terms of mortality, modesty and justice. Also, because the laughter of the gods is so powerful, they only laugh at one another and never laugh at humans, who would be destroyed if they did.[1]

We can apply some of our theories to understanding the humour in this passage. There is an incongruity between what is expected, that Hebe or Ganymede would pour the nectar, and what actually occurs, with Hephaestus pouring it (Kant, Darwin). A cripple is someone whose gestures are mechanical, fossilized and reduced to typical movements through a loss of the élan vital (Bergson) and note that the Greeks felt no such compunction as do we about laughing at others. They never said "There but for the grace of God go I," or "You should walk a mile in his shoes before you judge him."[2] Moreover, the laughter in this passage breaks out at a moment of crisis, namely the argument between Zeus and Hera. Thus Hephaestus' actions

---

[1] L. Woodbury, [doctoral dissertation summary] *HSCP* 55 (1944) 114-17.

[2] Not that this is actually advisable, as the first thing you would need to do is steal his shoes.

provide an insignificant channel for carrying off the inertia of the emotional charge (Spencer).

The second passage we will consider is the comedy of character in *Iliad* Book Six lines 312-68 and 503-529:

> Hector came to Alexander's (a.k.a. Paris') beautiful
> house, which he himself had built with men who were the best
> in very-loamy Troy – carpenter men, that is,
> who made for him a bedroom,[3] house, and hall
> near Priam's and Hector's on the acropolis.
> There Hector went, dear to Zeus, and in his hand
> a spear he held of one and ten cubits. In front of the shaft shone
> a brazen tip, and it was run round with a golden hoop.
> Him he found in the bedroom fussing over his very beautiful armour
> (his shield and breastplate), and polishing his back-curved bow.[4]
> And Argive Helen too with serving-women
> sat, and the handmaids' very beautiful work she was directing.
>   Him Hector chided with a look in shaming words:
>   "Strange one, it isn't good that you keep this bile in your heart!
> The people are dying about the city and steep walls
> fighting, and for your sake the battle-cry and war
> burn round this town. You would quarrel even with another
> whom perhaps you might see returning from hateful war.
> But up! Lest soon the city glow with ruinous fire!"
>   Him then answered godlike Alexander:
>   "Hector, since you have reproached me in measure and not beyond
>   measure,
> therefore I'll speak to you, and you store it up and listen to me.
> Not so much from bile at the Trojans or resentment
> have I been sitting in my bedroom, but I wanted to give myself up to grief.[5]
> Yet even now my wife, having addressed me with soft words,
> has urged me into war. And this seems to me as well
> to be better. Victory comes to men in turn.
> But come now, wait while I put on the armour of Ares,
> or else go, and I will come after – but I think I'll overtake you."
>   So he spoke. Him shining-helmeted Hector did not address,
> but Helen spoke to him with soothing words:
>   "Brother-in-law of me (who am a dog, maker of evils, chilly one!),
> would that on that day when first my mother bore me,

---

[3] The most important room in the Alexander establishment in mentioned first.

[4] Note Paris' vanity. He has been polishing his armour in his wife's boudoir while other men die cleaning up his mess. He talks a good game, but...

[5] As excuses go, this seems pretty lame. (There is a relationship between sorrow [*achos* in Greek] and anger, or "bile" [*cholos*]; but the person who is sad and then grows angry in this poem is not Paris, but Achilles, whose very name means "Sorrow of the People.")

an evil tornado of wind had come along and swept me away
to the mountain, or on a wave of the loud-roaring sea,
and a wave had carried me off, before these evils had come to pass.
Yet since the gods have ordained these things at least like this,
then would that I were wife of a better man
who knew the reproach and many shameful reports of men![6]
But this man's wits aren't firm now, nor will they likely be
hereafter, and I think he'll pay the price for it.
But come on, here now! Sit upon this stool,
brother-in-law, since round your mind most of all toil has come round
for the sake of me (a dog!) and for Alexander's folly,
on whom Zeus has placed this evil fate so that even afterward
we will be a subject of song for men who are yet to be."[7]
    Her then did great flashing-helmeted Hector answer,
    "Don't seat me, Helen, loving though you are. You won't persuade me.
For already my heart urges that I rush back
to the Trojans, who yearn for me greatly while I'm gone.
But you at least bestir yourself, and let him also hurry,
so he might catch up with me while I'm still inside the city;
for I will go home so that I might see
my family, both my dear wife and infant son.
For I don't know whether I will come to them again returning,
or if already the gods will subdue me under the hands of the Achaeans."

Nor did Paris tarry long in his high-roofed house,
but he at least, when he had put on his famous armour, intricate, of bronze,
hastened through the city, trusting in his rapid feet.
As when some stabled horse, corn-fed at the manger,
having broken its tether, runs galloping on the plain,
wont to bathe in the fair-flowing river,
full of pride: he holds his head high, and about his withers
his mane waves, and he trusts in his caparison,
and lightly his knees bring him to the haunts and pastures of horses:[8]
so Priam's son, Paris from the top of Pergamus
shining in his armour like the sun came
laughing, and his swift feet bore him. And soon then
he overtook godlike Hector, his brother, when he was about
to turn back from the place where he had chatted with his wife.
    Before that, Alexander the godlike spoke to him:
    "Sir, indeed, I've held you back in your hurry
by my tarrying, and not come in good measure as you bade me!"
    Him answering, shining-helmeted Hector said:
    "Strange man! Not any man, you know, who is reasonable

---

[6] A better man than this... (You, for example). Helen tries to seduce her brother-in-law in front of her own (second) husband, adding incest to adultery. She's one to talk about modesty!

[7] Just picture her flipping through *People* magazine to see if there's any mention of her.

[8] In short, Paris just got laid.

would dishonour your work in battle, since you are strong.
But willingly you come, and are not unwilling. For my heart
grieves me in my breast when I hear shameful things about you
among the Trojans, who have much toil because of you.
But let us go. We'll take pleasure in these things some other time, if somehow Zeus
should grant that we set up for the heavenly gods who are forever
a punch-bowl free in our halls,
once from Troy we've driven the well-greaved Achaeans."[9]

The next passage we will consider is a piece of social satire found in Book Fourteen lines 153-269 and 292-351. The story relates to the fact that Hera sides with the Greeks while Zeus is pro-Trojan:

Hera of the golden throne looked with her eyes
as she stood on the shore of Olympus. Yet she saw
him puffing up battle that brings glory to men –
her own brother and brother-in-law [Poseidon] –, and she rejoiced at heart.
But Zeus on the topmost peak with many springs of Ida
she saw sitting, and hateful he was to her heart.
Then she was in doubt, was cow-faced lady Hera
how she might cheat the mind of goatskin-wearing Zeus.
This plan seemed best to her at heart,
that she go to Ida herself, well-dressed,
if perhaps he might long to sleep in love
beside her body, and on him sleep, harmless and warm
she might pour on his eyelids, and clever mind.[10]
So she stepped to go into her bedroom, which her own son had made,
Hephaestus, and he attached the close-fitting doors to the doorposts
with a secret lock that no other god could open.
There she, going in, put to the shining doors,
and with ambrosia first of all about her desirable body
she washed off all the dirt and anointed herself with shining oil,
immortal, sweet, that had been sacrificed to her.
When it wafted round the bronze-built house of Zeus,
the smell of it filled all earth and heaven both.
With it then anointing her beautiful body and hair,
combing her locks, with her hands she braided them
beautiful, immortal from her deathless head.
And she put on an immortal fine linen robe that Athena
had worked to make for her, and had put on much appliqué-work.
With golden brooches on her chest she pinned it
and belted herself with a belt fitted with a hundred tassels,
and ear-rings she put into her well-pierced lobes,
skillfully made with three bright drops. Much grace shone from her.

---

[9] Hector hides from his brother the knowledge of the fated doom of Troy that he has just now (in the passage in between that we did not quote) freely shared with Andromache, his wife.

[10] *Peukalimos*, a rare word, sometimes otherwise explained as "bitter."

With a veil over top, the shining one of goddesses veiled herself,
a beautiful one, brand new, that was white as the sun.
And under her shining feet she bound beautiful sandals.[11]

Yet when she had put about her body all this adornment,
she stepped to go from her bedroom, and, calling to Aphrodite
above all other gods, she spoke this word:

"Will you now obey me, dear child, in whatever I may say,
or would you deny it, since you bear a grudge in your heart,
since I'm with the Danaans, but you side with Troy?"

Her then answered Zeus' daughter, Aphrodite:

"Hera, elder goddess, daughter of great Cronus,
speak as you think best. My heart bids me,
if I am able, to accomplish it, at least it's accomplishable."

Her crafty-minded lady Hera addressed:[12]

"Now give me love and desire, with which you always
tame the immortals and mortal men.
For I'm going to the ends of the very beautiful earth
to see Ocean, father of gods and mother Tethys,
who reared me well in their home and cherished me,
having taken me from Rhea, when broad-browed Zeus put Cronus
under the earth and the unharvested sea.
Them I'm going to see, and I will put an end to their unceasing quarrels,
for now for a long time they have kept apart from one another
in bed and love, since bile has fallen into their hearts.[13]
If by advising the two of them with words in their own heart
I can cause them to share their bed in love,
always I would be called 'dear' and 'venerable' by them."

Her then addressed laughter-loving Aphrodite:

"It is not possible, nor is it right to deny your words:
for in the arms of Zeus, the greatest of all, you sleep."

She spoke, and took off her chest her stitched brassiere,
petit point, where all her charms are depicted.
Thereon is love and on it is desire and on it is pillow-talk,
an allurement that steals the mind even of those who think wisely.
This she put into her hands, and spoke a word, and named her out:[14]

"Here now, put this bra on your bosom,
petit point, on which all things have been depicted. Nor do I say
it will go unaccomplished, whatever you desire in your heart."

---

[11] Like a warrior, Hera arms herself for battle. She has special "armour" woven by Athena, just as Hephaestus will forge special arms for Achilles in book 18.

[12] This is a lie (to Aphrodite) in aid of a deception (of Zeus). Zeus, who ought to lie (or at least keep his mouth shut), will instead tell the truth about his love-affairs, and at great length.

[13] Hera attributes falsely altruistic motives to herself. Meanwhile if it's quarrelling couples you want, look no further than Hera herself and Zeus!

[14] We find it mildly disturbing that the Olympians share underwear.

So she spoke, and the cow-faced lady Hera smiled,
and smiling then she put it on under her bosom.
    Then Zeus' daughter, Aphrodite went home,
and Hera, hurrying, left the shore of Olympus,
and went to Pieria and lovely Emathia,
and hurried to the horse-herding Thracians' snowy mountain,
the topmost peaks. Nor did she touch the ground with her two feet.
From Athos she stepped over the wavy sea,
and came to Lemnos, city of god-like Thoas.
There she came upon Sleep, brother of Death,
and indeed she stretched out her hand and spoke a word and named him out:
    "Sleep, lord of all gods and all men,
both before you have heard my word, and still now also
obey. I will know for you gratitude all your days.
Put Zeus' two shining eyes to sleep for me under his lids,
as soon as I have lain with him in love.[15]
Gifts I'll give you: a beautiful throne, unperishable always,
golden. Hephaestus, my son, doubly lame
would labour to make it, and under it he'll place a stool for your feet,
on which you can put your shining feet whenever you're hosting a party."[16]
    Her answering, said sweet Sleep:
    "Hera, elder goddess, daughter of great Cronus,
another one of the gods whom are forever
I would readily lull to sleep, even the streams of River
Ocean, who is the origin of all things.
But Zeus, Cronus' son, I won't go near,
nor would I lull him to sleep, unless he himself tells me to, at least.
For already another time your orders got me into trouble,
on that day when that arrogant son of Zeus
sailed from Troy, having sacked the city of the Trojans.
And I calmed the mind of goatskin-wearing Zeus,
pleasantly having been poured over him, and you contrived evils for him in your
        heart,
having stirred up the blasts of tiresome winds upon the sea
and then drove him to well-built Cos
far from his friends. He, when he awoke, was furious,
and kept throwing the gods from their halls, and me most of all
he was looking for. And he would have thrown me unseen from sky to sea,
had not Night, tamer of gods, saved me – and tamer of men.
Her I reached in flight, and he desisted, angry though he was.
For he stood in awe lest he do things hateful to Night the swift.
Now again you order me to accomplish this other impossible thing."
    Him then answered the cow-faced lady Hera:
    "Sleep, why do you worry about this in your mind?

---

[15] Not everyone may think that supernatural aid is necessary to make a
male conk out after sex.

[16] She bribes Sleep. Remember the judgement of Paris in which she tried
to bribe *him* (unsuccessfully, because Aphrodite won the contest – again
with a bribe, having Helen as his wife). Despite his name, Sleep is no
dozy bargainer: offered a footstool, he holds out for a Grace to wed.

Do you claim that broad-browed Zeus will be as angry if you help the Trojans
as he was about Heracles, his son?
But go! And I to you on of the Graces will give,
a fairly young one, to be married to you and to be called your wife."

....

Hera swiftly went to the top of Gargarus
on lofty Ida, and cloud-gather Zeus saw her.
As he saw her, lust veiled his compact wits,
as when first they were mingled together in love,
going often into bed, hiding from their parents.[17]
He stood up before her, and said a word, and named her out:
      "Hera, what do you want that you come here from Olympus?
There are horses and chariots ready on which you could travel."
      Then the crafty-minded lady Hera said:
"I'm going to the ends of the very beautiful earth
to see Ocean, father of gods, and mother Tethys,
who reared me well in their home and cherished me.
Them I'm going to see, and I will put an end to their unceasing quarrels.
For now for a long time they have kept apart from one another
in bed and love, since bile has fallen into their hearts.
The horses at the foot of Ida with many springs
stand, who will bear me over dry land and wet.
Now for your sake I have come here from Olympus,
lest perhaps you be angry with me hereafter, if in silence
I leave for the home of deep flowing Ocean."[18]
      Her answering, addressed cloud-gatherer Zeus:
      "Hera, there too you can go – later.
But come, let us two turn to lie abed in love.
For never yet[19] has the desire for a goddess or a woman so
tamed the heart within my chest poured forth all around.[20]
Neither when I loved the wife of Ixion
who bore Perithous, a counselor equal to the gods,
nor when it was Danaë slender-ankled daughter of Acrisius,
who bore Perses, most renowned of all men;
nor when it was the daughter of Phoenix far-famed,
who bore me Minos and godlike Rhadamanthys;
nor when it was Semele; nor Alcmene in Thebes,
who bore Heracles, my strong-willed son
– Semele, by the way, bore Dionysus, a joy to mortals –
nor when it was Demeter the fair-haired queen;

---

[17] Like teenagers making out in the back of a car.

[18] Again, she attributes falsely altruistic motives to herself.

[19] He then offers her a list (remember the *Priamel* from Chapter II note
3?) of his liaisons which normally make her so angry (compare her
quarrel with him in Book One when she suspects that he and Thetis have
been up to something). This is not recommend as a technique for getting
someone into bed.

[20] It's almost as if his *desire* itself has just ejaculated.

nor when it was very famous Leto, nor when it was you yourself:
so much do I now desire you, and sweet yearning seizes me."
    Him the crafty-thinking lady Hera addressed:
    "Most terrible son of Cronus, what a word you have spoken!
If now you desire in love to go to bed
on Ida's peaks, where everything is visible:
how would it be, if someone of the gods who are forever
should perceive us two asleep, and going among all the gods,
should tell? I would not be able to go back to your house
having gotten out of bed, but it would be embarrassing.[21]
But if you really want to, and it is dear to your heart,
we *have* a bedroom, that my own son has made,
Hephaestus, and he attached the close-fitting doors to the doorposts.
There let us go to lie, since now bed is your pleasure."
    Her answering cloud-gathering Zeus addressed:
    "Hera, don't be afraid that either any of gods or of men
will see this at least; in such a cloud will I veil you,
golden, not even the Sun could make us out,
whose light indeed is the sharpest thing to see by."
    He spoke. And the son of Cronus took hold of his wife in his arms,
and beneath them the godlike ground produced new-blooming grass,
and the dewy lotus and crocus and hyacinth
thick-petalled and soft, which hold them up from the ground.
On it they lay, and they were covered by a cloud
beautiful, golden, and the glistening dewdrops fell.[22]

The fourth and final passage that we will consider is from Book
Nineteen, lines 380b-424, in which Achilles returns to battle after the death
of his best friend, Patroclus (not, we would have thought, the best place for
a comic episode, but there you are):

                  Having lifted his helmet,
[Achilles] set it strong upon his head, and it shone like a star
did the horse-hair helm, and its bristles shook around,
golden, that Hephaestus had put on the crest in abundance.
He tested by himself in his armour, godlike Achilles,
to see if it fitted him well, and ran with his glorious limbs:
and it was like wings to him, and lifted up the shepherd of the people.[23]
From its carrying-case he drew his father's spear,
heavy, great, stout, which no-one else of the Achaeans could
brandish, but it Achilles alone knew how to wield –
of Pelian ash-wood, which to his own father Chiron had given,

---

[21] Hera is a tease, like Myrrhina in Aristophanes' *Lysistrata* (see Chapter
IX above).

[22] The passage ends with the holy marriage (*hieros gamos*) of Sky and
Earth.

[23] Achilles preens himself in front of a mirror, in anticipation of Brad
Pitt.

from the peak of Pelion to be death for heroes.
His horses Automedon and Alcimus, his squires,
did yoke: about them they put the straps and into their
jaws they threw the bronze, and stretched back the reins
toward the built-tough chariot. He then, taking in his
hands, well fitting, the shining whip, leapt behind the two horses,
Automedon did. And behind him stepped helmeted Achilles,
shining in his armour like Hyperion the Sun,
and loudly he called the horses of his father:
    "Xanthus and Balius, far-famed children of Podarge,
otherwise plan and save your rein-holder
back into the host of the Danaans, when we leave off from war,
than when you left Patroclus out there dead."[24]
    Him from under the yoke addressed the foot-nimble horse,
Xanthus, and at once tossed his head, and his whole mane,
falling over the yoke-cushion beside the yoke, fell to the ground,
for the goddess, white-armed Hera made him speak:[25]
    "Yes, of course, now still at least we will save you, stout Achilles,
but (you know) near is the destructive day, nor (you know) are we
to blame,[26] but both great God and cruel Fate:
for neither by our slowness nor our sloth
did the Trojans take from Patroclus' shoulders his armour,
but the best of the gods, whom fair-haired Leto bore,
killed him in the front ranks and to Hector glory gave.
But we two indeed could run with Zephyr's breath,
which they say is the lightest thing. But for you yourself
it is fated by both a god and a man to be subdued."
    His voice, once he had spoken, the Furies checked,
and him, quite peeved,[27] swift-footed Achilles answered:

---

[24] This accusation is unfair. The death of Patroclus was Achilles' own fault; he never should have let him go alone into battle; now he unjustly blames the horses for his own failing.

[25] Does anyone remember Mister Ed and Wilbur Post from the 60s TV show? In addition to being a talking horse, Mister Ed gives us one of the classic egghead jokes of all time:

> Wilbur: I've been meaning to ask you, Ed. Just how *do* horses sleep standing up?
> Ed: We do?
> Wilbur: Didn't you know?
> Ed: How could I? When I'm asleep, my eyes are closed!

Does anyone remember Balaam's ass (Numbers 22.28-31)?

[26] The horse, rightly, sticks up for itself.

[27] Disturbed, it seems, not so much because his horse is talking to him (which would scare the hell out of us), nor even at the news of his impending death, but because the horse has made out that he knows more than Achilles.

"Xanthus, why do you prophesy my death? You don't have to.
Well now I myself know that Fate will kill me here
far from my own father and mother. But even so
I will not stop, before I've driven the Trojans off from fighting."
He spoke, and shouting, where the first men were he drove the single-
hoofed horses.

Humour and the Odyssey *(and* Battle of Frogs and Mice*)*

Next, we will consider three passages in the *Odyssey*. The first is in Book
Four in which Telemachus goes to the court of Menelaus and we hear Helen
and him recounting their version of the Trojan War. The Greeks fought for
ten years to get Helen back, not so that Menelaus might bring her back
home, but so that he could avenge his honour by killing her, and live happily
ever after. Yet (according to one of the lost epics of the epic cycle, *The Little
Iliad* [fr. 19 Davies, Bernabé]) when at the end of the war he stood before her
with drawn sword ready to kill her, she bared her breasts to him,[28] and her
beauty was so overwhelming that the sword wilted in his hand and he had
to forgive her (no doubt something else attached to him was not wilting, but
doing the opposite). How is this couple making out now, ten years later?
Helen has recognized Telemachus - whom she has never seen before – by his
hands and feet, which are so like Odysseus', and they have swapped stories
and wept. She has just poured some drugs for the three of them that she got
in Egypt – if nothing else the ancient Greeks knew how to have a good time
– when our passage begins (lines 240-89; Helen is speaking):

"I could not tell you everything, nor could I recount them,
so many are long-suffering Odysseus' struggles.
But such a thing is this that he accomplished and dared, brave man,
among the people of the Trojans where the Greeks used to suffer griefs.
Having marred himself with blows unseemly,
having thrown bad clothes about his shoulder, like a slave,
he entered the enemies' wide-wayed city.
As another man he was concealing himself,
a beggar, of whom no such was among the Achaeans' ships.
In his likeness he entered the Trojans' city, who were indifferent
all, yet I alone recognized what sort of man he was,[29]
and interrogated him. But he was cunningly evasive.
When indeed I had washed him, and anointed him with oil,
and put clothes upon him, and sworn a strong oath
that I would not reveal that Odysseus was among the Trojans
at least until he had gotten back to the swift ships and huts,
only then indeed to me did he explain the whole plan of the Achaeans.
Having killed many of the Trojans with the long-pointed bronze,
he went back to the Argives and brought back much intelligence.

---

[28] Like a Phryne *avant la lettre*, cf. Chapter V.

[29] As she has just recognised Telemachus, though she has never met him
before.

There other Trojan women loudly wailed, but my heart
was rejoicing, since already my heart had changed to return
back homeward, and I kept lamenting the ruin that Aphrodite
gave when she led me here far from my own father-land,
abandoning my child and bedroom and husband,
who did not lack for anything, either in mind or appearance."
    To her, replying, blond Menelaus spoke:
    "Yes indeed, all these things at least, wife, you have said according to
       measure.
Already I have learned many men's counsel and mind –
heroic men's, and I have travelled much over the earth,
but not yet have I seen such a thing with my eyes
as enduring-minded Odysseus' own heart.
And such a thing as this he accomplished and dared, brave man,
within the polished horse where all the best were sitting
of the Argives, to the Trojans bringing slaughter and fate.
You then went there (perhaps a divinity was leading
you, who wanted to hold out fame to the Trojans?)
and you as you went godlike Deiphobus followed.[30]
Three times you went around the hollow ambush, caressing it,
and naming out by name the best of the Danaans,
counterfeiting the voice of every Achaean's wife.[31]
I and Tydeus and godlike Odysseus,
sitting in the middle, heard how you called.
The two of us both wanted to start
either going out or answering immediately from within,
but Odysseus restrained us and held us back, eager though we were.
Then the others all were silent, sons of the Achaeans,
but Anticles alone wanted to exchange words
with you at least, but Odysseus squeezed his jaws together with his hands
ceaselessly strong, and saved all the Achaeans,
and kept on until Pallas Athena led you away."

The main thing to note in this passage is that what Menelaus says flat-out contradicts Helen's version of events, and accuses her of trying to kill him, yet he presents the story as though it were in support of her own account, "all this that you said is fair and orderly," which it *is* to the extent that both of them agree that Odysseus was pretty darn smart. There is thus no confrontation, no fighting, and they have apparently agreed to disagree on the matter of Helen's loyalties.

    The next passage to consider is from Book Eight lines 307-344, the story of Ares and Aphrodite. This passage is quoted in full in chapter VI, and we will not quote it here again (and there will be a test of long term-memory at the end of this chapter). From that passage there are two things of particular note. First there are two moments of laughter in that story: the one

---

[30] Deiphobus was a brother of Paris and Hector, who married Helen after Paris died, thereby becoming her *third* husband. His presence here serves to remind us that Helen is, after all, the archetypal slut.

[31] Helen is all things to all men; every man's ideal woman.

engineered by Hephaestus as punishment for Ares and Aphrodite, and the
second a dirty joke between Apollo and Hermes ("Would you mind being
looked at if you were getting it on with Aphrodite?" "What do you think?").
All the gods laugh except for Poseidon – special god of the Phaeacians, who
is therefore presented in a respectable light – who is too busy arranging for
the release of Ares and his payment of compensation to Hephaestus. The
second point is that the convention of subjecting couples engaged in
inappropriate sexual behaviour to public ridicule passed from the ancient
world into the middle ages, where it acquired the names *charivari* (French)
and *rough music* (English), which often consisted of banging pots and pans
under the window of the bridal chamber. This is the origin of our custom of
tying tin cans onto the cars of young couples heading off on their
honeymoon. We don't really thereby accuse them of inappropriate behaviour,
but just in case...

The last passage of the *Odyssey* to consider is Book Nine, the Cyclops-
episode. Once again, for the sake of our poor fingers, we won't type out the
whole book, but we will draw attention to three things. First, the Cyclops
drinks "unmixed milk" (line 297). This uses Homer's formulaic vocabulary
to advantage, because "unmixed" is an adjective usually applied to wine.
Greeks drank their wine diluted with water, in spritzers as it were, because
of the excessive heat; one who drank "unmixed wine" was a lush.[32] The
Cyclops, uncivilized shepherd that he is, drinks NO wine at all – which makes
it all that much easier for Odysseus to get him drunk and blind him. By
saying that he drinks "unmixed milk" Homer draws attention to this fact,
and also presents him as a kind of giant baby, a late-learner or *opsimath* (for
Greek adults did not drink milk).

The second thing is line 366 with the famous Nobody-trick. This is in fact
a manifold pun. Odysseus' name comes from the verb *odyssomai*, which
means "I am hated" (*Od.* 19.407-409; Odysseus is hateful in the sense that
he brings destruction to almost everyone whom he meets). The Nobody trick
works in any language, and in fact that story has been found all over the
world, told by people who never could have had any knowledge of Homer,
but it works especially well in Greek, for the word for Nobody, *Outis*, actually
does sound a bit like Odysseus. Now there is a special feature of Greek, which
is that it has two words for "no," one for negating statements of fact (the *ou*
of *Outis*) and the other (*me*) for negating commands, wishes, or
suppositions.[33] When Polyphemus and Odysseus speak of Nobody in the
latter contexts, they involuntarily change the name to *Metis*. Now this is very
interesting, because there is a homonym in Greek, *metis*, which means "plan
or stratagem." This makes a particularly nice pun, because the Nobody name
IS Odysseus' stratagem for getting out of the cave alive! (Note that the whole
naming thing is central to this book, because once Odysseus has blinded the
Cyclops and is sailing away, he stands on the deck of his ship and shouts out
his real name: Odysseus, son of Laertes, of Ithaca, postal code.... This proves

---

[32] Cf. Chapter III note 39 and Chapter VI note 15.

[33] Latin likewise has two (*non* and *ne*), ditto Biblical Hebrew (*lo* and *al*).

to be a very bad move indeed, because it makes it very easy for Poseidon, who happens to be the Cyclops' dad, to track Odysseus down and punish him for blinding his son.)

The last thing to note in this book is that the Cyclops himself has a kind of gallows humour, in that when asked by Odysseus for a guest-gift, he replies (line 369) that his gift to Odysseus will be to eat him last.[34] This horrible threat, jestingly masquerading as a gift, will come back to haunt the Cyclops, because the last person he eats in the story is indeed nobody at all – for all the men have escaped.

So far we have looked at comedy in the epic. However, comedy could itself BE the epic. Much as most major cultural phenomena have a counter-culture just waiting to satirize, parody, and otherwise make fun of them, ancient epic was exactly the same, and the Greeks were not above parodying their own epic stories.

There is a tiny epic poem that was attributed to Homer in antiquity called *Batrachomyomachia* (*The Battle of Frogs and Mice*), whose contents are pretty much made clear by the title.[35] Note that the title is very long, what the Romans call a "sesquipedalian" word (a foot and half long one). Such words are often funny, especially when, as here, they serve to describe something intrinsically trivial (rather like using a phrase such as "explore the possibilities of static movement in three dimensional space while efficiently exchanging oxygen for carbon dioxide" to represent stretching and yawning). This poem is a parody of the *Iliad* describing an incident 'round the pond when a frog treacherously drowns a mouse and the mice-army gathers to seek revenge. There is a council of war on both sides and an arming-scene (the frogs take up bulrushes as spears, the mice put nut-shells on their heads as helmets, etc.). There is a council of the gods in which Athena expresses her contempt for both sides (on the one hand the frogs keep her up nights with their croaking, on the other the mice nibble at her weaving), and the gods in the end decide to stay neutral. Battle is joined and the mice are on the verge of winning, when Zeus pities the frogs and sends the crabs to join them, thereby tipping the scales in their favour. This can be read as a parody of the *Iliad* with the Frogs in the role of Trojans (their treachery prompts the war) and the Mice as Greeks (they mount the invading army), but it can also be read as a kind of proto-Aesopic fable or a story like the Egyptian satirical papyri from Chapter IV showing animals charmingly engaged in human pursuits.

---

[34] J. A. Thorson, "Did you Ever See a Hearse Go By? Some Thoughts on Gallows Humor," *Journal of American Culture* 16 (1993) 17-24.

[35] This little poem charmed even the chronic depressive Giacomo Leopardi (who was fond of writing things like "in the immensity of the infinite my thought drowns, and shipwreck is sweet to me on such a sea"). He returned again and again to his translation of the poem over his lifetime.

The Cercopes and Satyr-Plays (especially Euripides' Cyclops*)*

Zenobius of Athos 2.85 (Miller, *Mélanges* 367 = Archil. fr. 178 West), in discussing the rather colourful proverb "you have met with a black-rumped man," writes about a pair of trickster brothers called the Cercopes:

> The phrase occurs in Archilochus. For Heracles was hairy and black-rumped. They say that the mother of the Cercopes told them to watch out for a black-rumped man. Afterward when they were caught by Heracles and their feet were tied to one another, he held them hanging head downward. When they saw his black bum, they laughed. When he asked them why they were laughing, they told him of their mother's prophecy and in this way, so they say, they met with his mercy.

The brothers didn't stop their nuisance-ways there, however, and eventually to get rid of them, Zeus turned them into monkeys. This story is often illustrated in art, as in a metope from the temple of Hera at Paestum (modern Foce del Sele) near Naples, Italy and an Attic red-figured krater now in Munich.

We see various kinds of humour at work in this story: Heracles' hanging the Cercopes upside down is a physical manifestation of the humorous principle of inversion, we see how laughter defeats strong emotion (after laughing, Heracles let them go), and we see, of course, that, mischievous little busy-bodies that they are, monkeys are always funny.[36]

Next to the monkey-like Cercopes it seems fitting to consider satyr-plays, that genre of plays presented by tragedians after their three tragedies in the festival of Dionysus. A satyr-play is like a tragedy in that it deals with a story from Greek myth, but differs from it in that its chorus consists of satyrs, with their leader Silenus. Satyrs are a mythic species of almost humans, reminiscent of our Sasquatch. They are short, with permanent erections and horses' ears and tails. They live in the woods and are exclusively male (they rape nymphs, thereby begetting new satyrs). In drama they are inevitably enslaved by someone and yearn for freedom to worship Dionysus, the liberating god of wine. They always behave in some way like animals, though by no means always necessarily like the horses to which they owe their ears and tails.

The satyr-play accompanying Aeschylus' *Oresteia* was the *Proteus*, of which only one full line survives: "beaten about my ribs with a winnowing-fan like a wretched, hungry woodpigeon" (frs. 210-15 *TrGF*). Although this line is not overly helpful in reconstructing the story, we know from the title that it was based on the passage in *Odyssey* Four in which Menelaus, returning home from the Trojan War is blown off course and washes ashore in Egypt. There he must disguise himself as a seal and wait until Proteus, the old man of the sea, comes to shepherd his flock of seals. He must then leap out and wrestle with him (which is hard, because Proteus, like all water-gods, is a shape-

---

[36] See J. Kirkpatrick and F. Dunn, "Heracles, Cercopes and Paracomedy," *TAPA* 132 (2002) 29-61.

shifter). When Menelaus has finally wrestled him down, Proteus tells him how to get home. (There actually were seals in the Mediterranean in antiquity, by the way, although they are extinct now.) In this play the satyrs apparently join the seals in the flocks of Proteus and when Menelaus defeats the slippery god, he also coincidentally liberates them.

The first half of a satyr-play by Sophocles, called the *Ichneutae* or *Trackers* was found in the sands of Oxyrrhynchus, Egypt. Enough of the text survives (frs. 314-18 *TrGF*) for us to know that it was modelled on the story of the *Homeric Hymn to Hermes*. The four-day-old Hermes has stolen his brother Apollo's cattle, and Apollo goes looking for them using some satyr-slaves as tracking-dogs (hence the title of the play). They sniff around the orchestra, looking for the missing cattle. The end is missing, but we can intuit the basic outcome: the cattle are found, Hermes invents the lyre in compensation for his theft, the satyrs are freed from their servitude and go off rejoicing to worship Dionysus (and no doubt get laid).[37]

The only complete satyr-play we have is the *Cyclops* of Euripides. It tells the story of the Cyclops as we know it from *Odyssey* book nine, except that the Cyclops has – you guessed it – enslaved some satyrs. When Odysseus and his men come and are kidnapped by the Cyclops they blind him using the good old-fashioned Homeric tricks of the "Nobody" name and a hot pointy stick, and then sail off to freedom taking the satyrs with them.

Although they were technically tragedies, the satyr-plays were meant to be funny, at least in places. From the *Cyclops* we can see some of the humorous techniques available to the writer of satyr-plays. First there is slapstick in the mechanical movements of the one-eyed monster, who is deformed, gluttonous (when he wants a change of menu, Silenus says in effect at line 247, "oh no, not *lion* again!") and cowardly, and winds up playing "blind man's bluff" with Odysseus. Then we have Silenus in his role as comic cook serving the wine to himself rather than to his master with a comic delaying-tactic scene reminiscent of Cinesias and Myrrhina in Aristophanes' *Lysistrata*. There is sex humour in the wish to gang-rape Helen (lines 177-87; Euripides apparently found this funny – remember, this was a culture that thought cannibals were hilarious), the Cyclops' claim that he doesn't need anyone, not even Zeus, because he can masturbate all by himself – if that is the meaning of lines 327-28; the point is disputed. And then there's his threat to rape Silenus (whom he calls his "Ganymede", lines 581-84), who happens to be at least as ugly as Socrates. There are no good jokes in this play at all, except for the Nobody-trick, which is inherited from Homer and already known to the audience, and it only gets three lines (548-51).

Euripides breaks the dramatic illusion once interestingly with Odysseus' lines (375-76):

Oh Zeus, what can I say? I've seen dreadful things within the cave – unbelievable things –, like those in human myths and not in reality!

---

[37] This fragment is the inspiration for Tony Harrison's 1988 play, *The Trackers of Oxyrrhynchus*.

And, finally there is one great moment of literary parody, when Silenus says (lines 186b-87):

> Would that nowhere any longer
> the female sex existed – except for me alone!

This is a take off on Euripides' own *Hippolytus*, whose title-character is famously misogynistic (616-50, cf. *Med.* 573-74), yet by adding the last four words, Silenus reverses the sense entirely to mean, "I wish all other *men* in the word would sod off!"

Chapter XI – A Funny Thing Happened on the Way to the Agora

Old Comedy and Aristophanes' Clouds

"Comedy" derives its name from *-edy* meaning "song" (also found in the word "trag-edy") and *komos*, which Christopher Carey rather well translates as a "pub crawl."[1] This type of comedy normally ends in a joyful party or *komos*, often a wedding-feast in which the hero marries some glorious abstract principle like Peace or Kingship, leaving the melodrama of the later adultery, divorce, and cliched attempted murder for the poorly written Hollywood sequel. The Old Comedy of Aristophanes is not the comedy that would follow, however – it's a genre that dies out with Aristophanes and his contemporaries.

So far we have examined the fundamental elements of comedy, but we have spent relatively little time actually showing how these elements interact and come together. Indeed, a single joke alone does not make a play (although there are some comedy screenwriters who seem to believe that to be the case). Now, we are going to look at four different comedies of Aristophanes, and examine how these elements are brought together.

In *Clouds*, a story of Strepsiades attempting to learn how to weasel out of his debts from the great *eiron* and *alazon* Socrates, the final *komos* is unusually dark, consisting of Strepsiades and Pheidippides burning down the Thinkery. There are two other obligatory elements in Old Comedy as well as the *komos*: the *agon* and the *parabasis*. *Agon* means "contest" and, as mentioned in Chapter VIII, is the source of our English word "agony" (what you feel during a contest, especially a wrestling-match, or, for that matter, while watching a really slow game of baseball). The *agon* in Old Comedy is a rhetorical debate between the *alazon* and *eiron* in which – because of his unparalleled skill with words the *alazon* inevitably wins. The *eiron* is the good guy, however, and must ultimately triumph, which he does by driving the *alazon* away by force in a slapstick, Keystone Kops style of rout, also known as an "exodus." The *parabasis* is a moment in which the chorus take off their masks, "step aside" (*parabainein* in Greek) from their roles, and address the audience directly in the person of the poet.[2] There are two of these in *Clouds*, although at least one and possibly both were added to the play after the performance in preparation for publication in book-form as a kind of pamphlet.

The one other stereotypical feature of Old Comedy is that the chorus often represents animals. We actually have a *Frogs*, *Birds* and *Wasps*, and we know of other titles of lost comedies with animal-choruses, such as *Ants*. This

---

[1] C. Carey, *Lysias: Selected Speeches* (Cambridge, 1989) 163 ad 14.25.

[2] This was known as *Opsimathy*, or "late learning." This was a culturally acceptable way for adults to learn new things, even if the parabasis was often like a prepaid political message.

may be influenced by the Egyptian humour mentioned in chapter IV, where animals have taken on a human aspect and human activities.

Let us consider some of the humorous techniques that Aristophanes uses in *Clouds*. There is slapstick in the doorway-scene and above all in the burning of the Thinkery (though Aristophanes himself claims on line 543 that he is above that sort of thing). There is also a lot of "low humour":

Sex: A man can't be in bed without masturbating (line 734); Strepsiades chases one of his creditors, Amynias, away with the threat of buggery (lines 1299-1300).

Scatology: Pheidippides farts in his sleep (line 9); Strepsiades likewise (line 390); a gnat sings through its anus (line 157); a gecko shits on Socrates' head (line 169); rain is Zeus pissing through a sieve (line 373); Strepsiades used to toilet train the infant Pheidippides by holding him out into the street (line 1384).

Bugs: After waking up Pheidippides, Strepsiades says that he is thrashing around because he was bitten by a "bumbailiff" (Greek *demarchos*) out of the mattress (line 37); Socrates performs a scientific experiment to see how many of its own feet a flea can jump, using wax booties (lines 143-53); Socrates' student expounds on a theory of whether a gnat sings through its mouth or its anus (line 157).

There are some puns, like Strepsiades' claim that the earth is a tandoor, a sort of Indian cooking pot, and we are the coals (*anthrakes*, punning on *anthropoi* and *andres*, the two Greek words for "people," line 97 – it is actually funny in Greek, take our word for it) or the pun on thunder (*bronte*) and farting (*porde*) on line 394, or on the two meanings of *tokos*, "interest" and "child" on line 1156.

There are several breakings of the dramatic illusion, quite apart from the two parabases. Socrates has to tell Strepsiades to look in the wings to see the arriving chorus (line 326). And Lesser Argument forces Greater Argument to admit that the audience consists mostly of assholes (line 1325; see Chapter II).

There are various types of parody of life: the sophistic movement (passim), Strepsiades considers himself lucky to have married beyond his social class, failing to notice that his wife is damaged goods (from the Greek perspective, at least), Strepsiades suggests using witchcraft to steal the moon in order to avoid paying interest on his debts (lines 749-50), and the Greater and Lesser Arguments are both brought on stage in cages like fighting cocks.

Finally, there is one particularly interesting piece of literary parody whereby the prologue in which Strepsiades convinces Pheidippides to do a horrible thing to save his father and the exodus in which the two burn the Thinkery together is a send up of Sophocles *Women of Trachis* 972, 1181-1202 and 1243-1251, in which the dying Heracles extracts a favour from his son,

Hyllus:[3]

> Hyllus: Alas, Father, what should I do you for you, poor man?
>   What should I contrive? Alas!
>
> ....
>
> Heracles: First of all, put your right hand in mine.
> Hyl: Giving it over to what excessive oath?
> Her: Won't you give it more quickly, and not disobey me?
> Hyl: There. I'm holding it out, you can't deny it.
> Her: Swear, then, by Zeus who begot my head.
> Hyl: To do what, indeed? About this too you must speak.
> Her: Indeed to fulfil the deed of which I will speak.
> Hyl: I for my part swear, taking Zeus as witness.
> Her: If you should depart from it, pray to get sufferings.
> Hyl: I won't get any, for I will do it. Even so, I'll pray.
> Her: You know the peak of Oeta [sacred] to loftiest Zeus?
> Hyl: I know it, since I've often stood upon it as a sacrificer.
> Her: There then you must carry my
>   body with your own hand and with whomever of your friends you need.
>   Cut much wood of deep-rooted
>   oak, and also cut many a manly
>   wild olive-tree. Put my body on it,
>   and, taking the gleam of a pine torch,
>   burn it. Let me not see a tear of weeping,
>   but unmoaning and unweeping, if indeed you are
>   my son, do this. If not, may I remain for you
>   even below, being forever a heavy curse!
>
> ....
>
> Hyl: Woe is me! What a great dilemma I'm in!
> Her: Yes, for you don't think it right to listen to him who begot you.
> Hyl: Should I have been taught, then, to be impious, Father?
> Her: It's not impiety, if you will please my heart.
> Hyl: Do you really order me to do these things with justice?
> Her: I do. I call upon the gods as witness to my words.
> Hyl: Well, then, I'll do it. I won't refuse, now that you've revealed
>   the deed to the gods, for never could I
>   appear bad, if I am obeying you, Father.

Aristophanes' Birds, Lysistrata, and Frogs

Aristophanes' *Birds* follows the typical shape of Old Comedy, again as in *Clouds*, with two *parabases*, an *agon*, and a *komos*. It is the story of two Athenians named Peisthetaerus and Euelpides who, sick of the city, found one of their own in the sky with the birds – and end up cutting off the supply of sacrifices to the gods in the process.

---

[3] See R. D. Griffith, "Strepsiades' Bedroom, Wife and Sufferings: Three Notes on the Prologue of Aristophanes' *Clouds*," *Prometheus* 19 (1993) 135-42, esp. 141-42.

We find slapstick humour in the suggestion that Euelpides bang Tereus'[4] rock with his head rather than with his foot (line 55), clearly implying that Euelpides' head is hollow for lack of brains, which is an insult, but it may impugn his manhood more than his intelligence (according to the Greeks, we think with our diaphragm; our brain is a repository of semen); this particular rock is Tereus' doorway, and doorway scenes are usually funny in Aristophanes. More slapstick can be found in the idea of Euelpides' climbing up a ladder with a hod and falling off (line 840), and in Peisthetaerus' dealings with the various alazons who come to Cloudcuckooland from Athens (lines 859-1465) – they pop in from all directions with a new one showing up each time an old one has been beaten off, in a mechanistic device that Douglas MacDowell aptly calls "jack-in-the-box" clowning.[5]

There are sex jokes – for example Peisthetaerus' fantasy about a sexual utopia where men will blame you for *not* trying to hit on their sons on lines 137-42 (this may seem odd, but remember that ancient Greek sexuality had no stigma against homosexual pedophilia). And there are jokes at the expense of the Nightingale, who is probably a flute-girl with her *aulos* (the Greek two-bodied oboe held on with a neck-brace like a folk guitarist's harmonica); she is probably wearing nothing else but a few feathers in her hair.[6] The Athenians in the play want to open her beak (the *aulos*), kiss her and have sex (lines 672-74).

Bugs, such a source of petty irritation in other Aristophanic plays, are here replaced by birds, who keep threatening to peck Pisthetaeros and Euelpides. The modern equivalent would be "nibbled to death by ducks."

There is, of course, scatological humour when Euelpides soils himself from fear (line 66), and the birds' account of why wings are useful – you can fly home to use the bathroom during a boring tragedy, and still be back in time for the comedy, which is an interesting commentary on the audience's reaction to tragic plays (lines 785-89).

There are puns. Lots of puns. The whole story is really based on the saying "go to the crows!" (line 28) – just as the Widow of Ephesus story from Petronius is really based on the saying "go to the cross!" There is a very untranslatable pun on *polis*, *polos* and related words when Pisthetaeros declares that the heavens revolve on a sort of pole (lines 179-80). Then there are *sesquipedalian* (a very long and convoluted word meaning "big") words such as the name of the new city itself, Cloudcuckooland (*Nephelokukkugia*).

There is parody of life in all the *alazons* who try to invade the new city upon its founding providing laws and services that nobody in the city actually

---

[4] A mythological figure who raped his sister-in-law and then, to keep her quiet, cut out her tongue. They were both turned into birds, and Tereus himself became a very obnoxious looking one.

[5] D. M. MacDowell, *Aristophanes Wasps* (Oxford, 1971) 149 ad 136-229.

[6] It's possible that this is a man wearing a sort of naked female body suit, but it is also quite possible that it isn't – it could be an actual naked woman. Courtesans in Athens were flute-players.

needs, and in the idea that Peisthetaerus would convict his new fellow-citizens of treason in order to have an excuse to execute and barbecue them (lines 1583-85).

And, there is literary parody, again, as in *Clouds,* at the expense of Sophocles, for the Tereus of Aristophanes' play is none other than the title-character of Sophocles (now lost) *Tereus* (581-95b *TrGF*, cf. Ar. *Av.* 100-101).

Now we'll deal with sex.[7] Let us turn to look at Aristophanes' *Lysistrata.* As mentioned earlier in the book, the play revolves around a group of women who decide to put an end to war by denying sex to their men. In the play, we have the familiar form of the *agon*, which segues into a *parabasis*, and the *komos*.

The title is (uncharacteristically for a comedy) the name of an individual. It is a "speaking name" meaning "she who unties – i.e. demobilizes – the army" and is probably a reference to the priestess of Athena, Lysimache, whose name meant "She who dissolves the battle."[8]

Here again (lines 1218b-20), as in *Clouds* line 453, Aristophanes swears off slapstick, and here again, as in *Clouds,* he uses it freely, especially in the encounter between the chorus of men trying to burn the women out of the acropolis and that of women dousing them with water (lines 254-386).

We have lots of sex jokes, mainly around sexual frustration and its various remedies such as dildos and masturbation,[9] but it is the frustration of the males that is more pertinent, as shown by the exempli gratia scene with Cinesias and Myrrhina ("speaking names" again, for Cinesias is a "mover and shaker" and Myrrhina is "Little Miss Perfume"), where Myrrhina tells her husband that she'll make an exception for him, and in a long, drawn out scene that we examined in Chapter IX, leaves him with lots of furniture and a raging erection, but no sex. This is again a jack-in-the-box episode with Myrrhina popping back into the scene-building every two minutes to get some new stage-property.

There is no scatology and no bugs either. Apparently people being driven crazy by the lack of sex is enough low-brow humour for this one.

Verbal humour is confined mainly to pointing out the difference between the Athenian and Spartan dialects. There are some long words too.

For literary parody, which seems to us the highest form of humour, we

---

[7] Woohoo! We're dealing with sex...we're dealing with sex!
Um...er...sorry. We get carried away sometimes.
Breasts.

[8] But, she can't be named in public, being a woman, and because if she was mentioned by name, her brothers would visit Aristophanes at night and explain the finer points of etiquette to him with a really big stick.

[9] And, we'd give you examples, but you know, maybe we shouldn't. After all, we are sadists. Well, okay, we will tell you this - there are lots of REALLY titillating examples that would put you into such a state of arousal that you'd feel the irresistible need to pop in a porno this very minute. And no, we still won't tell you what they are.

turn to lines 138-39:

> How totally wide-arsed[10] is our whole sex!
> Not without reason are there tragedies about us:
> we're nothing but Poseidon and a skiff.

This seems to be a reference to Sophocles (now lost) *Tyro* (frs. 648-49 *TrGF*) in which Poseidon disguised himself as the mortal Enipeus and seduced that man's girlfriend, Tyro. She gave birth to twins, Pelias and Neleus and exposed them on a skiff. But of course children exposed in myth always survive (these were reared by kindly shepherds) and come back and meet their parents, which happened in this play in a famous recognition-scene.

Our last example is the much mentioned but so far untouched *Frogs*. This play is unusual partly because it is not certain that there were, in fact, frogs in the chorus in *Frogs*.[11] The other unusual thing is that the *agon* is a debate between Aeschylus and Euripides, both of whom are portrayed as *alazons*: Aeschylus the bombastic-warmonger (Aristophanes passionately hated the Peloponnesian War and railed against it all the time) and Euripides the swivel-tongued sophist. The only *eiron* present really is a right-thinking everyman even though he is a god – Dionysus. This is a unique case where the *eiron* is not a participant in the debate, but the judge (and the jury is still out on whether or not this is a judicious improvement).

There are various elements of slapstick in the play, such as the corpse-scene of lines 167-80, in which the corpse turns out to be a surprisingly good bargainer, and would "rather come to life again" than accept Dionysus' offer to carry his bags to Hell.[12] Then there is the appearance of the bogey-monster Empusa engineered by Xanthias in lines 285-311, which so terrifies Dionysus that he has to ask for a sponge, the Greek equivalent of toilet paper, at line 479, on which more can be seen below. Finally there is the scene where Aeacus decides to make the real god "please stand up" by whipping both

---

[10] Allowing oneself to be anally penetrated was a reprehensible sign of effeminacy. The fact that the speaker is herself a woman, and is talking about women, may be part of the joke.

[11] The chorus-members are later needed to represent those who died after being initiated in the Eleusinian Mysteries; while actors in Greek theatre often played multiple roles with mask- and costume-changes, it would be highly unusual for a chorus to enter as one "character" then leave the orchestra and re-enter in another role; on the other hand, could Aristophanes really have resisted the temptation to put cute little green frogs into his play? Would he really have thrown away this opportunity for special effects in order to have a chorus dressed wholly in rags?

[12] This is a reversal of the commonplace saying, "I'd rather drop dead," but a logical one – to the Greeks, resurrection was one of the greatest crimes anybody could commit against the gods, and was usually rewarded with a lightning bolt where the sun doesn't shine.

Dionysus and his slave Xanthias on the premise that real gods don't feel pain in lines 605-73. This is funny in part at least because the premise is totally wrong: gods *do* feel pain as the stories of Prometheus and the eagle eating out his liver, or Diomedes wounding Aphrodite's wrist, or Psyche burning Cupid's shoulder with oil from her lamp show.

There are various sex-jokes. For example, Dionysus' desire for Euripides is phrased in sexual terms, with Heracles trying to figure out if Dionysus' lust is for a woman, a boy, or a man (lines 55-56); or the chorus longing for the woman whose breast peeps out of her rags in line 412b. Although the play begins with Dionysus telling Xanthias to lay off the old jokes about shitting and farting, these are plentiful in the play, as when Dionysus' anus croaks like a frog during his rowing-duel with the frog-chorus in lines 236-38, or when he soils himself and has to ask for a sponge in line 479, which was mentioned above, and on which there is more below.[13] There are no bugs; though there are those pesky frogs (an improvement, or at least a move up along the food chain; perhaps there were bugs, but the frogs ate them).

Verbal humour is had with various sesquipedalian words. For example, the "bubblousblustifications" in line 249 is all one word in Greek; ditto "Trumpetspearpointlongbeard, grinningpinebender" of line 966, which is supposed to be typical of Aeschylean style. We also have a contrary to expectation joke when Dionysus fears that Euripides will fall and break open his head and his *Telephus*, a terrible play, will ooze out (line 855).

There is breaking of the dramatic illusion when the criminals of Hell turn out to be the audience in lines 273-76, and when Dionysus appeals to his own priest for help from the boogie-monster in line 297.

There is satire of life in the very opening tableau of the play with the slave riding on a donkey carrying a sack of provisions on his own back, accompanied by Dionysus (easily recognizable by his effeminate appearance – clean-shaven face, long silk nightie and Persian slippers) wearing over his clothes the borrowed gear of Heracles (cave-man club and lionskin).

This play is especially rich in literary parody, as befits a play in which two main characters are poets. Fun is poked on line 304 at Euripides' *Orestes* 279, where the title character begins to recover from the madness inflicted on him by the Furies and says, "The storm is over and the calm has stilled the waves."[14] This is funny because in the premier performance the actor Hegelochus in the title role slipped up and said, "The storm is over and the clam has stilled the waves."[15] Again when Dionysus soils himself and has to

---

[13] Why are you surprised that we keep tempting you like this? As we've said before, we're SADISTS.

[14] This is R. Lattimore's highly imaginative translation for this wholly untranslatable line; see W. Arrowsmith, R. Lattimore and D. Parker, *Four Plays by Aristophanes* (New York 1964) 506.

[15] It's much funnier in Greek, because the screw up involved the word *galene*, "calm" mispronounced as "weasel" – Greeks didn't keep house-cats and used weasels as domestic mousers with the consequence that all

ask for a sponge in line 479 he says *enkechoda: kalei theon* ("I have shit myself: call upon the god"), which is a pun on the libation-offering given after a meal, *ekkechutai: kalei theon* ("It has been poured forth: call upon the god"). At line 1214 Dionysus utters an Aeschylean death-cry (from *Agamemnon* 1345) upon Aeschylus' sabotage of Euripides' prologues by his constant insertion into them of the words "lost his little bottle of oil." Finally Dionysus breaks his promise to bring Euripides back to life, choosing to take Aeschylus instead and when Euripides reproaches him replies in line 1471 with a notorious line from Euripides' *Hippolytus* (612): "my tongue swore, but my heart remains unsworn."

Visual Representations

Taking a break from the literary humour, it is worthy to note for a moment that the Greeks also had visual humour. Like the Egyptians mentioned in Chapter IV, there are remains of pottery that mirror our modern day mugs illustrated with Far Side cartoons.

Here are some examples illustrating various kinds of Greek humour:

1. *Heracles, Eurystheus and Cerberus from an Attic red-figure vase circa 530 in the Louvre.*

Eurystheus has sent Heracles on a suicide-mission to fetch the three-headed hound of Hell, and Heracles has just successfully completed his mission and proudly brought the thing into Eurystheus' living-room. Far from being pleased, the king is scared out of his wits and has jumped into a storage-jar

---

of our cat-superstitions were transferred to the weasel. Having a weasel cross your path in Greek, therefore, was the height of BAD luck; so Hegelochus has inadvertently reversed the meaning of the line.

for safety;[16] this theme was also treated by the Athenian painter Scythes.[17]

2.   *Heracles and the Cercopes on a metope from Paestum circa 550 BC.*

We saw this in a textual reference in the previous chapter; but hey, monkeys are always funny, why not look at them again?

3.   *A woman holding a penis-bird as a pet from an Attic red-figure vase.*[18]

---

[16] He can only pray that the dog is house trained.

[17] J. Boardman, *Athenian Red Figure Vases: The Archaic Period*. P. 221 (plate 89).

[18] J. Boardman, "The Phallos-Bird in Archaic and Classical Greek Art," *Rev. Arch.* (1992) 228-42.

The idea of a penis detached from its owner and outfitted with wings is surreal; that a woman keeps such a thing as a pet inverts the normal order of this patriarchal society. Okay, we might not find it quite as funny, but the Greeks did. The bird = penis equation had a long subsequent history. Catullus poem 2 reads as follows:

> Sparrow, my girl's pet,
> with whom she often plays, whom on her bosom she holds,
> to whom the tip of her finger she gives, when you seek it,
> and teases out sharp pecks,
> whenever my shining desire
> wants to make I-know-not-what dear joke
> and little consolation for her sorrow,
> and I think that then her heavy longing grows still:
> if only I could play with you as Herself does,
> and take away the sad cares of my mind!

Various scholars have argued that the "sparrow" is a euphemism for the poet's penis:[19] the sparrow is associated with Aphrodite, goddess of sex (Sappho fr. 1.10 Lobel-Page) and its Greek name is slang for "penis" (Ar. *Lys.* 722-23).[20] What sense do we then make of Catullus poem three, in which the sparrow dies?

---

[19] A. Pomeroy, "Heavy Pettings in Catullus," *Arethusa* 36 (2003) 49-60, , with biblliography.

[20] J. Henderson, *Aristophanes: Lysistrata* (Oxford, 1987) 165.

4.   *A herm with a bird sitting on his phallus.*

And we complain about pigeons defiling *our* statues!

5.   *A door-bell from Pompei now in the gabinetto segreto in the Naples Museum.*

6.   *A penis horse on an Attic red-figure vase (ARV 157, 84).*

Presumably a species related to the penis-bird (no matter what, it's an animal that's got balls).[21] (This image gives new meaning to the children's nursery-rhyme "Ride a cock-horse to Banbury Cross.")

7.   *Bluebeard from the Old Parthenon, in the Athens Acropolis Museum.*

We put this guy here to illustrate the phenomenon of the "archaic smile." E. A. Gardner comments:[22]

> Yet when we look at the Typhon, at once the most characteristic and the best preserved of all this series, it is almost impossible to resist the impression that the sculptor must have revelled in the absurdity of the monster he was creating. Nor need we resist this impression on archaeological grounds. A humorous treatment of the subject, sometimes tending to caricature, is by no means uncommon upon early vases, and especially upon a class of vases which, though found in Italy, almost certainly come from Asia Minor, and which otherwise show many affinities with these architectural sculptures.

---

[21] On horses as images of the penis, see J. Henderson, *The Maculate Muse* 2nd ed. (New York and Oxford, 1991) 127, 165 and 177.

[22] E. A. Gardner, *A Handbook of Greek Sculpture* (London, 1897) 161-62.

8.   *The Hermes of Praxiteles (ca. 350 B. C.) in the museum at Olympia.*

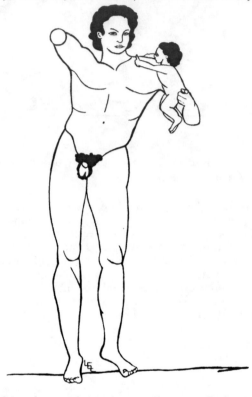

There is nothing funny about this at all. We include it just to show the pin-headed little Dionysus, evidence that the Greeks could conceive of babies only as tiny, that is defective, adults. This relates to our discussion earlier of the laughter of Hector and Andromache at their baby in Chapter III.

9.   *Gold cup from Royal Tomb IV at Mycenae in the National Museum, Athens.*

This gives you some idea of what Homer had in mind when he described the cup of Nestor (*Iliad* 11.632-37):

> And beside him was a very beautiful cup, which the old man had brought
>   from home,
> pierced with golden studs. There were four
> ears (= handles) on it, and two doves on each,
> golden ones, were feeding. Under it were two stands.
> Another man, labouring, might start to move it off the table,
> when it was full, but Nestor the old man labourlessly lifted it.

And the reason we're showing you this is because of what's next.

10. *A little clay drinking cup from tomb 168, Pithecusae, Ischia circa 750 B.C. with the following incised inscription (454 Hansen, CEG):*

> [I am] the good-drinking cup of Nestor.
> Whoever drinks from this cup, will immediately
> be seized by the yearning of beautiful-crowned Aphrodite.

The owner's name was possibly (but not likely) Nestor. Then there is the inscription. The first line appears as a simple owner's inscription until we get to the rare, poetic and pretty inappropriate word "good-drinking" (*eupoton*), since Homer's Nestor had a cup that was very hard to drink from, being too heavy to lift, and all. The second line appears like a curse, and such curses against theft were common on household objects, although a curse against drinking from a cup would be unusual and inhospitable in the extreme. The third line shows that the curse is really a blessing. The humour is thus of the defeat-of-expectation sort, combined with the bathetic comparison of Nestor's magnificent golden cup with this modest clay mug.[23]

---

[23] P. A. Hansen, "Pithecusan Humour: The Inhterpretation of Nestor's Cup Resonsidered," *Glotta* 54 (1976) 25-43; see, however, C. A. Faraone, "Taking the 'Nestor's Cup Inscription' Seriously: Erotic Magic and Conditional Curses in the earliest inscribed hexameters," *CA* 15 (1996) 77-112.

11. *A thin boy laughs at a fat boy on an Attic red-figured drinking-cup (ARV 2nd ed. 166, early 5th cent. B.C.).*

The Greeks had no compunction about laughing at physical deformities, especially when they are placed on display. The message: fat boys should not go to gymnasia, where they would be exposing their bodies to ridicule.

Compare that scene with these two passages of Greek literature – Pindar's description of the losers in the great games (*Pyth.* 8.83-87):

> For them (the losers) neither was a homecoming
> as cheerful (as yours) decided at the games,
> nor about them as they came to their mothers did laughter sweet
> bring grace, but through back-alleyways, aloof from their enemies,
> they skulk, bitten with misfortune.

And Aristophanes' *Frogs* describing the annual torch-race in the Panathenaic games (1089-98):

> By Zeus, I withered away
> laughing at the Panathenaea
> when a certain slow man was running bent over,
> white, fat, left behind
> and having a hard time. And then the Cerameans
> at the gates struck his
> belly, ribs, flanks, bum,
> and he – beaten by their outspread hands –
> farted softly,
> blew on his torch, and kept trying to get away.

These passages bring to mind the episode involving Hephaestus in *Iliad* 1, as well as other real-life insults (to take just one of many examples: Archedemus, a demagogue in the last years of the Peloponnesian war, was universally referred to as "blear-eyed" according to Lys. 14.25 and Ar. *Ran.* 588). The Greeks were unable to think, "there, but for the grace of God, go I."[24]

12. *Pygmy Zeus from the Theban Kabeireion.*

He is, or thinks he is, Zeus (note the thunderbolt, and compare the myths about those who would be Zeus, e.g. Salmoneus). Note his enlarged (suggesting anti-heroic) and circumsized (suggesting barbaric, and non-Greek) penis. Well, they thought it was funny.

---

[24] R. Garland ed., *In the Eye of the Beholder: Deformity and Disability in the Graeco-Roman World.* (Ithaca 1995).

Chapter XII – The Roman Wit

Latin Verbal Humour and Petronius' Satyricon

The word "Classical" is used to refer to both Greek and Roman culture, suggesting that the two were the same, or at least similar enough to warrant using the same word for each. In many cases, there are similarities, but this really is an oversimplification. And, as often happens between different cultures, senses of humour varied.

While Greek poetry was composed orally and recited in public for aural consumption, Roman literature (like our own) was a literate product, committed to paper and intended for consumption by a reading audience. This enabled Roman writers to play word games far more subtle than Greeks could use. Additionally, Latin was an inflected, that is conjugated and declined language, allowing meaning to depend not on the order of words, but on the endings of those words – and allowing for certain word games that English isn't capable of producing. Here are four examples:

1. *saxo cere comminuit brum*
    "He split his brain in two with a rock"

This is allegedly from a battle-epic by the early poet Ennius (*Annals* fr. 609 Vahlen = Spuria 5 Skutch). The joke is that the word for "brain," *cerebrum* is here actually split in two by the word for "split in two," in a perfect case of form following function. The technical name for this literary device is "tmesis."

2. *in lignis flamma latet*
    "Flame hides in logs"

This is from the versified physics-textbook by Lucretius (1.871) in which he is expounding the theory of Democritus that all things are made up of atoms, and seemingly very different things have the same atoms in them, just arranged differently. So wood and fire are the same atoms in a different combination. This is funny because the Latin word for "fire," *ignis* actually IS hiding in the "logs" (*lignis*).

3. *parturient montes, nascetur ridiculus mus*
    "The mountains go into labour and give birth to a ridiculous mouse."

Horace, *Art of Poetry* 139 is describing bombastic poets whose work is full of sound and fury signifying nothing (not unlike many of the recent summer blockbusters). The last two words are a joke on form (the technical term is clash of ictus and accent, and there are parallels, e.g. Verg. *G.* 1.182), but it's funny because there are so few really little words in Latin, and *mus*, "mouse" is perfect in form for the tiny creature it describes.

4.   *Pindarum quisquis student aemulari,*
      Iulle, ceratis ope Daedalea,
      nititur pinnis, vitreo daturus
                 nomina ponto.

"Whoever is eager to imitate Pindar, Iullus, relies on wings waxed by the skill of Daedalus, destined to give their names to the glassy sea."

Horace again (*Odes* 4.2.1-4), this time apologizing to his friend Iullus for not writing odes in the manner of the great Greek lyric poet, Pindar. Whoever tries, he says, will be a quack and crash and burn like Icarus in the story of Daedalus and Icarus. The joke here is that the name *Pindarus* occurs broken apart and floating on the rest of the sentence *PINnis, vitreo DAtuRUS* just as the body of Icarus broke apart on reentry into the atmosphere and floated on the surface of the sea henceforth called "Icarean." (The technical name for this is "anagram").

The Romans wrote what could be considered some of the earliest novels. And, like the Greeks, the Romans didn't necessarily take themselves seriously in what they wrote.

Let's look at Petronius' *Satyricon*. Petronius was the "arbiter of elegance" at the court of Nero (Tac. *Ann.* 16.18), meaning that he had to organize entertainments for dinner-parties, etc. Knowing as he did about GOOD taste, he chooses in this work to satirize its opposite. The work is composed in *prosimetrum*, a random alternation of prose and verse that fits the odds-and-sods nature of the content, flaunting the Roman convention that prose and poetry should never meet[1] (remember Homer's *Margites* and the mishmash of metres in which it was composed).

Although the work is in Latin, the title is Greek and means "pertaining to satyric things." It does, however, recall satire, the only genre of literature native to Rome, and which, as we said way back in Chapter I, can be seen as a kind of sausage (the name is related to our word "satisfy" and has to do with being *stuffed* full of odd things; compare our word "farce," which was originally the French word for "stuffing"). Horace, one of the greatest Roman writers of satire, describes the purpose of the genre (*Sat.* 1.1) as *ridendo dicere rerum*, "telling the truth through laughter."

But if those associations lie in the background of the name, its basic meaning recalls satyrs (those Sasquatch-like horny wild men of the woods) and the only genre of literature peculiar to them, the satyr-play. Satyr-plays could be defined as dramas based on the *Odyssey* due to their plot, and Petronius' novel has both qualities.

Encolpius is hounded over the Mediterranean by the garden-god Priapus, as Poseidon persecuted Odysseus in the *Odyssey* or as Juno pursued Aeneas in the *Odyssey*'s highbrow adaptation into Latin, Vergil's *Aeneid*. Encolpius meets various people with highfalutin Homeric names: Agamemnon the rhetorician (chapter 2) and his side-kick Menelaus (chapter 27), and Circe

---

[1] Or talk. Or shake hands. Or have sex and have strange, mutant babies. The Romans just didn't have a sense of humour about those things.

the beautiful nymphomaniac (chapter 127). These low-lives with the high-sounding names call to mind the cup of Nestor from Pithecusae. Encolpius, like Odysseus, uses pseudonyms, calling himself at one point (chapter 127) "Polyaenus," a name with the *poly-*, ("many") element that Homer often uses in describing Odysseus (man of many wiles, who saw many places and knew the minds of many men), and it fittingly could be translated either as "one of whom many tales are told" (i.e. "famous one" or as "one who tells many [mutually incompatible] tales," (i.e. con-man). Unlike the *Iliad* with its strong hero Achilles, the *Odyssey* with its crafty hero Odysseus, or the *Aeneid* with its dutiful hero Aeneas, Encolpius is defined by his naivety (chapters 7 and 41). This work is the ultimate comic inversion, for the hero (our sympathies are drawn to him by the first-person narrative) is the *alazon* both as parasite and as sophist, not, an *eiron* like the usual comic hero. The hero-*alazon* is pitted against any number of other quacks, such as the nouveau-riche poseur, Trimalchio.

The Satyricon as Drama

The generic qualities of drama can be seen from the Greek word for actor, *hypokrites*, and its Latin counterpart, *histrio*. Actors are hypocritical and histrionic, and Encolpius and friends, as con-men running sham projects and scams of all sorts are all of that.

Compare, for instance, the fake-deaths. Trimalchio's dinner party takes the Roman idea of a *memento mori* (skeleton reminding the party-goers to eat, drink and be merry for tomorrow we die) to the nth degree, by ending with a sham funeral at which the guests, parasites that they are, outdo one another in their lamentations and displays of grief (ch. 78). This false funeral ends in a false fire-alarm rather as that earlier comedy of quackery, Aristophanes' *Clouds* ends in a burning down of the Thinkery. Encolpius offers to commit suicide like so many of Euripides' virgin heroines (famously Iphigeneia and Macaria) who offer to die for the good of the state. Encolpius is no maiden in any sense and no-one honours his offer (ch. 97). The boy-toy Giton is obsessed with slitting his throat and commits a theatrical suicide with a dulled practice razor, with which he later volunteers to castrate himself (chs. 94 and 108).

There are various, as it were, stage-properties in the novel, with a reference to painting the face with wine-lees, the earliest form of theatrical mask (ch. 22); Fortunata dancing the *cordax* (perhaps similar to the Can-Can) in ch. 52; a theatrical machine, which Encolpius expects to see bursting out of the wall at any moment (chs. 54 and 75); and the props that Eumolpus et al. plan to use to catch legacy-hunters in Croton (ch. 117).

One of the commonest elements of a drama, especially a tragedy is the recognition scene, and we get one here on ship-board when Lichas recognizes Encolpius, not by some typical recognition-token such as a scar, but by his penis (ch. 105). Of course, Encolpius has a very particular penis because it is impotent due to the curse of Priapus, or, as he calls it, his Achilles' heel (just a long, flaccid one) in ch. 129. He gives it a talking to (ch. 132):

"What do you say," I said, "you shame to all men and gods? For you aren't fit to name in serious conversation. Did I deserve this from you that, when I found myself in heaven, you have dragged me into Hell? – that you have made a public mockery of my years, flowering in their first prime, and laid on me the weakness of extreme old age? I beg you: give me back a brief demonstration!"

This talking to doesn't work, and Encolpius' member hangs its head like a dropping poppy. When he gets a temporary reprieve from his impotence he calls it Protesilaus (ch. 140), with reference to the myth of the first Greek to die at Troy (the gods brought him back to life for one day so that he could finish his interrupted honeymoon).

The novel contains allusions to specific dramas, such as the *Ajax mad* (ch. 59) and to the *Odyssey*, or perhaps a satyr-play version thereof such as Euripides' *Cyclops*, in the story of Giton tying himself under the hotel-bed to escape detection by the magistrates (ch. 97).

Finally, there are allusions to Platonic dialogue, which is after all a kind of drama, in the speeches of the freedmen at Trimalchio's dinner-party (chs. 41-46; which echo the speeches in Plato's *Symposium*) and in the host's story of the unbreakable glass which parodies the myth of Thoth as told in Plato's *Phaedrus* (274c-275b). Thoth thought he was so great because he had invented the art of writing, which would be a recipe for remembering, but when he showed it to pharaoh, the latter was angry, saying that Thoth had invented a recipe not for remembering, but for forgetting, because once people could write things down, they wouldn't bother trying to remember them any more.[2] Trimalchio's story goes as follows:

> But if things made of glass didn't break, I would myself prefer them to gold. Now, however, they're worthless. But there once was a craftsman who made a glass bowl that couldn't break. He was taken before Caesar, therefore, with his gift, pretended to hold it out to Caesar, and dropped it on the pavement. Caesar couldn't have been more scared. But the other picked up the bowl from the ground. It had been dented like a bronze vase. Then he drew a little hammer from the fold of his toga, and fixed the bowl at his own sweet leisure. This done, he thought he occupied the throne of Jupiter, until finally Caesar said to him, "Does anyone else know this recipe for glass?" Watch now: after he'd said "No," Caesar ordered him to be beheaded, because if it should become known, we would value gold like mud.

Encolpius' side-kicks: Trimalchio and Eumolpus

As in a number of comedies, one of the main sources of humour is the sidekick. Encolpius has two of them, and we will finish our examination of the *Satyricon* with a look at them both.

Trimalchio is characterized as a *nouveau-riche* by his profligate waste, as for example with all the spilled wine (which itself may be a satirical version

---

[2] Yes, we know we mentioned this before, but we like the story. Deal with it.

of a corrupted libation), the lavish display of his wealth (e.g. ch. 48), the inept display of his wealth (e.g. ch. 50), his vulgarity (e.g. chs. 50 and 61) and especially his pretension to culture (e.g. chs. 62-64).

Eumolpus is a bad poet – people are always stoning him to shut him up (chs. 99, 101), yet when he's not really trying to impress, he tells the wonderful "widow of Ephesus" tale, which we quoted in Chapter II. This is a type of story called a "Milesian tale" after the city in Asia Minor. These are remarkable stories, sometimes funny, sometimes supernatural, told about anonymous characters (a little in the manner of our "there once was a man from Nantucket…" limericks).[3] Perhaps the most wonderful thing about the story is the gentle parody that it offers on the love story of Dido and Aeneas from Vergil's *Aeneid* book 4 (which the widow's serving-woman appositely but surprisingly – how many maids can quote Shakespeare? – quotes).

Trimalchio, by the way, can also tell a very good story when not trying to impress. His story of the unbreakable glass is a beautiful parody of the invention of writing story from Plato's *Phaedrus*.

When the group moves to Croton, Eumolpus plays a dying rich man in hopes of getting entertained by *captatores* – "legacy hunters." Now he and Encolpius have taken over the roll of Trimalchio in their turn.

Seneca's Apocolocyntosis

While the *Satyricon* was a very important work, it was far from the only case of Roman humour. In earlier chapters we have seen a number of examples from Rome to illustrate Greek types and archetypes, such as the numerous poems by Catullus. In the case of Seneca, we have another Roman poet preparing another very Roman work of satire.

The most important thing about this work is its title, a nonce-word (made up word) in Greek, serving as a title for this Latin text (just as *Satyricon* is a Greek name for a Latin novel). The word is based on the term "apotheosis," which means transformation from a man to a god. In traditional Greco-Roman religion the only person to achieve apotheosis was Heracles/Hercules, but as the Roman empire expanded and came into contact with eastern cults where the gods were regarded as divinities, the emperors got jealous and started to ask the senate to decree that they became gods after their deaths (apparently the senate really was that powerful – or it had no ego problems whatsoever; we will leave it to the reader to decide).

---

[3] Here's another example (from Phlegon of Tralles, *de mirabilis* 1; H. J. Rose, "Antigone and the Bride of Corinth," *CQ* 19 (1925) 147-50: A young bride died and six months later a male guest came to stay at her parents' house. For three nights in a row a girl, whom he thought to be a prostitute visited this guest. The guest made some comment and on the third night the dead girl's mother intruded upon her guest and found that the supposed prostitute was in fact her daughter. The girl reproached her mother for her meddling and departed. The parents rushed to the tomb and upon opening it found not their daughter's body but a ring that the guest had given her.

The first emperor to be treated in this way was Julius Caesar, to whom the senate voted the posthumous title of *Divus Iulius* – Julius the god. This idea is greatly offensive, especially to Greek sensibilities, and in the eastern part of the empire where Greek was the lingua franca, the Latin *divus* was translated as *hemitheos*, "half-god." Now a half god is not at all like a half pint. A half pint is still beer, but a half god is no god at all, but a mortal; he or she is half a god only in the sense that half of his or her parents (i.e. one of them) was divine. Such a person may have special qualities, but immortality, the distinguishing mark of divinity for the Greeks and Romans, will not be among them. These considerations problematised the notion of imperial apotheosis.

Furthermore, Seneca was a philosopher who adhered to the Stoic school, one of the two great schools of thought of this period. The rival Epicureans taught that the gods have withdrawn beyond the flaming walls of the world, leaving us to our fate, indifferent, paring their nails, as Stephen Dedalus would say.[4] The Stoics, however, believed that God had an active concern for His creation, and that we had a duty to serve Him. God, for the Stoics, was not only ethically but also physically perfect, and since the most perfect shape was the sphere (they thought angles were a sort of imperfection – go figure), God must be a sphere. The various "gods" – Zeus/Jupiter, Hera/Juno, et al. – were just projections of certain qualities onto the surface of this sphere as onto a movie-screen so that God could accommodate Himself to our feeble human perceptions (think of Plato's cave here).

Now for the Stoic Seneca, if the emperor could be apotheosized (big "if"), he would have to be transformed into a sphere. Now that's actually not too far off for Claudius, who was pretty round to begin with. Into what sphere would he most plausibly be turned? Maybe a pumpkin (Greek *kolokunte*), which owing to its hollowness, signified an empty head, as Italians say *zucca secca* or French say *Il n'a rien dans la citrouille*. A hollow head for the ancients would mean either one lacking in intelligence or one lacking in sexual vitality (remember our discussion about how to interpret Euelpides knocking the Hoopoe's door with his head in Aristophanes' *Birds*) – either way, a big insult.

These and more are the ideas that Seneca manages to get across with the title of his satire. It is perhaps as much an attack on the idea of apotheosis per se as it is an attack upon Claudius. Nevertheless Claudius comes in for some pretty devastating digs: he breathes his last, for example, not out his mouth, but from the other orifice (ch. 4). He limps (ch. 1), which Seneca expresses to devastating effect by quoting a line from Vergil (*Aeneid* 2.724) about the child Ascanius trying to keep up with his father – in Claudius' case his left foot can't keep up with his right. He also stutters, so that the gods have to call the world-traveller Heracles to see if he can identify him. Finally, he is very stupid, and doesn't know that he is dead until he sees his own funeral in ch. 12 (bringing new meaning to the phrase "he would be late for his own funeral").

---

[4] J. Joyce 1916 *A Portrait of the Artist as a Young Man* (Harmondsworth, 1960) 215.

Beyond that, there's not too much to comment on in the work, besides the parody that it affords of historians (who pedantically cite their sources, promise to be impartial, etc.) of poets (for this work, like Petronius, is written in *prosimetrum*) and of myth: Claudius is condemned to throw dice from a leaky dice-cup, like the Danaids carrying water in their sieve.

We will end this chapter with a late Latin schoolboy joke that hearkens back to the Egyptian paintings showing animals performing human feats, with which we began Chapter IV. This joke takes the form of the last will and testament of one M. Grunnius Corocotta, a pig, as dictated to the butcher before his "execution" in which he plans for the disposition of the various cuts of his meat.[5] The text reads:

> Here begins the piglet's will.
> M. Grunnius Corocotta[6], a piglet, has made his will. Since I was not able to write with my hand, I have dictated it to be written.
> Mageirus[7] the cook said, "Come here, over-turner of the house, digger-up of the floor, runaway little piglet! Today I am going to separate you from Life."
> Corocotta the piglet said, "If I have done anything, if I have sinned in any way, if I have broken a little jar with my feet, I beg you, Mr. Cook; I ask for my life – yield to him who begs to you."
> Mageirus the cook said, "Over here, boy! Bring me from the kitchen the butcher's knife, so I can make this piglet bloody."
> The piglet was caught by the slaves and led on the sixteenth day of Lucernina, when cabbage is plentiful, under the consulship of Tandoor and Peppersauce. When he saw that he was going to die, he asked for the space of an hour, and begged the cook that he might be able to make a will. He called his relations to him, so that he might give something to them from his provisions. He said:
> > To my father, Boar Lardy, I give and bequeath to be given thirty bushels of acorns. To my mother, Veturina Scrofa[8], I give and bequeath to be given forty bushels of Spartan wheat, and to my sister, Quirina[9], whose wedding I will not be able to attend, I give and bequeath to be given thirty

---

[5] See E. Champlin, "The Testament of the Piglet," *Phoenix* 41 (1987) 174-83, who cites further bibliography.

[6] G. Anderson, "The Cognomen of M. Grunnius Corocotta: A *Dissertatiuncula* on Roast Pig," *AJP* 101 (1980) 57-58 explains the name thus: *Grunnius* means "grunter", and *Corocotta* is a (rare) word, meaning "hyena, which also happens to sound like *choiros coctus*, Greek/Latin for "roast pig."

[7] Greek for "butcher."

[8] Scrofa, meaning "breed-sow" actually *was* a real Roman surname! Roman last-names often tended to be insulting; see A. Corbeill, *Controlling Laughter: Political Humor in the Late Roman Republic* (Princeton, 1996) 57-98.

[9] Quirinus/a is the most ancient and August Roman name. It also happens to sound a lot like Greek *choirine*, "piggy"!

bushels of barley. From my entrails I will give and donate to the shoemakers my bristles, to those who quarrel my skull, to the deaf my ears, to the argumentative and talkative my tongue, to the drunkards my intestines, to the mincemeat-makers my thighs, to the women my loins, to the boys my bladder, to the gays my muscles, to the runners and hunters my heels, and to the burglars my hooves. I give to Him Who Must Not Be Named, the chosen cook a cake and pestle that I used to carry with me: may he tie it to his neck from Treveste to Trieste. I want a monument to be made for me, inscribed with golden letters:

M. GRUNNIUS COROCOTTA (A PIGLET)

LIVED FOR 999 ½ YEARS.

IF HE HAD LIVED FOR ½ A YEAR MORE,

HE WOULD HAVE BEEN A THOUSAND.

Those who love me best, consuls of my life, I ask that you do well by my body. Season it well with good condiments: nuts, pepper and honey, that my name may be remembered forever. Masters, nieces and nephews, who are present at my will, order it to be signed.

Lardy signed, Morsel signed, Cabbage signed, Sausage signed, Porkrind signed, little Celsus signed, Wedding-pig signed.

Here ends the piglet's will on the sixteenth of Lucernina, under the blessed consulship of Tandoor and Peppersauce.

Coda: A Funny Thing Happened on the Way to the Longship

Those Zany Barbarians

In our study of Greek and Roman humour so far, there has been a historical trend of conquest and assimilation. First, the Mycaeneans were conquered by the Dorians, who moved in and took over the culture. Then, the Greeks as a whole were conquered by the Romans, who proceeded to copy large parts of the culture wholesale. But, in the fifth century AD, this pattern comes to an abrupt halt. The Roman Empire was conquered by a number of different tribes of Germanic barbarians, and secular Greek and Latin literature in Western Europe seemed to disappear overnight.

But, the fact that this trend isn't continued is rather odd, because the Germans absolutely adored the Roman Empire – they wanted nothing more than to be a part of it, love it, and call it "George." However, the Empire did not have a similar love of them. The Germanic tribes, many of which volunteered to become Roman citizens, were kept at arm's length as *foederati*, or Federated People, relegated to the edge of the Empire on the grounds that if they paid Rome taxes and defended the Empire, Rome would leave them alone. This was not what they signed up for, and discontented customers with lots of weapons are never a good thing.

But who were these Germans, and what did they find to be funny? How was it that the comic works of Greece and Rome passed right over them and into centuries of historical oblivion in the Western World?

Unfortunately, the stories of the fifth century Germans are not recorded – theirs was an oral rather than a written, literary culture. But, there are a number of clues as to who they were, including written accounts in their own words.[1]

The first account of the Germans comes from the great Roman historian Gaius Cornelius Tacitus (c.56-117 AD). Tacitus, a Roman Senator and a primary source for anybody studying emperors such as Claudius and Nero, travelled through the outskirts of the German frontier around 96-98 AD, recording what he saw. While he tells us a great deal, it is important to remember that he did have a slant. Disgusted at what he viewed as the moral degradation of Rome, he held the Germans up as morally pure, even though they were pesky barbarians who didn't even know how to live in cities (*Germ.* 16a):

> It is well-known that no cities are inhabited by the tribes of the Germans, nor even do they allow their dwelling-places to be joined together. They dwell separate and scattered, as a fountain, a field, or a woodland pleases them. They situate their villages, not in our manner, with connected and well-ordered buildings. Each person surrounds his own house with space, whether as a precaution against the threat of fire, or through ignorance of how to build.

But, while Tacitus wrote with an agenda, he also told us a great deal

---

[1] And this is not a contradiction. Seriously. We'll bet you $20 it isn't.

about the Germanic tribes, particularly in terms of their code of law, which at first may seem to be similar to the Roman system, but has some interesting features of its own (*Germ.* 12):

> It is allowed in the assembly to make an accusation, and even to propose capital punishment. There is a difference of penalties according to the crime. Traitors and runaways they hang from trees. Cowards, deserters, and those infamous in [the treatment of] their body they drown in mud and bogs with wickerwork holding them down. The difference between executions stems from this, that crimes ought to be shown as they are punished, shameful things concealed. But for lighter crimes also [there is] punishment in due measure. Those convicted are fined a number of horses and sheep. Part of the fine is paid out to the king or state, part to him who laid claim to it, or to his relations. In these same assemblies princes are also chosen, who give laws throughout the towns and villages. Each one has a hundred companions from the ordinary people as his council and [guarantee of] authority.

It is in the fines that we start to see a very different picture. While Tacitus recorded that the king received half, the other half went to the family of the victim, which starts to separate the culture of the Germans from the society-oriented Greeks and Romans. To make matters more interesting, murder is not a capital crime (*Germ.* 21a):

> It is necessary to take over both the enmities and the friendships either of one's father or of one's relatives. But they do not carry on unresolved. Indeed, even murder is absolved by a certain number of cattle and sheep, and the whole household receives satisfaction, the more usefully for the public good, because enmities are more dangerous [when they are] joined with freedom.

All things considered, the picture that Tacitus paints is not of a culture where the society comes first, but instead one where the individual does. The crime of murder being considered a matter between families rather than for the state is a clear indicator of this. However, there is even more evidence to support the view of the Germans as being oriented around the individual rather than the society – we have their law codes in their own words.

As we mentioned above, the Germans loved the Roman Empire. So, when they conquered the Western Roman Empire and established the various barbarian kingdoms, they kept the Roman civil service intact. And, while the Germans themselves had an oral culture, the Roman bureaucracy was, like all bureaucracies, dedicated to generating paperwork. Since one of the roles of the Latin civil service was to aid in the interpretation of the law (particularly important, since everybody was considered to carry their own law around with them, and SOMEBODY needed to keep track of it all), the Germanic law codes were written down, leaving us with a written record of the legal system of the Germanic tribes in their own words. Where Tacitus implied that the Germans had culture that placed the individual over society, the law codes state it beyond a shadow of a doubt.

The most famous of these law codes is Salic Law, the laws of the Salian

Franks,[2] recorded around the year 500. In Salic Law, every individual had a monetary value, and if a crime was committed against that individual, a fine, known as a *wergeld* (literally "man-price"), would be levied. This fine varied between a dizzying array of circumstances, depending on the status of the victim, whether a pregnancy was involved, if a pregnancy had occurred earlier in life, and even the nature of the offence (which could be anything from name calling to out-and-out murder). For example, the Salic Law states:

> If any one shall have killed a free Frank, or a barbarian living under the Salic law, and it have been proved on him, he shall be sentenced to 8000 denars.
> (Henderson, trans.)

What is particularly telling is what is to happen with the wergeld once it is paid. Unlike Tacitus, who states that the state gains a share of the money, Salic Law is very clear that it all goes to the family:

> If any one's father have been killed, the sons shall have half the compounding money (wergeld); and the other half the nearest relatives, as well on the mother's as on the father's side, shall divide among themselves.
> (Henderson, trans.)

While these codes of law may not seem funny (okay, some of the Salic Law is funny – but it's not meant to be), they tell us a great deal about what the sense of humour of the Germans was. As we have seen in the previous chapters, Greek and Roman humour was based on character, or more specifically, people acting in ways that go against the norms of society. Laughter is, to the Greeks and Romans, a corrective. This is perfectly reasonable in a culture where the society is all-important. However, the Germans did not have such a society, suggesting that the humour is very unlikely to be character based. Instead, it is more likely to be situational.

But how can we confirm this? We can reconstruct the humour of the barbarians, in part because while the fifth century Germans themselves were an oral culture, their descendants were not, and did write some of the stories down centuries later. The trick is to find the right branch of Western literature to look at. The keys to our search lie in Old English and Old Icelandic literature,[3] in particular two epics – *Beowulf*, probably committed to parchment in the form we have now around the 11th century, and the

---

[2] Of whom the most famous descendent would be Charlemagne, but since he doesn't actually contribute anything to humour, this entire footnote is nothing more than name dropping to show off how smart one of the authors is.

[3] Which is itself unique, as in Iceland there was a literary society where farmers wrote for an audience of farmers, giving a unique vision of what it was like to be an ordinary person in the Viking Age. For more information, see Robert Kellogg's introduction to *The Sagas of Icelanders* (London, 2000) xxxviii-xliii.

Völsunga Saga, written between 1200-1270.[4]

We begin with *Beowulf* because of the action of the poem or, more to the point, because we can date the action of the poem. One of the characters, Beowulf's uncle Higelāc, is a historical figure who is recorded by Gregory of Tours to have died in 525 AD.[5] This places the action of the poem within 50 years of the fall of the Roman Empire in 476 AD.

The story of *Beowulf* is a very old and famous one. King Hrothgar of the Spear-Danes has a problem – this large, angry monster named Grendel comes into his hall of Heorot every night and eats everybody there, no doubt raising insurance prices along the way. Beowulf the Geat comes into Heorot, wrestles Grendel, rips the monster's arm off, and then goes on to kill Grendel's mother, return home to Geatland, become the king, and die while fighting a dragon.

What is very important about the action of *Beowulf* is a story that is told by a storyteller after Beowulf kills Grendel about a dragonslayer named Sigemund the Wælsing, who has a nephew named Fitela (lines 874-897). The fact that it is a story within a story suggests that it is a well-known one to the cultural milieu in which *Beowulf* appears. What is even more telling is that the same characters appear in the Völsunga Saga as Sigmundr and Sinfjotli the Völsungs. The discrepancy between the two stories is that it is Sigmundr's son, Sigurðr,[6] who kills the dragon Fafnir, suggesting that the story has evolved over the centuries. However, it is a common story shared between the two cultures, with a setting and date of action in Europe just after the fall of the Roman Empire. And thus, we can turn to Iceland and Anglo-Saxon England for our reconstruction of barbarian humour.

Wordplay and Stupidity

One of the first things that comes to mind when examining the literature of the Anglo-Saxons and the Norse is the comical use of wordplay, in particular, **understatement**.[7] Understatement can be used in a number of different ways, but the greater the understatement, the more comical it

---

[4] For more information about this, see J. Byock's introduction to his translation of *The Saga of the Volsungs* (Berkeley, Los Angeles and London, 1990).

[5] There is some debate as to the actual date. We are using George Clark's assessment. See G. Clark, *Beowulf* (Boston, 1990) 44.

[6] Contrary to popular transcription, the letter ð is not a "d," but instead a "th" sound.

[7] Puns and the more linguistic types of humour that appear in Old Icelandic and Old English we have disqualified from our reconstruction, on the grounds that there is enough of a possibility that the language has changed between the Gothic of the Barbarian Kingdoms and the Icelandic and English of the Norse and Anglo-Saxons that what works in the newer languages may not have worked in the older ones.

becomes, and the Anglo-Saxons and Norse were not afraid to understate matters dramatically. Our first example is heroic understatement from *Beowulf* as Beowulf is describing his struggle with Grendel to Higelāc (line 2137):

> For a while there was between us a sharing of hands;

Beowulf's comment suggests a friendly handshake, but most friendly handshakes don't involve a gory dismemberment where the other guy's arm is ripped off at the shoulder. Part of what makes this line work as humour is that the reader, who has already read about how Grendel died, knows that this is a gross understatement, even if Higelāc doesn't quite yet.

Humorous understatement was often used in the narrative of Icelandic sagas, describing an object or situation in terms of not being the exact opposite object or situation. For example, Snorri Sturluson's *Edda* contains a story in a section called *Gylfaginning* (literally "The Tricking of Gylfi") where Thor and his entourage are travelling through Jotunheim, the land of the giants. As night falls, they seek shelter in what appears to be a barn, but with strange chambers inside. When the morning arrives, Thor discovers to his horror not only that he has been sleeping in a glove, but that the owner has come to claim it:

> When the day came, Thor went outside and saw where a man lay not far from him in the forest, and he was not little.

Not only is there a disparity between the statement and the reality, it is a gigantic one – a massive giant with hands as big as a barn is described as not being small. It's very much like saying that a hundred-foot tall tree is no twig.

With description routinely made comical by reference in a way that is ridiculous, it is not surprising that a side-note of this sort of wordplay is the quaint saying, as found in the 11th century *Durham Proverbs*, some of which are comical because they turn from the ordinary to the ridiculous. Just to list a couple (proverbs 44 and 45, respectively):

> "Far and wide things are not well, said he who heard screaming in hell."

> "Belong to him who might call for you, said he who saw hunger leave town."

With such a sardonic sense of humour, it is hardly a surprise that while the Greeks and Romans tended to find stupidity by itself pathetic rather than funny, the Germans appear to have found it hilarious. In fact, a survey of Anglo-Saxon and Old Icelandic literature even reveals that there are sub-classes of stupidity, all used to comic effect.

If, for example, you wanted to make a joke that played on stupidity, you could pretend to be stupid when you are not by asking a stupid question. This is **feigned stupidity**, and our first example is from *Beowulf*, where Higelāc greets Beowulf upon his return home from fighting Grendel in the land of the Spear-Danes and asks (lines 1987-1990):

> What befell you in your journey, beloved Beowulf,
> when you suddenly resolved to seek battle
> far over the salt water,
> to fight at Heorot?

Higelāc is anything but a fool, and yet he still asks about an obvious outcome. If Beowulf had fared badly, he would have been eaten by Grendel, and not been there to answer the question. It is similar to being caught in a terrible thunderstorm, coming home, getting inside, being able to hear the crashing thunder outside and the rain hammering at the windows, and promptly being asked if it's raining outside. Higelāc knows better, and he is making a joke, playing on the idea of a stupid question to do it.

One does not need to feign stupidity merely through asking a question. You can, if you want, make a suggestion and word it in a way that sounds very stupid. Such an example appears in *Egil's Saga* in chapter 46, where Egil Skallagrimson, who with his men has just escaped from a farming community with his life while the entire village is feasting in the local mead hall, celebrating that they're going to be torturing some Vikings to death in the morning, manages to find the treasure room and take all of the community's valuables with him. They reach the treeline, safe from the villagers, and then Egil turns to his men and says:

> This raid is very bad and not honourable. We have stolen the farmer's wealth such that he does not know about it. Such shame will never befall us; let's go back to the villagers and let them know what has happened.

Egil's men have a completely logical reaction to this idea – sheer and utter horror. However, they are unable to stop him from turning around and sprinting towards the hall. Egil's way of telling the farmers about this deed is to burn down the hall with everybody inside[8] – his actions are therefore calculated, and not stupid, even though the way he suggests it sounds like he's about to earn a Darwin Award.

But, while feigned stupidity is funny, there are plenty of cases of **honest stupidity**. Sometimes, people do or say things that are just plain dumb – and it's funny.

Our first example is from *Njál's Saga*, chapter 77, where one of the characters, Gunnar, is about to be murdered in his home by a group of men led by Gizur. Gizur and his men surround Gunnar's home, but they have a problem – they don't know if Gunnar is actually home. So, they send a man named Thorgrím to climb onto the roof and take a look:

> Gunnar saw a red tunic through the window and thrust out with his spear into his middle. Thorgrím's feet slipped and he lost his shield, and he fell from the

---

[8] Egil is what we would know today as a "homicidal maniac." But we love him anyway.

roof. Then he went to Gizur and the group, where they were sitting on the field. Gizur looked at him and said, 'Is Gunnar home?'

Thorgrím replied, 'Find that out yourself, all I've learned is that his spear is home.' Then he fell down dead.

Gizur's question is honestly quite stupid. More to the point, there is very little evidence that he is trying to be funny, if for no other reason than if he is trying to be cute, it is at exactly the wrong time, and therefore it remains a stupid thing to say. Thorgrím's answer, while trite, serves a humorous purpose of its own – it sticks it back to Gizur, a type of humour that we will discuss in detail below.

Honest stupidity also exists outside of dialogue. One of the more interesting examples comes from *Völsunga Saga*, chapter 20, right after the hero Sigurðr has eaten the heart of the dragon Fafnir, thus gaining the dragon's wisdom.[9] Immediately after, he sets out to find the beautiful warrior maiden Brynhild. When he finds her, here is how he identifies her:

> Sigurðr went within the rampart and saw that there slept a man, dressed in full armour. He first took the helmet off of the man's head and saw that it was a woman. She was in a coat of mail, and it was so tight it was as though it had grown into her flesh.

So, rather than notice the two breasts attached to her chest, or the shapely figure visible through the skin-tight armour, the dragon-heart-enhanced Sigurðr checks to see if she has a beard. At least this is an isolated incident, and Sigurðr is actually quite intelligent through most of the saga.

But identifying a woman via checking for beards is far from the strangest moment of stupidity that appears in the Icelandic Sagas. The *Saga of the People of Vatnsdal* has a moment in chapter 33 with a character named Berg the Bold, who manages a show of strangeness that would put any Greek or Roman quack to shame:

> One had a cloak over him and a long gown of good cloth; they watched what this man did; he drew his sword and sliced off the bottom, which had become dirty while riding, and cast it away – it was the width of a hand – and speaking such that they could hear, he declared that he had no wish to drag it behind him soiled.

When the other characters see and hear about this, they consider him a show off, a fool, or very arrogant. However, this is an isolated incident – when at the end of the section his identity is revealed, he has lost his momentary quackiness (he does not, however, lose his arrogance).

Victimization

If you are faced with stupidity, or somebody who is just not so clever as

---

[9] At least, that's what the birds say, and everybody knows you can trust them, right?

you are, the funny thing to do is to find a way to stick it to them. When it comes to our reconstructed culture of the fifth century, this is an entire genre of humour, that we call **victimization**.

The easiest way to victimize somebody is to do something clever, or beat them to something, and then brag about it. For an example of this, we turn not to literature, but to archaeology, in particular, to the Maeshowe barrow in the Orkneys. To understand why the Vikings were in the barrow in the first place, you need to understand that unlike our society, where social status is based on the acquisition of wealth, social status in the time of the early Germans, the Viking Age, and to a degree the centuries after in the Scandinavian world, was based on how much you could give away. Gifts were part of the social bonds of society, and any gift given had an obligation attached to it.[10]

As a result, the whole of this northern society required a constant influx of treasure, and a popular way for people to go out and make a name for themselves, as well as get gifts to give away, was to go on a Viking expedition. On these expeditions, the Vikings would raid monasteries,[11] villages, engage in trading, and break into burial mounds, also known as barrows, and take everything that wasn't nailed to the ground, and a few things that were. The neolithic barrow at Maeshowe appears to have been a frequent stop for 12th century Norse crews, at least according to all the graffiti they left.[12] The roughly 30 pieces of graffiti range from the very crass – "Thorny fucked. Helgi carved" – to outright boasting – "Only Hókon carried treasure out of this mound."[13] It's the boasting that interests us, as Hókon's inscription may very well be a response to another inscription: "That will be true, which I say, that treasure was brought away. For three nights treasure was brought away, before they broke this mound." Either way, between the two of them they well and truly stick it to anybody coming into the barrow: he got there first, he got all the treasure, and every Viking broke in after him is screwed.

While bragging about getting there first may have been the easiest way to victimize somebody, it was far from the most common. The **practical joke** was alive and well in the Germanic world, even in mythology. Our first example is from a story of the gods, also known as the Æsir, from the

---

[10] For more information, see J.M. Hill's *The Cultural World of Beowulf* (Toronto, Buffalo and London, 1995) 86-87.

[11] After all, what's a monk going to do? Pray at you?

[12] M.P. Barnes, *The Runic Inscriptions of Maeshowe, Orkney* (Uppsala, 1994) 39-42. There has been a lot of debate about when exactly the barrow was broken into, but the runic carvings suggest that it happened sometime between 1100 and 1200. For a more detailed examination of this date, and the scholarship around dating the Maeshowe runes, see Barnes, chapter 2.

[13] For a full list of the graffiti, along with translations and commentary on each line, see Barnes, 61-219.

Gylfaginning in Snorri's *Edda*. The gods are very concerned about a child of Loki known as the Fenriswolf, which has been prophesied to one day kill the god Oðin. This is a concern to the gods, so they decide to trap the wolf, telling it that if it can break the fetter they make, it will be a matter of great glory for the wolf. The Fenriswolf falls for it once, breaking the fetter. Then the gods make another fetter, and the Fenriswolf tries a second time. But, by the third time, the wolf has started to wisen up, and demands that one of the gods gives a token of safe conduct by putting his hand in the wolf's mouth:

> But every Æsir looked at each other and now their minds were troubled, and no one wished to put their hand forward, before Tyr put forward his right hand and placed it in the wolf's mouth. And when the wolf kicked off, then the band hardened, and the harder it was that he struggled, the tighter was the band. Then all laughed except Tyr. He lost his hand.

The gods are laughing because they have just tricked the Fenriswolf, and thereby victimized him. However, Tyr is not laughing, in part because having your hand bitten off by a big pissed-off wolf at least calls for a bit of aspirin, but also because while the Æsir have stuck it to the Fenriswolf, the Fenriswolf (and to a degree, the gods through the wolf) has stuck it to Tyr. Tyr has become part of the practical joke, and is therefore one of the victims being laughed at.

If the Norse were anything, they were heavy drinkers, and alcohol was as good a tool for a practical joke as anything. For an example of alcohol-based humour, we will turn to *Egil's Saga*, chapter 44, at a point in which Egil is serving with Olvir and his men, and the Vikings find themselves at the home of a man named Bard, who is a servant of King Eirik. Needing rest and hospitality, they accept shelter from Bard, who tells them that there is no decent drink available, and instead fills them up on bread, butter, and curds. Shortly after the meal is over, King Eirik and his entourage arrive, and a party begins, wherein Bard brings out all the ale and mead that he told Olvir he didn't have. Olvir's Vikings are invited in, and the practical joke begins, leading to one of the great vomit scenes in Icelandic literature:

> Then they were brought ale to drink. There were many toasts drunk and the horn had be drunk off in each toast. But as the evening dragged on many of the companions of Olvir became incapacitated; some vomited there in the room, while some made it out of the door. Then Bard kept going to bring them drinks.

This is the beginning of a lengthy and detailed vomit scene that ends in violence and the death of Bard. After all, in a practical joke involving alcohol, the homicidal maniac with the sword gets the last laugh.

Perhaps the perfect example of both victimization and stupidity is the *Þrymskviða*,[14] or Thrym's Poem, found in the *Poetic Edda*. Almost everybody involved either shows a moment of comic stupidity, or gets it stuck to them somehow by somebody, or both:

---

[14] The character Þ is a "th" sound named "thorn."

Angry was Thor when he awoke
and missed his hammer;
his beard shook, his hair tossed,
the son of Earth groped around.

And these were the first words that he spoke:
'Hear now Loki, what I now say,
what nobody knows anywhere on earth
or in heaven: the Æsir's hammer is stolen!'

They went to the beautiful dwelling of Freyja[15]
and these were the first words that he spoke:
'Will you lend me, Freyja, the feather coat,
so I might find my hammer?'

Freyja said:
'I'd give it to you, even if it were made of gold,
I'd grant it to you, even if it were made of silver.'

Then Loki flew – the feather coat resounded –
until he came out of Asgarð,[16]
and he came into the home of the giants.

Thrym sat on a mound, the lord of the ogres,
plaiting golden collars for his dogs
and was trimming the manes of his horses.

Thrym said:
'What's with the Æsir, what's with the elves?
Why have you come into the land of the giants?'

Loki said:
'Bad news among the Æsir, bad news among the elves;
have you hidden Thor's hammer?'

Thrym said:
'I have hidden Thor's hammer
eight leagues under the earth,
no man will ever get it back again,
unless I am sent Freyja as a wife.'

Then Loki flew – the feather cloak resounded –
until he came out of the land of the giants
and he came into Asgarð;
Thor met him in the middle of the grounds,
and these were the first words that he spoke:

---

[15] Think the Norse version of Aphrodite, but with a bigger sexual appetite.

[16] The home of the gods, where Oðin holds his court, and a very nice herring restaurant can be found at Main and Third.

'Have your labours been rewarded?
Declare all your news in the air:
tales often fail the sitting man
and the man lying deals in falsehoods.'

Loki said:
'I had difficulty and success:
Thrym has your hammer, the lord of the ogres;
no man will ever get it back again
unless he's sent Freyja as a wife.'

Then they went to find the beautiful Freyja,
and these were the first words which Thor spoke:
'Dress yourself, Freyja, in a bride's head-dress.
The two of us shall drive to the land of the giants.'

Then Freyja was angry and snorted,
all the hall of the Æsir trembled from the shock,[17]
the great necklace of the Brisings[18] fell asunder –
'I'll be known to be the most man-crazy woman,
if I drive with you to the land of the giants.'

At once all the Æsir came to the Assembly,
and all the goddesses came to the discussion,
and the powerful gods debated,
how Thor should recover his hammer.

Then Heimdall said, the whitest of the Æsir –
he can see into the future, as can the Vanir:[19]
'Thor should be put into a bridal head-dress,
have him wear the great necklace of the Brisings.

'Let keys jingle about him
and let women's skirts fall down to his knees,
on his breast spread out jewels,
and neatly put a head-dress on his head.'

Then said Thor, the strong Æsir:
'The Æsir will call me a womanish coward,
if I let you put me in a bridal head-dress.'

Then said Loki, son of Laufey:
'Be silent, Thor, with those words;
The giants will soon be settling in Asgarð

---

[17] The Norse gods did nothing small.

[18] A mythological necklace that Freyja wears that eventually ends up in
the hands of somebody from *Beowulf*. How this happens is unclear.

[19] Rival gods to the Æsir, who among other things can see into the
future. They make a really good casserole, too.

unless you recover your hammer.'

Then they dressed Thor in a bridal head-dress
and in the great necklace of the Brisings,
they let keys jingle about him
and women's skirts fall down to his knees,
on his breast jewels were spread out,
and a head-dress put neatly on his head.

Then said Loki, son of Laufey:
'I will go with you to be your handmaid,
we two will drive to the land of the giants.'

At once the goats were driven home,[20]
hurried into the harness, they would run well.
The mountains broke, fire burned from the earth,
Oðin's son was driving to the land of the giants.

Then said Thrym, lord of ogres:
'Stand up, giants! And strew the benches[21]
now that Freyja is being sent to me as a wife,
Njarð's daughter from Noatun!

'Golden horned cows wander here in the grounds,
all-black oxen that would delight a giant;
I have a great number of treasures, a great number of jewels,
I think I only lacked Freyja.'

They came there early in the evening,
and ale was put on the table before the giants;
Thor ate an ox, eight salmon,
all the dainties meant for the women,
the husband of Sif[22] drank six casks of mead.

Then said Thrym, lord of ogres,
'Where have you seen a bride eating more keenly?
I have not seen any woman take bigger bites,
nor any maiden drink more mead.'[23]

The very wise handmaid sat before him,
she found an answer to the giant's speech,

---

[20] Thor's chariot is powered by goats. We think it's because they're less
picky about what they eat than horses.

[21] Part of getting ready for a party – skins and cushions are strewn on the
benches so that people can sit comfortably.

[22] Thor's wife – part of the comedy here is that Thor is already married as
this happens.

[23] Arguably, at this point, Thor needs it.

Freyja ate nothing at all for eight nights,
so madly eager was she for the land of the giants.'

He bent under the head-dress, wishing to kiss her,
but instead he sprang back along the whole length of the hall:
'Why are Freyja's eyes so terrible?
I think fire burns from them.'[24]

The very wise handmaid sat before him,
she found an answer to the giant's speech:
'Freyja did not sleep at all for eight nights,
so madly eager was she for the land of the giants.'[25]

In came the hateful giantess,
she dared to ask for Thor's bridal gifts:
'You, give the red rings from your hands,
if you want to win my love,
my love, all my favour.'

Then said Thrym, lord of ogres:
'Bring in the hammer to hallow the bride,
lay Mjollnir[26] on the maiden's knee,[27]
consecrate us together by the hand of Var[28]!'

Thor's heart laughed in his chest,
when the one stern of heart recognized the hammer.
First he struck Thrym, lord of ogres,
and smote all the race of giants.

He struck the old giantess,
she who had asked for the bridal gifts;
she got a blow instead of money,
and a hammer stroke instead of many rings.

---

[24] Apparently, Thrym does not find the revelation that Freyja has a thick beard to be disturbing. We find this very disturbing. (Cf. Chaucer's *The Miller's Tale* 550-54, where in the dark Absolon kisses the wrong – the hairy – end of his girlfriend, and is surprised to find that she has a beard.)

[25] The fact that Thyrm accepts this excuse twice suggests, among other things, that he can't count. There's no indication that more than a day or two has passed since he stole the hammer in the first place.

[26] The name of Thor's hammer. Come to think about it, the Norse named just about everything.

[27] Because, obviously, any girl would be thrilled to have a big-assed heavy hammer put in her lap as a wedding present.

[28] A discouraged goddess who keeps track of promises men and women make each other.

Thus Oðin's son got the hammer back again.

The poem almost speaks entirely for itself. You have multiple moments of stupidity, first from Thor for having his hammer stolen in the first place, and then from Thrym, who manages to lose all of his intelligence when confronted with Thor dressed as Freyja. There's victimization, first of Thor by Thrym, then of Freyja by Thor (albeit not a successful one), then of Thor by the rest of the gods when he has to cross-dress, then of Thrym by Loki, and then of the giants by Thor. The last lines even contain a semblance of understatement, describing what the old sister of Thrym got instead of wedding gifts.

But, while people are victimized in the sagas, this does not mean that you couldn't use a joke to victimize the person hearing it. For an example of this, we turn to Anglo-Saxon England, although this time not to *Beowulf*. Instead, we turn to an ecclesiastical source, the *Exeter Riddles*, written down by monks in the 11th century. There are over ninety riddles, many of which are very sexually graphic and ribald, and have both a sexual and non-sexual solution, of which the correct answer is considered to be the non-sexual one. Riddle number 44 reads:

> Wondrous it hangs by a man's thigh
> beneath the husband's clothing: a hole is in front.
> It is stiff and hard; it has a good firmness.
> When the man[29] lifts his own vestment
> over the knee, he wishes to greet
> with the head of his hanging object that intimate hole
> that he, equally long, had often filled up before.

The riddle works on a number of different levels. The graphic description builds up an expectation of a sexual answer, but while the listener may answer penis, the actual solution is "a key," thus deflating expectation. But, there is more to it than that. It's important to remember that the teller of the riddle is a monk, while the listener may be a monk or lay person. By telling the riddle and misleading the listener, the teller has led the listener into sin, and by doing so played a practical joke on them, as well as asserted moral superiority.[30] This makes the listener part of the joke – the monk, double

---

[29] The Old English word here is *esne*, which can mean a labourer, slave, servant, retainer, youth, or man (Clark-Hall, 107) – and each different meaning modifies the riddle slightly. Translating riddles into a language that has double-entendres is difficult when the original is in a language with triple-, quadruple-, and quintuple-entendres.

[30] After all, HE knew it was a key – the listener is the dumb twit who couldn't keep his mind out of the gutter.

entendre fully intended, has stuck it to the listener.[31]

The humour of the Germans who conquered the Roman Empire and their descendants was situational, rather than character based. Part of this was due to the fact that the society of the Germans simply didn't operate in a way that would make character-based humour funny. And so, while the Church preserved the Christian heritage of the Roman Empire, the secular literature, and humour, was left to the east, where the Empire did not fall.

But, in the 12th century, contact between the Christians and Muslims in Spain, particularly in Cordova, resulted in an influx of classical works back into the west. This was known as the Twelfth Century Renaissance, and it is during this period that Europe regained its classical heritage. It was also in this period that countries like England and France began to become nations, and a balance was struck between the importance of the individual and the importance of society. When Boccaccio and Chaucer wrote their respective *Decameron* and *Canterbury Tales*, for their humorous episodes they drew not only on the situational humour of the early Germans, but also on the multitude of quacks, ironists, suckers, and other comic characters that would be all too familiar to the ancient Greek or Roman. It had taken around 700 years, but classical humour had come home.

---

[31] There is some argument that this may have been a way of expressing homoerotic desire without getting in trouble with the abbot. This is stretching it, though. Among other things, it requires the abbot to be a moron. For more on this, see D.K. Smith's "Humour in Hiding: Laughter Between the Sheets in the Exeter Book Riddles," 79-98 in J. Wilcox ed., *Humour in Anglo-Saxon Literature* (Cambridge, 2000).

Conclusion – By R. Drew Griffith

The only real category of humour I have noticed that we have that the ancients seemed to lack – though the Germanic tribes made up for this! – is that of laughing at someone simply because they are dumb. All of the stock characters we have considered in this book are cunning in some way, even if their various obsessions lead them to do stupid things. The cult of stupidity for its own sake (what one might call the Forrest Gump syndrome) seems to be a modern invention.

All of the kinds of character that we have looked at have their own types of speech, which suffer a bit in translation: the poseur or quack has his fluent nonsense (*phlyaria*), the ironist his mockery (*chleuasmos*), the parasite or flatterer his wheedling-words (*thruptesthai*) and the clowns their invective (*psogos*). There are other kinds of potentially comic speech as well, the blustering (*paphlasma*) of demagogues and other bullies, the gossip (*huthlos*) of, well, gossips and the endless prattle (*lalia*) of chatterboxes.

I want to end this book by talking about three aspects of ancient humour that survive into the modern day. The first is within theatre. The great Greek comic character types made their way into Rome in the Atellan farces with their stock characters (recognizable by masks and gestures; one was called Dossenus, the hunchback, which suggests a certain kind of gestural language). These Atellan figures eventually morphed into the Italian *Commedia dell'Arte* whose fixed masks included such quacks as Pantalone, the miser, Dottor Graziano, the *mendicus medicus* or sham-doctor and Capitano Scaramuccia, the vainglorious soldier. The good-guys (read ironists) were the lovers Pedrolino (French Pierrot Lunaire) and Colombina. The clowns were Harlequin with his piebald pants, Pulchinello the humpback (direct descendant, perhaps, of Dossenus) and Rosaura his wife. The parasites were the servants, who were always called Gianni ("John"), just as our archetypal chauffeur is always called "James," except that in the Veneto dialect Gianni is Zanni. Pulchinello becomes our English Punch, Rosaura is Judy and Capitano Scaramuccia the cop who tries in vain to keep Punch in line: so too the antics of the Zanni survive in English in our word "zany." This is a pretty impoverished survival, but there it is nonetheless.

Secondly, I want to mention four laughter words from Greek that we still use today: *hilarity*, which originally comes from the idea that when you prayed to the gods, you not only wanted to get their attention, but you wanted to assure that they would be in a good mood. You waited when a god came to see whether or not he or she was smiling – if so, it was okay; s/he was "propitious" or "well disposed" toward you (in Greek *hilaros*). Another word is *sarcasm*, from the Greek for tearing the flesh like a dog, said of witty comments that really hurt. Then again there is *sardonic* describing the bitter smile of Odysseus in *Odyssey* 20.302, which allegedly gets its name from a poisonous Sardinian plant, and the folk-belief that those who have the misfortune to eat this herb die grimacing. Finally there is the word *hysteria*, which originally describes the condition in women caused when the womb (*hystera* – literally the hind-parts), craving moisture, wander through the body displacing other internal organs including the diaphragm (what the Greeks thought of as the "brain") and so producing mental derangement. Greek seems never to have associated this word – as we do – with laughter or with males, even though the laughter of Penelope's suitors at Theoclymenus' prophecy is actually a perfect example.

The last thing I want to talk about are the two laughter-festivals that we celebrate, both of which have ancient antecedents. Easter is inextricably linked to Passover, which, though it is linked to the vernal equinox, is timed by the lunar calendar and so changes every year as a "moveable feast." Forty days before Easter Christians traditionally begin a fast, foregoing certain foods, notably meat. So the day before the fast begins they hold a great feast and eat as much meat and fat as possible. This is the French *Mardi gras* ("Fat Tuesday") and it tells you something about Anglophone culture that our counterpart to that glorious celebration is having pancakes for breakfast. Anyway on Shrove Tuesday, or *Mardi gras* one takes away the meat, in Latin *carnem levare* or more simply says "Bye-bye, meat" *carne, vale*. This is the occasion for carnival, in which in a temporarily topsy-turvy world a beggar is crowned king and entertained at public expense for a day, before being kicked out – a survival of the ancient scapegoat rituals. April first, of course, is a fixed not a moveable feast, yet it usually comes at or around the end of the lenten fast and allows all the bottled up energy to be released in various high jinx. It is perhaps a survival of the ancient Hilaria festival, which was the end of the Megalensia (actually celebrated beginning 25 March) to mark the resurrection of the eastern god Attis, not so different in some ways from the point of Easter. This is the feast that seems to have been the inspiration for the "god of Laughter" episode in Apuleius' *Metamorphoses*.

As I look back over this book, I am struck by how many of the things that we find funny today were laughed at in antiquity. I hope that you will go away from this book having learned a little about the ancient world, but more about the processes of humour in our own lives. And if you have learned anything about antiquity, I hope it is that the Greeks and Romans didn't take themselves too seriously, in spite of what the stodgy label "Classics" might suggest.

Afterword – By Robert B. Marks

Speaking as a writer, it's not often that you get to work on a project like this. In this case, I feel especially honoured – my academic work has been in Medieval Studies and English Literature for the most part, with an occasional touch of the Classical. To be able to work on a textbook about ancient humour, well, it has been a joy and a privilege.

My own involvement in this has been mainly editorial. Some of the comments and clarifications are mine, but for the most part, it's all been the work of R. Drew Griffith. While I helped bring the text into focus and add a few touches of my own, it is his expertise, work, and research that made it possible.

And, just to finish up on the right note, credit where it is due. A special thanks to the Classics department of Queen's University for supporting the project, as well as to the many friends and peers, both of Professor Griffith and myself, who have looked at the text and offered comments to help make it better. In particular, thanks to Professor George Clark, Dept. of English, Queen's University, for taking a look at the Coda, and a thanks to Professor Andrew George, School of African and Oriental Studies, University of London, for pointing us in the right direction for Babylonian humour. And, also a special thanks to the ancient humour class of January to April 2006 and 2007, on whom several of the drafts of this textbook was inflicted - er - tested.

A Note on Translations and Illustrations

All Greek, Latin, Hebrew, and Egyptian passages were translated by R. Drew Griffith. All Old English and Old Icelandic passages were translated by Robert B. Marks. Any errors in translation or visual representation are therefore our own.

All Akkadian/Babylonian translations are taken from *The Babylonian Gilgamesh Epic*, edited by Professor Andrew George, and are used with permission. Any errors in translation in this case are his own damn problem.

Anybody pointing out these errors will be hunted down and... thanked. Yes. That's it. Thanked.

Works Cited

Abel, D. H. 1943. "Genealogies of Ethical Concepts from Hesiod to Bacchylides," *TAPA* 74: 92-101.

Amory, F. 1981-82. "Eiron and Eironeia," *CQ* 33:49-80.

Arrowsmith, W., R. Lattimore and D. Parker. 1964. *Four Plays by Aristophanes*. New York.

Austin, R. G. 1964. *P. Vergili Maronis Aeneidos Liber Secundus*. Oxford.

Barnes, M. P. 1994. *The Runic Inscriptions of Maeshowe, Orkney*. Uppsala.

Barth, F. 1966. *Models of Social Organization* = *Royal Anthropological Institute Occasional Paper* 23. Glasgow.

Baudelaire, C. 1855. "De l'essence du rire," 975-93 in Y. G. le Dantec, Pléiade edition. Paris, 1961.

Bayerschmidt, C.F. and Hollander, L.M., trans. 1998. *Njal's Saga*. Hertfordshire.

Bergson, H. 1900. *Laughter: An Essay on the Meaning of the Comic*, C. Brereton and F. Rothwell trans. New York, 1911.

Bergson, L. 1971. "Eiron und Eironeia," *Hermes* 99: 409-22.

Bond, G. W. 1952. "Archilochus and the Lycambides: A New Literary Fragment," *Hermathena* 80: 3-11.

Branham, R. B. 1994. "Defacing the Currency: Diogenes' Rhetoric and the Invention of Cynicism," *Arethusa* 27: 329-59.

Bremmer, J. 1983. "Scapegoat Rituals in Ancient Greece," *HSCP* 87: 299-30.

– 1997. "Jokes, Jokers and Jokebooks in Ancient Greek Culture," 11-28 in J. Bremmer and H. Roodenburg eds., *A Cultural History of Humour*. Cambridge.

– 1999. "Fosterage, Kinship and Circulation of Children in Ancient Greece," *Dialogos: Hellenic Studies Review* 6: 1-20.

Brown, C. G. 1989. "Ares, Aphrodite and the Laughter of the Gods," *Phoenix* 43: 283-93.

– 1991. "Stepsiades' Wife: Aristophanes, *Clouds* 41ff," *Prometheus* 17: 29-33.

Brown, P. G. McC. 1992. "Menander's *Kolax* and Parasites and Flatterers in Greek Comedy," *ZPE* 92: 91-107.

Büchner, W. 1941. "Über den Begriff der Eironeia," *Hermes* 76: 340.

Burkert, W. 1983. *Homo Necans*, P. Bing trans. Berkeley, Los Angeles and London.

– *Babylon, Memphis, Persepolis: Eastern Contexts of Greek Culture*. Cambridge, Mass and London.

Byock, J., trans. 1990. *The Saga of the Volsungs: The Norse Epic of Sigurd the Dragon Slayer*. Berkeley, Los Angeles and London.

Campbell, D. 1967. *Greek Lyric Poetry*. Glasgow.

Carey, C. 1989. *Lysias: Selected Speeches*. Cambridge.

Carter, L. B. 1986. *The Quiet Athenian*. Oxford.

Clark, G. 1990. *Beowulf*. Boston.

Clark Hall, J.R. 1960. *A Concise Anglo-Saxon Dictionary, 4th Ed*. Toronto, Buffalo and London.

Cohen, D. 1985. "A Note on Aristophanes and the Punishment of Adultery in Athenian Law," *Zeitschrift der Savigny-Stiftung für Rechtsgeschichte, Romantische Abteilung* 102: 385-87.

Corbeill, A. 1996. *Controlling Laughter: Political Humour in the Late Roman Republic*. Princeton.

Cornford, F. M. 1934. *The Origin of Attic Comedy*. Cambridge.

Dalley, S. 1989. *Myths from Mesopotamia: Creation, the Flood, Gilgamesh, and Others*. Oxford.

Darwin, C. 1872. *The Expression of the Emotions in Man and Animals*, P. Eckman ed. New York and Oxford, 1998.

Davidson, J. 1997. *Courtesans and Fishcakes: The Consuming Passions of Classical Athens*. Hammersmith and London.

Devereux, G. 1970. "The Nature of Sappho's Seizure in Fr. 31 LP as Evidence of her Inversion," *CQ* 20: 17-31.

Derrida, J. 1981. *Dissemination*, B. Johnson trans. Chicago.

Dodds, E. R. 1964. *The Greeks and the Irrational.* Berkeley and Los Angeles.

Douglas, M. 1975. *Implicit Meanings.* London.

Dover, K. J. 1978. *Greek Homosexuality.* Cambridge, Mass.

Ehrenberg, V. 1947. "Polypragmosyne: A Study in Greek Politics," *JHS* 67: 46-67.

Einarsson, B. ed. 2003. *Egils Saga.* Exeter.

Foster, B. R. 1974. "Humor and Cuneiform Literature," *JANES* 6: 69-85.

Freud, S. 1905. "Jokes and their Relation to the Unconscious," *Standard Edition of the Complete Psychological Works* vol. 8. London, 1960.

Gardner, E. A. 1897. *A Handbook of Greek Sculpture.* London.

George, A.R. 2003. *The Babylonian Gilgamesh Epic: Introduction, Critical Edition, and Cuneiform Texts.* Oxford.

Girard, R. 1972. "Perilous Balance: A Comic Hypothesis," *MLN* 87: 811-26.

Graver, M. 1995. "Dog-Helen and Homeric Insult," *CA* 14: 41-61.

Griffith, R. D. 1993. "Strepsiades' Bedroom, Wife and Sufferings: Three Notes on the Prologue of Aristophanes' *Clouds*," *Prometheus* 19: 135-42.

– 1995. "In Praise of the Bride: Sappho Fr. 105(A) L-P, Voigt," *TAPA* 125: 55-61.

– 1996. "The Eyes of Clodia Metelli," *Latomus* 55: 381-83.

– 1996. *The Theatre of Apollo.* Montreal and Kingston.

Griffith, R. D. and G. D'Ambrosio-Griffith. 1991. "Il gioco della chelichelone," *Maia* 43: 83-87.

Guidorizzi, G. 1997. "The Laughter of the Suitors: A Case of Collective Madness in the *Odyssey*," 1-7 in L. Edmunds and R. W. Wallace eds., *Poet, Public and Performance in Ancient Greece.* Baltimore.

Hall, E. 1989. *Inventing the Barbarian: Greek Self-Definition through Tragedy.* Oxford.

Harris, E. M. 1990. "Did the Athenians Regard Seduction as a Worse Crime than Rape?," *CQ* 40: 370-77.

Harvey, D. 1990. "The Sykophant and Sykophancy: Vexations Redefinitions," in P. Cartledge et al. eds, *Nomos*. Cambridge: 103-121

Heidegger, M. 1971. *On the Way to Language*. P. D. Herz trans. New York and San Francisco.

Heller, J. 1961. *Catch-22*. New York.

Henderson, E.F. 1910. *Select Historical Documents of the Middle Ages*. London.

Hernderson, J. 1987. *Aristophanes: Lysistrata*. Oxford.

– 1991. *The Maculate Muse* 2nd ed. New York and Oxford.

Hill, J.M. 1995. *The Cultural World in **Beowulf***. Toronto, Buffalo and London.

Hobbes, T. 1651. *Leviathan*, C. B. Macpherson ed. Harmondsworth.

Houlihan, P. F. 2002. *Wit and Humour in Ancient Egypt*. London.

Jameson, F. 1972. *The Prison-House of Language*. Princeton.

Jones, C. P. 1987. "Stigma. Tatuoing and Branding in Graeco-Roman Antiquity," *JRS* 77: 139-55.

Kant, I. 1790. *Critique of Judgement*, J. C. Meredith trans. Oxford, 1952.

Kellogg, R. 2000. *The Sagas of Icelanders*. London.

Killeen, J. F. 1973. "Sappho Fr. 111," *CQ* 23: 198.

Kirk, G. S. 1963. "A Fragment of Sappho Reinterpreted," *CQ* 13: 51-52.

Kirkpatrick, J. and F. Dunn. 2002. "Heracles, Cercopes and Paracomedy," *TAPA* 132: 29-61.

Klaeber, Fr. 1922. *Beowulf and The Fight at Finnburg*. Lexington.

Lattimore, R. A. 1942. *Theme in Greek and Latin Epitaphs = Illinois Studies in Language and Literature* 28. Urbana.

Lavelle, B. M. 1986. "The Nature of Hipparchos' Insult to Harmodius," *AJP* 107: 318-31.

Lefkowitz, M. R. 1981. *The Lives of the Greek Poets*. London.

Lloyd-Jones, H. 1967. "Sappho fr. 111," *CQ* 17: 168.

Lorenz, C. 1963. *On Aggression*, M. K. Wilson trans. New York.

Lowe, J. C. B. 1985. "Cooks in Plautus," *CA* 4: 72-102.

MacDowell, D. M. 1971. *Aristophanes: Wasps*. Oxford.

– 1985. "The Meaning of *Alazon*," 287-92 in E. M. Craig ed., *Owls to Athens* = Festschrift K. J. Dover. Oxford.

Markovich, M. 1963-64. "On Sappho fr. 111 L.-P.," *Humanitades* 5-6: 223-27.

– 1972. "Sappho fr. 31: Anxiety Attack or Love Declaration," *CQ* 22: 19-32.

– 1986. "Demeter, Baubo, Iacchus, and a Redactor," *Vigiliae Christianae* 40: 294-301.

McGlathery, D. M. 1998. "Petronius' Tale of the Widow of Ephesus and Bakhtin's Material Bodily Lower Stratum," *Arethusa* 31: 313-36.

Milano, L. 2004. "Food and Identity in Mesopotamia: A New Look at the *Aluzinnu*'s Recipes," 242-56 in G. Grottanelli and L. Milano eds., *Food and Identity in the Ancient World*. Padua.

Montiglio, S. 2005. *Wandering in Ancient Greek Culture*. Chicago and London.

Morris, D. 1967. *The Naked Ape*. New York.

Nesselrath, H.-G. 1985. *Lucians Parasitendialog: Untersuchungen und Kommentar*. Berlin.

Noel, E. 2005. *The Odyssey: Breadbox Edition, Book I*. Somewhere in the ether-realm.

O'Higgins, L. 2003. *Women and Humour in Classical Greece*. Cambridge.

Olson, S. D., and A. Sens. 2000. *Archestratos of Gela: Greek Culture and cuisine in the Fourth Century B. C. E.* Oxford.

Omitowoju, R. 2002. *Rape and the Politics of Consent in Classical Athens*. Cambridge.

Osbourne, R. 1990. "Vexatious Litigations in Classical Athens: Sykophancy and the Sykophant," in P. Cartledge et al. eds., *Nomos*. Cambridge: 83-102.

Pirandello, L. 1908. *On Humor*, trans. A. Illiano and D. P. Testa. Chapel Hill, 1960.

Pratchett, T. 1983. *The Colour of Magic*. Gerrard's Cross.

Quinn, K. 1973. *Catullus: The Poems*, 2nd ed. London.

Ribbeck, O. 1876. "Ueber den Begriff des *eiron*," *Rh. Mus.* 21: 339-58.

– 1882. *Alazon*. Leipzig.

Richardson, N. J. 1974. *The Homeric Hymn to Demeter*. Oxford.

Risden, E.L. 2000. "Heroic Humor in Beowulf," in J. Wilcox, ed. *Humour in Anglo-Saxon Literature*. Cambridge.

Rives, J. B. 2007. *Religion in the Roman Empire*. Oxford.

Rose, H. J. 1925. "Antigone and the Bride of Corinth," *CQ* 19: 147-50.

Roy, J. 1991. "Traditional jokes about the punishment of adulterers in ancient Greek literature," *LCM* 16: 73-76.

Säve-Sönderbergh, T. 1957. *Four Eighteenth-Dynasty Tombs = Private Tombs at Thebes*. Oxford.

Schaps, D. 1977. "The Woman Least Mentioned: Etiquette and Women's Names," *CQ* 27: 323-30.

Scodel, R. 1992. "The Wits of Glaucus," *TAPA* 122: 73-84.

Sedgewick, G. G. 1948. *Of Irony: Especially Drama*, 2nd ed. Toronto.

Shear, L. 1984. "Semonides fr. 7: Wives and their Husbands," *EMC* N.S. 3: 39-49.

Shippey, T.A. 2000. "'Grim Wordplay': Folly and Wisdom in Anglo-Saxon Humor," in J. Wilcox, ed. *Humour in Anglo-Saxon England*. Cambridge.

Smith, D.K. 2000. "Humor in Hiding: Laughter Between the Sheets in the Exeter Book Riddles," in J. Wilcox, ed. *Humour in Anglo-Saxon England*. Cambridge: 79-98.

Spencer, H. 1860. "The Physiology of Laughter," *MacMillan's Magazine* 1: 395-402.

– 1901. *Essays*. London.

Square, A. (= E. A. Abbott). 1884. *Flatland: A Romance of Many Dimensions*, 2nd ed. (rpt. Oxford 1974).

States, B. L. 1971. *Irony and Drama: A Poetics*. Ithaca.

Storey, I. C. 2003. *Eupolis: Poet of Old Comedy*. Oxford.

Sturluson, S. 1996. *Edda*. A. Faulkes Trans. London.

Thalmann, W. G. 1988. "Thersites: Comedy, Scapegoats and Heroic Ideology in the *Iliad*," *TAPA* 118: 1-28.

Thomson, J. A. K. 1927. *Irony: An Historical Introduction*. Cambridge.

Thorson, J. A. 1993. "Did you Ever see a Hearse go by? Some Thoughts on Gallows Humor," *Journal of American Culture* 16: 17-24.

Tylawsky, E. I. 2002. *Saturio's Inheritance: The Greek Ancestry of the Roman Comic Parasite*. New York.

Vatnsdœla Saga, in Sveinsson, E.Ó. ed. 1958. *Íslenzk Fornrit, vol. VIII*. Reykjavik.

Vellacott, P. 1975. *Ironic Drama: A Study in Euripides' Methodology and Meaning*. Cambridge.

Vlastos, G. 1991. *Socrates: Ironist and Moral Philosopher*. Cambridge.

Walker, A. 1977. *Delphi*. Athens.

West, M. L. 1994. "Some Oriental Motifs in Archilochus," *ZPE* 102: 1-5.

Wilcox, J., Ed. 2000. *Humour in Anglo-Saxon Literature*. Cambridge.

Wilkins, J. 2000. *The Boastful Chef*. Oxford.

Woodbury, L. E. 1944. [doctoral dissertation summary: *quomodo risu ridiculoque Graeci usi sunt*] *HSCP* 55: 114-17.

– "The Gratitude of the Locrian Maiden: Pindar, *Pyth*. 2.18-20," *TAPA* 108: 285-99.

– 1980. "Strepsiades' Understanding: Five Notes on the *Clouds*," *Phoenix* 34: 108-27.

– 1991. *Collected Writings*. Atlanta.

Suggested Further Reading

Arnould, D. 1990. *Le Rire et les larmes dans la littérature grecque d'Homère à Platon*. Paris.

Barnes, H. E. 1964-65. "Greek Tragicomedy," *CJ* 60: 125-31.

Barnes, M.P. 1994. *The Runic Inscriptions of Maeshowe, Orkney*. Uppsala.

Bartalucci, A. 1988. "Considerazioni sulla festa del 'Deus Risus' nelle metamorfosi di Apuleio (2, 31-3, 18), " *Civiltà classica e cristiana* 9: 51-65.

Bennett, H. 1935. "The Wit's Progress – A Study in the Life of Cicero," *CJ* 30: 193-202.

Bonner, R. J. 1922. "Wit and Humor in Athenian Courts," *CP* 17: 97-103.

Burrows, R. Z. 1965. "Deception as a Comic Device in the *Odyssey*," *CW* 59: 33-36.

Clarke, H. W. 1968-69. "The Humor of Homer," *CJ* 64: 246-52.

Colakls, M. 1985-86. "The Laughter of the Suitors in *Odyssey* 20," *CW* 79: 137-41.

Dillon, M. 1991. "Tragic Laughter," *CW* 84: 345-55.

Feldman, A. B. 1961-62. "Lapsus Linguae in Latin Comedy," *CJ* 57: 354-55.

Flory, S. 1978. "Laughter, Tears and Wisdom in Herodotus," *AJP* 99: 145-53.

Fordyce, C. J. 1932-33. "Puns on Names in Greek," *CJ* 28: 44-46.

Friedländer, P. 1934. "Lachende Götter," *Die Antike* 10: 209-226; rpt. 1969. *Studien zur antiken Literatur und Kunst*. Berlin: 3-18.

Grene, D. 1937. "The Comic Technique of Aristophanes," *Hermathena* 50: 87-125.

Grimal, P. 1972. "La Fête du Rire dans le *Métamorphoses* d'Apulée," *Studi classici* = Festschrift Q. Cataudella. Catania. 457-65.

Grossman, G. 1968. "Das Lachen des Aias," *MH* 25: 65-85.

Halliwell, S. 1991. "The Uses of Laughter in Greek Culture," *CQ* 41: 279-96.

Hart, W. M. 1943-44. "High Comedy in the *Odyssey*," *CPCP* 12: 263-78.

Hawley, R. C. 1968. "The Antiphonal Muse: Comic Sub-Theme in the *Iliad*," *CW* 62: 81-82.

Hewitt, J. W. 1926. "The Comic Aspect of the Greek Athletic Meet," *CJ* 21: 643-53.

– 1929. "Humor in Homer and in Vergil," *CW* 22: 169-81.

Hunt, W. I. 1890. "Homeric Wit and Humor," *TAPA* 21: 48-58.

Jensen, R. 1921. "'Quid Rides?'," *CJ* 16: 207-219.

Kelsey, F. W. 1907. "Cicero as Wit," *CJ* 2: 3-10.

Lee, G. 1971. *Allusion, Parody and Imitation*. Hull.

Lelièvre, F. J. 1954. "The Basis of Ancient Parody," *G&R* 1: 66-81.

Levine, D. B. 1982-83. "Homeric Laughter and the Unsmiling Suitors," *CJ* 78: 97-104.

– 1983. "Penelope's Laugh: *Odyssey* 18.163," *AJP* 104: 172-77.

– 1984. "Odysseus' Smiles: *Odyssey* 20.301, 22.371, 23.111," *TAPA* 114: 1-9.

Lofberg, J. O. 1921. "'Unmixed Milk' Again," *CP* 16: 389-91.

Matthews, V. J. 1973. "Some Puns on Roman *Cognomina*," *G&R* 20: 20-24.

McCartney, E. S. 1919. "Puns and Plays on Proper Names," *CJ* 14: 343-58.

– 1931. "Ancient Wit and Humor," 191-211 in G. D. Hadzsits ed., *Classical Studies* = Festschrift J. C. Rolfe. Philadelphia.

McCarthy, B. P. 1943. "Sarcasm in the *Iliad*," *CW* 36: 215-16.

Miller, H. W. 1945. "Comic Iteration in Aristophanes," *AJP* 66: 398-408.

Nilsen, D. L. F. 1990. "Incongruity, Surprise, Tension, and Relief: Four Salient Features Associated with Humor," *Thalia* 11: 22-27.

Nye, I. 1914. "Humor Repeats Itself," *CJ* 9: 154-64.

– 1937. "When Homer Smiles," *CJ* 33: 25-37.

Plaza, M. 2006. *The Function of Humour in Roman Verse Satire*. Oxford.

Pulquério, M. de O. 1959-60. "O Significado do riso nos poemas homéricas," *Humanitas* 11-12: 45-65.

Rapp, A. 1947. "The Dawn of Humor," *CJ* 43: 275-79.

Robertson, D. S. 1919. "A Greek Carnival," *JHS* 39: 110-115.

Rome, C. A. 1946. "L'Humour chez Pindare," *BCH* 70: 524-32.

Sadler, J. D. 1982-83. "Latin Paronomasia," *CJ* 78: 138-41.

Schlesinger, A. C. 1937. "Identification of Parodies in Aristophanes," *AJP* 58: 294-305.

Shorey, P. 1927. "Homeric Laughter," *CP* 22: 222-23.

Sikes, E. E. 1940. "The Humour of Homer," *CR* 54: 121-27.

Süss, W. 1969. *Lachen, Komik und Witz in der Antike*. Zurich and Stuttgart.

Swanson, R. A. 1962-63. "The Humor of Catullus 8," *CJ* 58: 193-96.

Watson, W. L. 1970. "The Surname as a Brickbat in Cicero's Speeches," *CJ* 66: 55-58.

Wilner, O. L. 1951. "Some "Comical Scenes from Plautus and Terence," *CJ* 46: 165-70, 176.

Index

About the Authors

In 1987, Robert D. Griffith answered a call from his dog that he go to serve among the cutest of the rich, and moved to Kingston's student ghetto. There ever since, under the top secret code name of R. Drew Griffith, he has taught Classics at Queen's University, one of the two most prestigious universities in Kingston, Ontario. Among his courses is CLST 205: Ancient Humour (a.k.a. "Very Old Jokes").

Robert B. Marks is a professional writer and editor in Kingston, Ontario. He holds degrees in Medieval Studies and English Literature, and has close to 250 short publication credits, and two books published. And, every year he puts a pillow under a big red coat, colours his beard white, and delivers gifts to children around the world, for which he is currently wanted for breaking and entering in at least thirty countries.

Also from Legacy Books Press

The War that Changed the World, by John-Allen Price (Spring 2009)

Printed in the United States
95336LV00005B/112-264/A